Psychiatric and Developmental Disorders in Children With Communication Disorder

Psychiatric and Developmental Disorders in Children With Communication Disorder

Dennis P. Cantwell, M.D.
Joseph Campbell Professor of Child Psychiatry
Neuropsychiatric Institute
University of California at Los Angeles
Los Angeles, California

Lorian Baker, Ph.D.
Research Psycholinguist
Neuropsychiatric Institute
University of California at Los Angeles
Los Angeles, California

Washington, DC
London, England

Note: The authors have worked to ensure that all information in this book concerning drug dosages, schedules, and routes of administration is accurate as of the time of publication and consistent with standards set by the U.S. Food and Drug Administration and the general medical community. As medical research and practice advance, however, therapeutic standards may change. For this reason and because human and mechanical errors sometimes occur, we recommend that readers follow the advice of a physician who is directly involved in their care or the care of a member of their family.

Copyright © 1991 American Psychiatric Press, Inc.
ALL RIGHTS RESERVED
Manufactured in the United States of America on acid-free paper.
First Edition 94 93 92 91 4 3 2 1

American Psychiatric Press, Inc.
1400 K Street, N.W., Washington, DC 20005

Library of Congress Cataloging-in-Publication Data

Psychiatric and developmental disorders in children with
  communication disorder/Dennis P. Cantwell, Lorian Baker.
        p.   cm.
    Includes bibliographical references and index.
    ISBN 0-88048-357-1 (alk. paper)
    1. Speech disorders in children—Patients—Mental health.
  2. Language disorders in children—Patients—Mental health.
  3. Handicapped children—Development—Research.   I. Cantwell, Dennis P., 1939–   . II. Baker, Lorian.
    [DNLM: 1. Cohort Studies. 2. Language Development Disorders—complications. 3. Mental Disorders—in infancy and childhood. WM 475 P9745]
  RJ496.S7P8 1991
  618.92′855—cd20
  DNLM/DCL
  for Library of Congress   90-14486
                                                                              CIP

British Library Cataloguing in Publication Data

A CIP record is available from the British Library.

To Emy Davis and the memory of
Frederick W. Davis;
to Marshall Buck, Ph.D.;
and to Susan, Suzi, Denny,
Colleen, Erin, and Marianne Cantwell.

Contents

Acknowledgments

ABOVE ALL, WE ARE INDEBTED to the many, many children with communication disorder and to their parents who participated in the research described in this book. They gave selflessly of their time and energy, sharing with us their problems and successes, from which we learned so much.

We are also especially grateful to several professionals who shared their knowledge and expertise to help with this research. Among the many speech-language pathologists, child psychiatrists, statisticians, research assistants, and clerical/administrative workers who were involved with the research, we particularly wish to thank Dolores Adams, Rose Goupillaud, Howard Grey, Donald Guthrie, Richard Mattison, and Beth Phillips.

The preparation of this volume was aided by funds from the Catherine Davis Trust and by Grants 17371 and 35116 from the National Institute of Mental Health.

Finally, we wish to note that the order of authorship of this volume is arbitrary and does not reflect differential contributions to the work.

Introduction

IN THIS VOLUME WE PRESENT DATA from a large-scale epidemiologic research study of children with speech and/or language disorders. The main function of the volume is to provide specific insights into the development and functioning of speech- and/or language-disordered children. In addition, however, we present a considerable amount of information relevant to general, theoretical, and methodological issues in child psychiatry.

Two very important issues in child psychiatry, and their relevant data from the present study, are addressed in Chapter 4. First, the correlates of psychiatric disorder in the literature are discussed, exemplifying the many possible etiological or "risk" factors that may be involved in the pathogenesis of both psychiatric illness in general and specific childhood psychiatric diagnoses. Second, issues of the subclassification of childhood psychiatric disorders are discussed with particular reference to the distinction between "behavioral" and "emotional" types of psychiatric disorders.

Other data and material presented in this volume are also of relevance to child psychiatry. For example, issues pertaining to psychiatric research methodology are discussed in Chapter 2. And the methodology used in the present study (outlined in Chapter 2) provides an example of an appropriate framework for conducting psychiatric research.

The age and sex data obtained in the present study (and presented in Chapter 5) are of psychiatric importance for several reasons. The age data address the growing subdiscipline of developmental psychopathology and provide further, much-needed data on the age-specificity of childhood psychiatric symptoms and disorders. The data on sex differences are relevant to the poorly understood area of how biologically and/or environmentally based differences between boys and girls may be related to differential rates of psychopathology.

The development and functioning of speech/language–disordered children (see Chapters 3 and 6) are of particular interest to the discipline of child psychiatry for a number of reasons. For example, the ability to communicate thoughts and feelings to others forms a foundation for the acquisition of higher-level learning and the establishment of social and personal relationships. Thus, it is often stated that language is the one ability that makes us "uniquely human." For children, speech and language development impacts virtually all other aspects of development, such as general cognition, play, educational or academic achievement, peer relationships, and emotional and behavioral development.

As is discussed in more detail in Chapters 1 and 3, children with speech/language learning disorders comprise a sizable proportion of the general population. In addition, these children are at increased risk for the development of both psychiatric disorders and learning disorders (see Chapters 4 and 6). As a result, children with speech/language disorders are particularly likely to present for psychiatric evaluation and/or treatment. These children are also of concern to a number of other professionals, including child psychologists, social workers, school teachers, educational therapists, and speech-language pathologists. It is hoped that this book will provide valuable insights for all of these professionals as well as for the parents of speech/language–disordered children.

1 Speech and Language Disorders: Definitions and Background

LANGUAGE IS DEFINED HERE as an arbitrary system of symbols and rules used to convey meanings. Language is composed of a number of subsystems including the following:

1. A *phonological* system that provides the rules for combining and selecting the speech sounds of a language. For example, some examples of phonological rules in English are that words cannot begin with the "ng" sound and that the sounds "b," "n," and " f " cannot occur contiguously.
2. A *semantic* or *lexical* system that specifies the meaningful units or vocabulary of a language. For example, in English, "-s" at the end of a word may signify "more than one"; "cat" signifies a feline animal.
3. A *grammatical* or *syntactic* system that provides rules for organizing meaningful units (or words) into sentences. For example, in English, "ball I threw" is not a grammatical sentence, even though it has a clear meaning.
4. A *pragmatic* system that provides rules for selecting particular forms of language for use in particular situations. For example, when to use informal expressions or slang, when to use a pronoun rather than a person's name, and when and how to "take turns" in a conversation.

In order to use these abstract systems known as language for communication, a number of relatively independent psycholinguistic processes must be employed by the speaker and listener. Three of the most basic of these processes are 1) speech (or the motor production of the sounds of a particular language); 2) expression (or the encoding, production, or formulation of ideas into the form designated by the rules of a particular language); and 3) reception (or the comprehension,

1

understanding, or decoding of a message).

Each of these processes consists of a number of steps that involve various cognitive, perceptual, and neuromotor functions. For example, production involves conceptualizing a thought and encoding it into words and sentences. Speech involves providing a phonological representation (in sounds and syllables) for the message and acting upon it with a motor-control program to coordinate the movements of the speech mechanism.

The exact nature of the psycholinguistic and neurolinguistic processes is not well understood at the present time. In fact, it is open to dispute as to whether linguistic activities or language structures are what is represented in the brain. The traditional neuropsychological model (e.g., Goodglass 1983; Goodglass and Kaplan 1972) assumes the former, whereas the neolinguistic model (e.g., Chomsky 1980) assumes the latter. Furthermore, the interrelationships between the subsystems of language are not well understood—neither with regard to normal linguistic functioning nor with respect to disturbed linguistic functioning.[1]

Definitions of Speech/Language Disorders

The term *speech/language disorder* is used in the present work to refer to a delay or deviance in the acquisition of speech or language, or both. Speech/language disorders in children are manifested by a wide range of signs that can occur singly or, more commonly, in clusters. Table 1-1 lists the signs, along with definitions and examples where relevant, that may be found in children with speech/language disorders.

It is important to note that a number of these features do not necessarily designate abnormality in and of themselves; the features must be considered with regard to the mental age of the child and with regard to the speech and language functioning of other children in the speech community who are at the same age level. For example, it is not abnormal for a 2-year-old to omit many speech sounds, to

---

[1] Readers interested in exploring these dilemmas in more detail are referred to the following works: Arbib et al. 1982; Bresnan 1983; Chiat and Hirson 1987; Coltheart 1987; Coltheart et al. 1987; Fletcher 1987; Fodor 1983; Fodor et al. 1974; Garfield 1987; Grodzinsky 1986; Gruber and Segalowitz 1977; Kean 1982; Keller and Gopnik 1987; Parisi 1987; Segalowitz 1983; Selkirk 1984; Sproat 1986; Wang 1982.

repeat utterances he or she hears, or to produce sentences with many words missing. However, such behaviors would be an indication of abnormality in a 6-year-old.

As indicated above, the various abnormalities or signs occurring in children with speech/language disorders may be found singly or in clusters. Unfortunately, there are only a few studies that have provided any empirical data as to how these signs cluster together to form specific syndromes or speech/language disorders (Aram and Nation 1975; Beitchman et al. 1989a, 1989b; Feagans and Appelbaum 1986; Martin 1980; McKinney 1984; Wilson and Risucci 1986; Wolfus et al. 1980; Wren 1982).

Furthermore, there is no consensus on the terminology or the conceptual framework to be used for describing children with abnormal speech and/or language development. Such children have been labeled as having "delayed," "disordered," "retarded," "handicapped," or "deviant" speech and/or language development.

To date, speech/language delays or disorders have been subclassified using a number of different models based upon linguistic, psychological, clinical-descriptive, and/or medical-etiological concepts. For example, clinical-descriptive classification systems (e.g., Orton 1937) have subgrouped speech/language disorders into subtypes such as stuttering, motor speech deficits, dyslexia, and word deafness. Linguistically oriented classification systems (e.g., Aram and Nation 1982; Bloom and Lahey 1978; Tomblin 1978; Wiig and Semel 1980) have subgrouped disorders into such categories as encoding or expressive language deficits, decoding or receptive language deficits, vocabulary deficits, syntactic deficits, semantic deficits, and/or language-use deficits. Etiologically based classification systems (e.g., Chase 1972; DeQuiros 1974; Ingram 1972; Morley 1957; Myklebust 1954; Pirozzolo et al. 1981) have included such subtypes as hearing loss, neurological abnormalities, structural abnormalities, psychiatric disorders, and mental retardation. Psychologically oriented classification systems (e.g., Aram and Nation 1982) have included categories such as speech-perception disruption, auditory-processing disruption, semantic-comprehension disorder, syntactic-comprehension disruption, language-integration disruption, semantic-formulation disruption, syntactic-formulation disruption, developmental verbal apraxia, speech-mechanism disorder, and phonological disorder. In addition, information-processing theory, neuropsychology and computer modeling of language processes, and brain imaging are currently being studied and will hopefully provide further insights into a coherent theory of speech/language development and disorders (Keller and Gopnik 1987).

Table 1-1. Common signs of speech/language disorder

Speech disorder signs

Articulation that is inaccurate compared with that of other speakers of the same
dialect at the same age level. (Articulation is the movement and placement
during speech of the lips, tongue, jaw, epiglottis, and/or vocal cords in order to
form speech sounds.)

Omissions of speech sounds (e.g., saying "ka" for "car," "ow" for "house," "scisso" for
"scissors," or "bu" for "blue").

Substitutions of one speech sound for another (e.g., saying "thithorth" for "scissors,"
"wabbit" for "rabbit," "shobel" for "shovel," "fum" for "thumb," "leap" for "leaf,"
or "dis" for "this").

Reversals in the order of speech sounds within words (e.g., saying "aminal" instead
of "animal").

Abnormalities in intonation. (Intonation is the melodic pattern of tone of voice and
loudness of syllables that is used to signal meanings in utterances. The most
common abnormality in intonation is using either a monotone or a "sing-song"
tone of voice.)

Additions of sounds or syllables in words (e.g., saying "crouge" for "rouge").

Vocal quality that is continually congested or nasal sounding, harsh, breathy, or
hoarse.

Stuttering. (Stuttering consists of disruptions in the flow of speech including
repetitions or prolongations of words or sounds, hesitations, or pauses within or
between utterances.)

Apparent difficulty saying words (e.g., making faces, grimacing, clenching fists,
appearing embarrassed, hesitating, or speaking unduly slowly).

Language disorder (semantic or lexical) signs

Frequent misnaming of items, using related but incorrect words (e.g., saying
"finger" for "thumb").

Vocabulary limited in terms of both the number and kinds of words known and the
frequency with which different words are used.

Overuse of nonspecific vocabulary (e.g., using words like "this," "that," "thing,"
"stuff," or "you know" instead of saying the object name).

Use of jargon. (Jargon consists of strings of sounds or made-up words that
apparently have meaning to the child.)

Difficulty understanding concepts, particularly those having to do with space, time,
comparisons, abstractions, or relationships.

Inability to retain knowledge of new words learned.

Use of functional descriptions instead of nouns (e.g., saying "sit on" for "chair").

Inability to recognize that words can have more than one meaning.

Difficulty understanding figurative language, puns, idioms, or proverbs.

Word-finding difficulties (e.g., producing the correct word, but only after long
hesitations, "uhms," and "ers").

Language disorder (grammatical or syntactic) signs

Limited verbal output (e.g., few spontaneous remarks, or preference for using
gestures rather than speech).

Simplified grammatical structures (e.g., shortened sentences and limited varieties
of sentences and grammatical structures).

Table 1-1 *(continued)*

Omissions of words from utterances.

Incorrect grammatical forms (e.g., "Me want a drink," "I have three toy," "I have two foots," "I throwed a ball").

Abnormal course or history of language development (e.g., late linguistic milestones, mixed developmental stages, sudden loss of acquired language).

Difficulty ordering words to form sentences (e.g., mixed up word order, sentences restarted again midway through).

Difficulty understanding verbal language (e.g., may respond incorrectly. to instructions, may frequently ask "Huh?" or "What?").

Difficulty remembering or repeating verbal information.

Difficulty attending to auditory information.

Difficulty discriminating between similar words or utterances.

Language disorder (pragmatic) signs

Failure to respond to the communication of others (e.g., not responding to own name, using mainly egocentric or self-directed speech).

Failure to initiate, reinforce, or sustain conversations with others.

Off-target verbal responses (e.g., tangential, irrelevant, inappropriate, or bizarre responses).

Idiosyncratic word usage.

Poor topic maintenance (e.g., excessive adherence to a single topic, perseveration or continuing references back to an earlier topic, failure to take turns in conversation).

Excessive verbal output (e.g., a series of obsessive questions or long, rambling sentences).

Immediate or delayed echolalia. (Echolalia is the repetition, or "echoing," of words or phrases previously heard.)

Failure to use language for a variety of functions (e.g., asking for things, asking questions, telling stories).

Speech or language style inappropriate for environment (e.g., failure to use polite forms and greetings).

Prevalence of Childhood Speech/Language Disorders

There is a wide range in the prevalence estimates for childhood speech/language disorders. A summary of the relevant epidemiologic literature is provided in Appendix 1. There it can be seen that the prevalence estimates for the various types of childhood speech/language disorders vary greatly. For example, the prevalence estimates for childhood speech disorders range from a low of less than 1% to a high of more than 33%; those for language disorders range from less than 1% to 17%.

These discrepant estimates are due to a variety of factors, most notably a lack of consensus on definitions and classifications of the disorders. Thus, some of the prevalence estimates include those speech and language impairments associated with hearing loss, mental retardation, and/or organic abnormalities, whereas some of the estimates exclude such cases. Other reasons for the discrepant estimates include the lack of a clear onset for most speech and language disorders, the unavailability of normed tests that encompass various age levels and dialect groups, and the difficulty in obtaining representative samples of children.

The available data summarized in Appendix 1 indicate that the prevalence rates for speech/language disorders vary according to several factors. These factors include the sex distribution of the sample, the ethnicity of the sample, the locale of the study, the professional training of the diagnostician, the age-range of the sample, and the types of disorders being studied. The currently available data suggest that speech/language disorders are more common in boys than in girls (Beitchman et al. 1983; Gillespie and Cooper 1973; Mills and Streit 1942; Stewart et al. 1979), more common in blacks than in whites (Stewart et al. 1979), more common in the southern United States than in other regions (National Center for Health Statistics 1981), and more common in younger children than in older children (Carhart 1939; Dickson 1971; Gillespie and Cooper 1973; Hull et al. 1971; Mills and Streit 1942). Prevalence rates for speech/language disorders are higher when the diagnoses are made by speech therapists or school teachers than when made by medical doctors (Calnan and Richardson 1976; Pronovost 1951). With regard to the different types of speech/language disorders, the studies indicate that speech disorders are more common than language disorders and that the most common type of speech disorder is an impairment in articulation not associated with organic abnormalities.

Significance of Childhood Speech/Language Disorders

Role of Language in Child Development

Despite the absence of firm prevalence figures, it is clear that childhood speech/language disorders affect a large number of children—several million in the United States alone (Jenkins 1978; National Institute of Neurological Diseases and Stroke 1972). The impact of such disorders upon these children and their families is significant and reaches across many areas of development.

Beyond the obvious function of language as a means of communication, evidence suggests that language plays critical roles in other areas such as concept development, problem solving, play, structuring the environment, socialization, establishing self-concept or self-image, learning to read, and acquiring an education (Baker and Cantwell 1982). Thus, it is probable that the child with a deficit in language development is likely to have a number of other difficulties as well.

Cognition, concept development, problem solving, and play. The degree of interdependence between cognitive development (or concept development and problem solving) and language development has long been open to controversy (Bates et al. 1979; Bruner 1973; Chomsky 1967, 1968; de Zwart 1973; Golinkoff and Gordon 1983; Kohlberg et al. 1968; Luria 1961; Mead 1934; Piaget 1952, 1955; Piattelli-Palmarini 1980; Vygotsky 1962). In general, it is clear that nonlinguistic cognition does not have a one-to-one correlation with linguistic development but that there is nonetheless a relatively strong correlation between the two.

Much of the data on cognitive development have originated from observations of developmental trends in children's play. There is, for example, considerable evidence that the development of various linguistic forms parallels the development of various corresponding cognitive stages (Bates et al. 1979; Casby and Ruder 1983; Fein 1978; Gopnik and Meltzoff 1986; Luria and Yudovich 1959; McCune-Nicolich and Carroll 1981; Raph and Nicolich 1978; Rosenblatt 1980). In particular, it has been observed that immature play forms (i.e., single-object play) are associated with single-word linguistic structures, whereas complex pretend or symbolic play is associated with complex multiword linguistic structures. Similarly, cognitive development in the structural concepts of constructive play (i.e., sequencing, proximate space, functional space, linearity, hierarchicality) parallels the acquisition of spatial, temporal, and causal linguistic units (Goodson and Greenfield 1975; Johnston 1981; Johnston and Johnston 1984).

Experimental studies have also shown an association between perceptual analogical reasoning, verbal analogical reasoning, proportional metaphor comprehension, and receptive vocabulary development (Nippold and Sullivan 1987). Furthermore, there is experimental evidence suggesting that language may provide a tool for conceptual analysis and thereby promote the acquisition of novel cognitive tasks (Rosenthal et al. 1972).

Despite the fact that there have been numerous associations documented between cognitive and linguistic functions, the directionality of these associations remains unclear. Specifically, uncertainty remains as to whether language development underlies cognitive development, whether cognitive development underlies language development, or whether some other less-direct relationship between the two entities exists. Similarly, just as causality has not been established between the development of linguistic and nonlinguistic skills, causality has also not been established between linguistic dysfunctions and disorders or lags in nonlinguistic cognition.

Nonetheless, it is a likely hypothesis that lags or disorders in linguistic cognition result in lags or disorders in areas of nonlinguistic cognition. Supporting such a hypothesis are data indicating that children with language problems are likely to have difficulties with certain specific types of thought operations. In particular, impairment appears likely in cognitive operations involving the formation of mental images or inner pictures (Hermelin 1978; Inhelder 1976; Johnston and Ramstad 1983; Roth and Clark 1987); solving of nonexplicit discrimination problems involving shape, size, and position (Nelson et al. 1987); and such concepts as seriation, spatial order, and conservation of space (Savich 1984; Siegel et al. 1981). With such impairments in concept development, the language-disordered child would have some difficulty in solving a number of different types of problems. Furthermore, there are some data indicating that language can affect recall (Loftus and Palmer 1974). Thus, it is possible that language-impaired children may also have difficulties with memory and recall for events.

Although some studies examining the play behaviors of language-disordered children have not found deficits (Kamhi 1981; Terrell et al. 1984), the majority of such studies have reported limitations in play skills. The specific aspects of play that have been demonstrated to be impaired in language-disordered children include symbolic play (Udwin and Yule 1983), especially when concrete props are not present (Lovell et al. 1968); integration of play behavior around a theme (Brown et al. 1975); planning (Callaghan 1983); and role playing (Callaghan 1983). Because play serves a number of functions for the child, the child whose play skills are impaired will be at a disadvantage in discovering and adapting to the environment, storing memories, relieving boredom, and interacting with people (Sheridan 1975).

Manipulating the environment, acquiring social skills, and developing a self-image. Language is an effective tool that allows the young child to manipulate the environment and to compensate for many of his or her own physical limitations. Thus, the small child can ask mother to get out-of-reach items; the clumsy child can ask daddy to mend things for him or her; the impoverished child can ask grandma to buy him or her things.

Requesting is among the earliest acquired functions of language. Even at the preverbal stages of language development, the regulatory function of language is very strong (Carrow-Woolfolk and Lynch 1982). Thus, toddlers express demands first by combining vocalizations with pointing and then later by using gestures of giving, pointing, or showing in order to draw attention to what is wanted. Finally, when language is more developed, request forms become more diversified and complex (Bruner et al. 1982).

The child with a language deficit is less able to make his or her needs and wants known, less clear and less persuasive in making requests, and therefore less successful in manipulating his or her environment. It has been hypothesized (Dukes 1981) that the child who lacks the verbal facility to manipulate the environment according to his or her desires may instead resort to physical aggression. At the very least, a lack of success in manipulating the environment would surely lead to frustration for the language-impaired child. Furthermore, it is also likely that repeated failures to achieve one's desires would result in diminishing levels of self-confidence for the language-impaired child.

Several authors have suggested, in fact, that self-image and self-confidence are acquired through linguistic interactions. Mead (1934), for example, proposed that the child develops a self-image by means of various self-directed communications in which he or she "tries out" different roles. In addition to providing for the rehearsal of explanations, language also allows for the development of social comparisons and the social understanding of subtle shades of meaning (Durkin 1986). A main function of language, and one that has considerable impact upon self-image, is in forming social relationships to bring the child love and a sense of being valued (Gemelli 1983). Being able to say the right thing at the right time is an essential skill for establishing and maintaining friendships.

The interactional function of language is present very early, but it becomes increasingly more important as the child grows. At 18 months of age, the child begins using language to express feelings, to answer questions, and to introduce new topics. Later, around the age of 3 years, the child begins acquiring abilities in the social modification of language. Two examples are *code switching* (i.e., using baby talk with infants, avoiding taboo forms with adults, using slang or "in" forms with peers) and *conversational rules*. Conversational rules underlie much of what we now call "social skills" and include such abilities as recognizing opportune times for conversation; making appropriate responses to questions, statements, and requests; showing tact; interpreting the feelings or attitudes of others; obtaining clarification when it is needed during conversational breakdowns; taking turns at interactions; and engaging in verbal bantering and humor. All of these abilities have been demonstrated to be somewhat impaired in language-disordered children (Donahue and Bryan 1984).

It is easy to imagine how children with such impairments would encounter social problems. Schwartz and Merten's (1967) anthropological examination of youth culture provides an example. These authors found that the proficient use of "in group" slang was a prerequisite for membership in adolescent cliques; thus, youngsters not proficient in slang were excluded from these social groups. Fine (1981) had similar findings with regard to the ability to engage in "ritual insults" by preadolescents. Other studies (Deutsch 1974; Donahue 1983; Gottman et al. 1975) have demonstrated that conversational skills are related to peer acceptance and popularity.

The path from social exclusion to psychic distress is also not difficult to imagine. Dukes (1981), for example, outlined a scenario in which a child's inability to say the right thing at the right time resulted in his not being selected for team sports, and continuing nonselection resulted in feelings of inferiority and poor self-image. It is also possible that a pure speech disorder (with normal language abilities) could also lead to scorn and social exclusion. Freeman and Silver (1989) observe, for example, that speakers with distorted articulation are often viewed as stupid, those with a lisp may be considered gay, and stutterers are often viewed as comical or crazy. As our review of the literature (discussed below) reveals, negative views of speech/language–impaired individuals are common among teachers and other professionals.

Academic achievement and educational success.   Lack of success in the educational setting is another path to a poor self-image. Mastery of language is necessary for educational success. The majority of scholastic problems are presented to a child in linguistic form whether the problem to be solved is verbal or nonverbal (Miller 1984).

In the school setting, an understanding of written language (reading) is a crucial part of the educational process. This is particularly true in the higher grade levels, where it is expected that students will learn material through independent reading. However, mastery of oral language is also essential for classroom success. It has been shown that the verbal interactions that occur in the classroom are qualitatively different than those in other settings (Blank et al. 1978), and that in order to learn, the student must have a high level of mastery in interpreting directions and making inferences from oral language (Vetter 1982).

As discussed above, language may also facilitate learning in other areas and cognition. The literature examining the relationship between language disorder and educational failure is discussed in more detail below.

Background Literature on Childhood Psychiatric Disorders and Speech/Language Disorders

It has been demonstrated that children with handicaps of all types, and especially those involving the brain, are at risk for the development of social and emotional problems (Rutter et al. 1970a). These children often suffer not only from the attendant frustrations of the handicap itself but also from adverse parental, community, and peer reactions. Considering the wide range of areas upon which language development impacts, it is not unexpected that children with language handicaps are particularly at risk for social and emotional difficulties.

The literature examining the adjustment of children with various types of speech/language disorders is summarized in Appendix 2. The majority of this research was done prior to the start of our study. However, some more recent references expand upon the results of our study, and these are included in the appendix for the sake of completeness.

The earliest clinical descriptions of childhood speech/language disorders generally assumed that emotional and/or behavioral problems were a necessary secondary complication. Thus, for example, Orton (1937) wrote that any single handicap affecting the ability to communicate would lead to some secondary behavioral problems.

The majority of the earlier works typically consisted of case reports or general speculations with very little objective data. Other early works consisted of "analyses" based upon unreliable measures and/or definitions of psychiatric disorders (often some type of projective test). Thus, many of these studies dealing with the behavioral or emotional adjustment of speech/language–disordered children must be discounted on methodological grounds. (The methodological issues and problems involved with these and other psychiatric studies are discussed in more detail in Chapter 2.)

The possible association between psychiatric disorders and speech/language disorders has been researched using several approaches, including descriptions of speech/language–disordered children, descriptions of psychiatrically ill children, descriptions of children with specific psychiatric illnesses, epidemiologic population studies, and surveys of professionals. These approaches are discussed below.

Descriptions of Speech/Language–Disordered Children

The most common research approach has been to describe or "analyze" the personality, behavior, or adjustment of a group of speech/language–disordered children. Studies using this approach have usually obtained their subjects from speech clinics or from speech classes in the public school system. As noted above, many of these works have consisted of case descriptions or summaries of material contained in patient charts (e.g., Caceres 1971; Demb 1980; Funk and Ruppert 1984; Gluck et al. 1965; Holroyd 1968; Ingram 1959; Morley 1973; Shriberg et al. 1986).

Other works describing children with speech/language disorders have used a variety of tools or tests. The children have been described both without reference to others and in comparison to control groups. Age- and/or sex-matched classmates with normal speech and language are most frequently chosen as control subjects. However, various studies have also used as control subjects children with orthopedic or physical handicaps (Clifford 1969; Harper and Richman 1978), children with different subtypes of speech/language disorders (Broad and Bar 1973), previously speech-impaired children who have subsequently recovered (Barrett and Hoops 1974), and psychiatrically ill children (Bartak and Rutter 1975; Gluck et al. 1965).

Among the tools that have been used to capture the personality characteristics or psychiatric adjustment of children are the following:

1. Teacher questionnaires or rating scales (e.g., English 1961; Klackenberg 1980; Lindholm and Touliatos 1979; Lolley 1975; Nelson 1953; Richman 1978; Richman and Harper 1978; Ruess 1965; Schweckendiek and Danzer 1970; Sherrill 1967)
2. Teacher interviews (e.g., Griffiths 1969)
3. Parental questionnaires or rating scales (e.g., Aram et al. 1984; Bartak et al. 1975; Baumgartner 1980; English 1961; Fitzsimons 1958; McWilliams and Matthews 1979; McWilliams and Musgrave 1972; Richman 1978; Ruess 1965; Schweckendiek and Danzer 1970; Simonds and Heimburger 1978; Tallal et al. 1989a; Wing 1969)
4. Parent interviews (e.g., Bartak et al. 1975; Beckey 1942; Grif-

fiths 1969; King et al. 1982; Solomon 1961; Spriesterbach 1973)
5. Children's self-rating scales (e.g., Clifford 1969; Kapp 1979; Sherrill 1967; Watson 1964)
6. Child interviews (e.g., Griffiths 1969; Simonds and Heimburger 1978)
7. Peer ratings (e.g., Muma et al. 1968; Sherrill 1967; Woods 1970)
8. School records (e.g., Bubenickova 1977; Schweckendiek and Danzer 1970)
9. Psychiatric observations (e.g., Paul and Cohen 1984; Paul et al. 1983)

Projective tests, personality inventories, and perceptual-cognitive tests are also among the different types of assessment tools that have been used with speech/language–impaired children. Specific examples of tests used are given in Table 1-2.

As Appendix 2 indicates, there are studies examining groups of speech/language–disordered children that date back almost 40 years. The results of these studies are somewhat contradictory, but the general pattern suggests that these children are "at risk" for behavioral and emotional problems.

Descriptions of Psychiatrically Ill Children

Another major approach to examining the relationship between speech/language disorders and psychiatric disorders is the study of a group of psychiatrically ill children.[2]

Samples of psychiatrically ill children have been studied in several ways. Some authors (e.g., Aimard et al. 1973; Chess 1944; Gemelli 1982; Glasner 1949; Ierodiakonou 1970; Livingood and Cohen-Sandler 1980; McHale 1967; Rousey 1974; Weber 1965; Wylie et al. 1965) have selected from the psychiatric clinic those patients with speech/language disorders. The authors then looked for consistent psychiatric or personality characteristics in those patients. Such studies have typi-

---

[2]Authors who have used this approach include the following: Aimard et al. 1973; Alessi and Loomis 1988; Alessi et al. 1990; Baltaxe and Simmons 1988; Cantwell and Baker 1980; Chess 1944; Chess and Rosenberg 1974; Cohen et al. 1988, 1989, 1990; Friedlander et al. 1974; Gemelli 1982; Glasner 1949; Grinnell et al. 1983; Gualtieri et al. 1983; Ierodiakonou 1970; Kotsopoulos and Boodoosingh 1987; Livingood and Cohen-Sandler 1980; Loomis and Alessi 1988; Love and Thompson 1988; McHale 1967; Mehrhof and Rousey 1971; Rousey 1974; Teja et al. 1972; Weber 1965; Wylie et al. 1965.

Table 1-2. Some assessment tools used with speech/language–disordered children

Test or inventory	Reference(s)
Bell Adjustment Inventory	Duncan 1947
Bender Visual Motor Gestalt Test	Broad and Bar 1973; Butler 1965
Bristol Social Adjustment Scales	Petrie 1975; Sheridan and Peckham 1973
California Test of Personality	Nelson 1953; Prins 1972
Children's Apperception and Thematic Apperception Tests	Broad and Bar 1973; Fitzsimons 1958; Ierodiakonou 1970; Varbiro and Engelmayer 1972; Wirls and Plotkin 1971
Dignan Ego Identity Scale	Garbee 1973
Draw-a-Person Test	Wirls and Plotkin 1971
Index of Adjustment and Values	Barrett and Hoops 1974
Manifest Anxiety Scale	Yanagawa 1973–1974
Michigan Picture Inventory	English 1961
Missouri Children's Picture Series	Richman and Harper 1979
Minnesota Multiphasic Personality Inventory	Harper and Richman 1978; Muma et al. 1968
Rhode Sentence Completion Test	English 1961
Rorschach Test	Ierodiakonou 1970; Moller 1960; Santostefano 1960; Wilson and Lamb 1974; Wirls and Plotkin 1971
Rosenweig Picture Frustration Study	English 1961
Wechsler Digit Symbol Subtest (Wechsler Adult Intelligence Scale)	Trapp and Evan 1960

cally involved relatively small groups of patients, most often stutterers. The most commonly used methodology for these studies was chart reviews; some authors, however, have used personality tests (Ierodiakonou 1970), and others have used parent interviews (Gemelli 1982; Glasner 1949).

The second and more recent approach is to screen or examine an entire pool of psychiatric patients in order to determine if there is an elevated prevalence of speech/language disorders. Authors using this approach have examined both psychiatric outpatients and hospitalized psychiatric inpatients. The outpatients have been drawn from psychiatric hospitals (Alessi and Loomis 1988; Alessi et al. 1990; Baltaxe and Simmons 1988; Cohen et al. 1989; Grinnell et al. 1983; Gualtieri et al. 1983; Love and Thompson 1988), from child guidance centers (Kotsopoulos and Boodoosingh 1987; Teja et al. 1972), and from private psychiatric practice caseloads (Chess and Rosenberg 1974).

Both the studies involving outpatients and those involving hospitalized psychiatric inpatients (e.g., Baltaxe and Simmons 1988; Cantwell and Baker 1980; Grinnell et al. 1983) have reported much higher prevalences of speech/language disorders than would be found in the general population. Interestingly enough, however, the speech/language disorders of many of these psychiatric patients were undetected prior to the systematic speech and language evaluations done for purposes of research (Cohen et al. 1989).

One difficulty with the studies of psychiatrically ill children is that these children are not necessarily representative of speech/language–disordered children in general. By definition, a child referred for psychiatric evaluation or treatment is likely to have significant behavioral or emotional problems. For example, our study (Cantwell and Baker 1980) clearly showed that language-disordered children presenting to the UCLA Neuropsychiatric Institute were not typical of language-disordered children presenting to a community speech clinic. Specifically, children in the Neuropsychiatric Institute sample were highly likely to have mental retardation and/or infantile autism and a pervasive developmental disorder (PDD). Nonetheless, when the mentally retarded/PDD children were separated out, there were some interesting discoveries to be made about those psychiatric patients with the more "pure" language disorders.

Specific Types of Psychiatrically Ill Children

The speech/language functioning of children with specific types of psychiatric diagnoses has also been studied. A number of psychiatric syndromes are characterized by speech and language dysfunctions. These include infantile autism/PDD; psychosis/childhood schizophrenia; and possibly attention-deficit hyperactivity disorder (ADHD) and conduct disorder.

Infantile autism, pervasive developmental disorder, psychosis, and childhood schizophrenia. Of the childhood psychiatric syndromes involving speech and language, the most strikingly involved are infantile autism/PDD, psychosis, and childhood schizophrenia. These disorders are characterized by speech and language pathology that may include *mutism* (Baltaxe and Simmons 1975; Kurita 1985; Lotter 1967), *abnormalities or delays in speech prosody* (Fay and Schuler 1980; Kanner 1971), *articulation errors* (Boucher 1976; Shervanian 1967), *grammatical and semantic production and comprehension problems* (Bartolucci and Albers 1974; Fay and Mermelstein 1982; Ferrari 1982; Hingtgen and Bryson 1972; Kanner 1946; Layton-Thomas and Baker 1981; Pierce and Bartolucci 1977; Schwartz 1981; Snow et al. 1987; Tager-Flusberg 1985; Weiland and Legg 1964), and, perhaps most dramatically, *deviance in pragmatics or language usage* (Cantwell et al. 1978; Paul and Feldman 1984; Wetherby 1986). Children with these disorders clearly suffer from widespread linguistic and psychiatric deficits. Their speech/language disorders are rather different from those of other speech/language–disordered children, and their psychiatric symptomatology is distinct from the symptomatology of other psychiatrically ill children.

Attention-deficit hyperactivity disorder (ADHD). Of the other childhood psychiatric disorders that may have speech and language components in their symptomatology, ADHD is among the more studied. Two general types of studies involving interactional analyses and cognitive-memory tests have both yielded evidence suggestive of linguistic dysfunction in ADHD children.

There is now a rather substantial literature examining interactions between ADHD children (on and off medication) and their parents, peers, and teachers, or between each other. These studies suggest that ADHD children have interactional abnormalities that include the following:

1. Excessive verbal output (Barkley et al. 1983; Campbell 1973; Copeland 1979)
2. Lack of attention to the speaker (Barkley and Cunningham 1980)
3. Lack of compliance with commands and requests (Barkley 1985)
4. Failure to modulate social communication behaviors with shifting task demands (Landau and Milich 1988)
5. Limited initiation of new themes (Patterson 1981)
6. Decreased frequency of response to questions (Tarver-Behring et al. 1985)

There is also evidence of a possible "verbal mediation" deficit underlying ADHD (Barkley 1981; Camp 1977). Cognitive testing of ADHD children with listening, semantic categorization, verbal memory, naming, and/or reaction-time tasks has demonstrated that these children may have deficiencies in verbal and semantic organizational strategies (Ackerman et al. 1986; Agrawal and Kaushal 1987; August 1987; Felton et al. 1987; Tant and Douglas 1982; Tarver 1981; Zentall and Gohs 1984). Observations of ADHD children during cognitive tasks have indicated deficiencies in organizational strategies, communicative effectiveness, and verbal fluency (Hamlett et al. 1987). Similar production deficiencies have been reported in another study, although their occurrence was specific to certain types of stimulus inputs (Zentall 1988).

Also, two studies (Neeper 1985; Thorley 1984) examining the characteristics of hyperkinetic boys found elevated rates of speech/language disorders. In addition, speech and language studies of psychiatrically ill children have found that ADHD is the most common psychiatric diagnosis in children with concurrent speech/language disorders and psychiatric disorders (Beitchman et al. 1986a; Love and Thompson 1988).

Conduct disorder and juvenile delinquency. Delinquency is a sociolegal category that does not have a clearly defined psychiatric status. However, it appears that there is a large degree of overlap between the legal category of juvenile delinquency and the psychiatric category of conduct disorder. This overlap is relevant to the present work because there is some suggestion that juvenile delinquents have increased rates of speech and/or language deficits. Specifically, Brickman et al. (1984), Cozard and Rousey (1968), Ollendick (1979), Voorhees (1981), Wolff et al. (1982), and Zinkus and Gottlieb (1983) have reported elevated rates of speech/language disorders, verbal IQ deficits, and/or expressive-receptive impairments in delinquent individuals. In addition, several authors have suggested that conduct disorder may involve deficits in language development, language use (Hogan and Quay 1984), and verbal mediation (Jurkovic and Prentice 1977; Richman and Lindgren 1981). Furthermore, there is some suggestion that adult criminals have elevated rates of speech and/or language dysfunctions (Belenchia and Crowe 1983; Wagner et al. 1983). The data, however, are currently rather speculative.

Epidemiologic Population Studies

The studies outlined thus far have examined the relationship between psychiatric symptoms and disorders and speech/language disorders in relatively small samples of children from speech/language or psychiatric clinic pools. Another way to examine the relationship between speech/language disorders and psychiatric disorders is with large-scale epidemiologic samples.[3]

One of the earliest studies of this type is the Isle of Wight study (Rutter et al. 1970a). Although the study was designed to investigate brain damage, not speech/language disorders per se, it did find a correlation between speech/language disorder and psychiatric disorder. In this study, brain-damaged children with psychiatric disorder had high rates of concurrent speech/language disorders (69% for articulation defects and 75% for retarded language development). However, brain-damaged children who were psychiatrically well showed significantly lower rates of speech/language disorders (50% for articulation defects and 30% for retarded language development). These results suggest that impairments in language development are significantly associated with the presence of psychiatric disorder.

Later studies have found similar correlations. For example, in Stevenson and Richman's epidemiologic study (Richman and Stevenson 1977; Richman et al. 1982; Stevenson and Richman 1976, 1978) of 750 3-year-old children, behavioral problems were present in 59% of those with language disorders but in only 14% of those with normal language. Jenkins et al. (1980) found that 18% of children with normal behavior had speech and/or language problems, as opposed to 35% of children with behavior problems. Silva et al. (1984) found that in their epidemiologic sample of 3-year-olds, those with speech delays had significantly more behavioral problems according to both parent and teacher reports than did the nonspeech-delayed 3-year-olds. Also, Beitchman (1985; Beitchman et al. 1983) found that in a 1-in-3 sample of kindergartners in Canada, psychiatric illness was present in 54% of the speech/language–disordered children but in only 12% of the nonspeech/language–disordered children.

Follow-ups of epidemiologic samples have also revealed that early speech and/or language problems are predictive of later psychiatric and behavioral problems. Two such studies are those by Fundudis et al. (1979) and Lerner et al. (1985). The Fundudis et al. study found that the association between speech/language disorders and psychiatric disorders held even after the extremely impaired children (i.e., autistic, mute, mentally retarded, or neurologically impaired) were separated out. These authors followed 102 children at age 7 years who

---

[3]Studies using this approach include those reported in Beitchman et al. 1983; Fundudis et al. 1979; Jenkins et al. 1980; Lerner et al. 1985; Richman and Stevenson 1977; Richman et al. 1982; Rutter et al. 1970a; Silva et al. 1984; Stevenson and Richman 1978.

had been speech/language retarded at age 3. They found that the speech/language–retarded children were significantly more impaired than the children who were not speech/language retarded according to teacher questionnaires, personality inventories, psychologists' evaluations, and psychiatrists' interviews. The Lerner et al. study was an 11-year follow-up of 3- to 5-year-old preschoolers. Using the Diagnostic Interview for Children and Adolescents parent and child interviews to establish psychiatric diagnoses, these authors found that the presence of psychiatric illness at follow-up was strongly associated with the presence of an early speech and/or language problem.

Surveys of Professionals

The final source of information regarding the possible association of psychiatric disorders and speech/language disorders is surveys of professionals in the field. Two studies that have obtained such data (Bennett and Runyan 1982; Blood and Seiden 1981) were somewhat dissimilar: one (Blood and Seiden 1981) surveyed speech pathologists regarding children who stutter, and the other (Bennett and Runyan 1982) surveyed school teachers regarding speech/language–disordered children. As with much of the literature, particularly when methodological approaches differ, the results of these two studies were contradictory.

Research Aims of the Present Study

Many of the studies in the literature suffer from methodological flaws (which will be discussed in more detail in Chapter 2). However, the weight of the literature clearly suggests that children with speech/language disorders are an at-risk group for emotional and behavioral problems. The studies, however, do not provide much insight into the possible mechanisms underlying such an association. Furthermore, the prevalence and types of psychiatric disorders found in children with speech/language disorders have not been reliably quantified.

Thus, the present study aimed to examine the prevalence and types of psychiatric disorders in children with speech/language disorders using a methodology designed to avoid the flaws found in other studies. As well as determining the prevalence and types of psychiatric disorders in children with speech/language disorders, a major goal of this study was to isolate those factors that are associated with psychiatric disorder. This is an area that has not been explored in the literature. Among the factors that were considered were the following:

1. Type, age of onset, severity, and duration of the speech/language disorder
2. Age and sex of the child
3. Neurological status of the child
4. Presence of hearing impairment and/or other biological-medical factors
5. Intellectual level
6. Educational level and history
7. Family structure and history
8. Demographic factors
9. Psychosocial factors (such as rejection by peers, lack of social integration, and impaired social relationships)

The particular hypotheses that were examined in our study were the following:

1. There is a high prevalence of psychiatric disorder in the speech- and language-disordered sample.
2. The types of psychiatric disorders found are those found in children of the same age in the general population.
3. There is a correlation between the presence of psychiatric disorder and the types of speech/language disturbance.
4. There is a correlation between types of speech/language problems and the types of psychiatric difficulty.
5. There is a correlation between certain aspects of the speech or language disturbance, such as severity and duration, and the type of psychiatric disorder.
6. Some environmental factors (such as family structure, socioeconomic class, medical problems, or psychosocial stress) may predict the presence of psychiatric disorder in certain subgroups of children.

Background Literature on Speech/Language Disorders and Learning Disorders

The literature summarized above suggests that children with speech/language impairments are at risk for psychiatric disorders. There is also evidence in the literature that children with speech/language impairments are at risk for learning disorders. The evidence comes from three different types of studies (see Appendix 3): 1) studies (concurrent or follow-up) of the academic achievement of children with speech/language disorders; 2) studies of the language functioning of children with learning disorders; and 3) follow-up population studies examining the development of learning disorders in large groups of children.

Academic Achievement of Children With Speech/Language Disorders

Few studies have specifically examined the learning of children with speech/language disorders. One problem is that the majority of speech/language–disordered children present while they are still in the preschool age-range. Hence, in order to obtain data on the academic achievement of these children, it is often necessary to do a follow-up study. Even with follow-up studies, the main focus is generally not learning status. Consequently, when learning is mentioned, it is often not systematically or operationally defined. Thus, many of the studies have relied upon impressionistic information derived from parent interviews or from reports of school placement. Studies presenting objective data such as the results of educational achievement tests are particularly rare. Part of the reason for this, however, is that there is no standard definition of learning disorder in use today. In fact, in a recent National Institute of Mental Health workshop, Karp (1987) reported that in 1984 there were more than 50 definitions of learning disorder in use across the United States.

Of the studies that have reported on the concurrent learning status of speech/language–disordered children, two dealt with stutterers (Bubenickova 1977; Williams et al. 1969), one dealt with "speech defective" children (Butler et al. 1973), two dealt with articulation-impaired children (Everhart 1953; Nelson 1953), four dealt with language-delayed or language-disordered children (Alessi et al. 1990; de Ajuriaguerra et al. 1976; Garvey and Gordon 1973; Gillam and Johnston 1985), and one dealt with children with cleft palate (Ruess 1965). Follow-up studies mentioning the learning status of speech/language–disordered children have included studies dealing with language disorders (Aram and Nation 1980; Aram et al. 1984; Fundudis et al. 1980; Hall and Tomblin 1978; Levi et al. 1982; Richman et al. 1982; Wolpaw et al. 1979), speech/language disorders (Griffiths 1969; King et al. 1982), articulation disorder (Hall and Tomblin 1978), and speech retardation (Klackenberg 1980; Sheridan and Peckham 1975, 1978).

The information available from these studies is generally quite consistent in indicating that some types of learning difficulties are common among school-age children who have or have had speech and/or language problems. It appears that the learning difficulties span a variety of areas including reading, spelling, written language, print matching, and arithmetic. The relative severity levels and frequencies of these different types of problems remain a mystery.

Linguistic Functioning of Learning-Disordered Children

The second relevant type of study involves the linguistic status of children with learning difficulties. The belief that learning-disordered children may have underlying linguistic deficits is one that is now gaining popularity. This belief is, in fact, reflected in United States Public Law 94-142 (1975), the Education of the Handicapped Act, which defines specific learning disabilities as "a disorder in one or more of the basic psychological processes involved in understanding or in using language."

There is now a relatively large literature confirming the presence of some type of language disorder among samples of learning-disordered children. The different types of language difficulties that have been identified tend to fall into four general areas: 1) syntactic and grammatical development, 2) semantic or concept development, 3) pragmatic usage, and 4) comprehension. However, linguistic difficulties have also been reported in learning-disordered children in overall language functioning (Reid and Hresko 1980) and in the phonological (or sound-system) area of language (Godfrey et al. 1981; Jerger et al. 1987; Snowling 1981; Wiig and Semel 1980).

With regard to syntactic and grammatical development, widespread deficits have been reported among learning-disordered students, including deficient or deviant overall syntactic development (Anderson 1982; Andolina 1980; Donahue et al. 1982; Hook and Johnson 1978; Hresko 1975, 1979; Lapointe 1976; Morris and Crump 1982; Olsen et al. 1983; Whitehouse 1983), difficulties retaining or recalling grammatical structures (Cambourne and Rousch 1982), and difficulties producing grammatical structures (Hresko 1979). In addition, more narrow difficulties involving specific syntactic structures have been reported among learning-disordered students. Examples of these include difficulties with verb-tense markers (Moran and Byrne 1977), delayed morphological acquisition (Vogel 1983; Wiig et al. 1973), difficulties with syntactic rules for pronoun reference (Fayne 1981), and deficits involving nonlexical grammatical markers (Kean 1984).

In the area of semantic development, difficulties have been reported with word finding, labeling, and naming tasks (Denckla et al. 1981; German 1979; Lewis and Kass 1982; Noel 1980; Pajurkova et al. 1976; Rudel 1980; Rudel et al. 1981; Wiig and Semel 1975), lexical diversity (Levi et al. 1984; Morris and Crump 1982), word association (Israel 1984), semantic memory (Cambourne and Rousch 1982; Klein-Konigsberg 1984; Lewis and Kass 1982; Lorsbach 1982), and semantic processing (Ceci 1982). In addition, semantic difficulties have been reported with certain specific types of words, including abstract nouns (Dean and Kundert 1981), pronouns (Fayne 1981), determiners (Kean 1984), and words referring to quantity and spatial concepts (Kavale 1982).

In the area of pragmatic usage, difficulties have been reported in general interactional skills (Moore and Simpson 1983), role-playing abilities (Dickstein and Warren 1980; Matthews et al. 1982), requests and persuasion tasks (Donahue 1981; Markoski 1983), dealing with limited information and/or requests for clarification (Donahue et al. 1980), initiation of conversations (Donahue 1983), and code switching or adapting to a listener (Knight-Arest 1984; Soensken et al. 1981).

The comprehension difficulties reported among learning-disordered students have included difficulties with nonverbal communication (Bryan 1977), comprehension strategies (Gambrell and Heathington 1981), auditory processing of language (Blalock 1982; Godfrey et al. 1981; Jerger et al. 1987; Klein-Konigsberg 1984), and general language-comprehension tasks (Byrne 1981; Fayne 1981; Gambrell and Heathington 1981; Lapointe 1976; Semel and Wiig 1975; Wiig 1976).

The language studies of learning-disordered children have produced some rather compelling evidence of linguistic dysfunctions. However, these studies have not proven the existence of linguistic dysfunctions underlying all cases of learning disorder. Because learning disorder is a generic term referring to a heterogeneous group of disorders, it is unclear whether the linguistic deficits are present in all learning-disordered children or only in children with certain subtypes of learning disorder. There are, however, two cluster-analysis studies of learning disorder that argue strongly for the importance of linguistic factors. Lyon and Watson (1981) used hierarchical cluster analysis to establish subgroups of learning-disordered children and found that some type of linguistic dysfunction was a key factor in approximately half of the learning-disordered children studied. Feagans and Appelbaum (1986), in a more detailed cluster-analysis study, found that using purely linguistic features, they could classify all their learning-disordered and nonlearning-disordered subjects into six clusters. These clusters were subsequently validated by different achievement profiles 3 years later.

Epidemiologic Follow-up Studies

The final type of study that provides information on the association between learning achievement and speech/language disorders is the follow-up of a large epidemiologic sample of children. Such studies have revealed correlations between early speech/language disorders and later learning problems (Calnan and Richardson 1976; Richman et al. 1982; Silva 1986; Silva and Williams 1983) and between later reading difficulties and earlier word-repetition difficulties (Mann 1984). Unfortunately, there are few large-scale follow-up studies that have examined the association between speech/language disorders and learning.

Research Aims of the Present Study

The literature indicates that there is a close relationship between speech/language disorders and learning disorders. Unfortunately, there are methodological problems with much of the research.

In the present study we examined the prevalence and types of learning disorders in children with speech/language disorders and tried to identify factors determining any association between the two disorders. Particular hypotheses that were examined in our study included the following:

1. There is an elevated prevalence of learning disorders in the speech- and language-disordered sample.
2. There is a correlation between the presence of learning disorders and certain types of speech/language disturbance.
3. There is a correlation between types of learning problems and psychiatric problems.

The methodology used in our research is described in detail in Chapter 2. The data obtained regarding the prevalence and types of psychiatric and learning disorders found in speech- and/or language-impaired children are presented in Chapter 3. The data pertaining to the correlates of psychiatric disorders and the correlates of learning disorders are presented in the subsequent chapters.

2 Research Methodology

AMONG ALL MEDICAL SPECIALTIES, psychiatry has traditionally had a poor reputation for research output, and, in particular, child psychiatry has been behind adult psychiatry in both quality and quantity of research. Part of this problem is related to certain difficulties specific to the field of child psychiatry (see Cantwell 1979). Such difficulties typically result either from the fact that it is a child who is the research subject or from limitations in available psychiatric assessment, diagnosis, and classification systems.

The child makes a particularly difficult research subject for a number of reasons. Because it is often difficult to communicate verbally with the child, many of the methods used in adult psychiatric research are inadequate. Even such basic tasks as making contact with the subject, engaging his or her cooperation, and maintaining his or her interest, are more difficult when dealing with children than with adults.

Furthermore, because the child is a growing organism actively developing in many spheres, the clinician effectively sees a "different child" at different points in time. This poses problems not only for longitudinal studies but also for "single-time" studies. For example, a behavioral pattern that is "normal" at one age may be "abnormal" at another; thus, age considerations are diagnostically relevant. Consequently, proper diagnosis requires both a developmental and a longitudinal approach.

Finally, because the child lives in a complex family and social environment that continually influences his or her behavior and development, multiple and complex variables must be considered in research. For practical and ethical reasons, most of these variables cannot be manipulated experimentally. Additionally, issues of patients' rights are more complex when dealing with children, both because of their limited comprehension of research and because of the unknown impact of experimental processes upon long-term development. Consequently, many kinds of study in the field of child psychiatry must be based on "experiments of nature."

Below, the sampling, assessment, diagnostic, and data-analysis problems that occur in child psychiatry research are discussed. Particular reference is made to how some of these problems have manifested themselves in the studies to date of speech/language–disordered children. Finally, the methodology of the present study of speech/language–disordered children is described with respect to how previous methodological weaknesses were avoided.

Research Issues in Child Psychiatry

Sampling Problems

A well-designed study of speech/language–disordered children requires the selection of a sample of children for study who are representative of the general population of speech/language–disordered children. A large-scale epidemiologic sample from the general population has the greatest likelihood of being representative. However, such an approach is both inefficient and expensive (Kraemer et al. 1987), because a very large number of nonspeech/language–disordered children must be tested in order to discover a much smaller number of disordered children.

As observed by Rutter (1989b), studies using samples of children obtained from a clinic setting are more likely to be unrepresentative because of referral bias. Such bias is most likely when a small number of patients are studied and/or when the clinic itself constitutes a very "biased" source (e.g., a specialty clinic oriented toward one particular type of patient). With regard to studies of speech/language–disordered children, samples drawn from a psychiatric or child-guidance clinic represent a common type of sampling bias (as mentioned in the discussion of the literature in Chapter 1). Other types of bias that were seen in the literature were socioeconomic-class bias, age bias, and treatment bias. The selection of children from a private patient caseload often produces a socioeconomic-class bias, because patients from lower socioeconomic classes often cannot afford private treatment. Selection of samples from school settings may also result in socioeconomic-class bias, as well as in the age bias inherent in the particular type of school. Additionally, bias may occur after subjects have been selected through refusals to participate or as a result of dropouts during a study. Small sample size was also a common source of methodological weakness in the reviewed studies of speech/language–disordered children. Studies using small samples may be weak not only because the narrower range of children studied may be less representative but also because a small number of children cannot provide data on a wider range of variables (such as age, severity, or types of disorders). Furthermore, smaller samples do not have the power to detect small differences or to estimate their significance.

Rutter (1989b) also criticized psychiatric clinic samples (which, by definition, contain patients who are already psychiatrically ill) as requiring dependence upon retrospective recall in order to examine the possible risk factors associated with psychiatric illness. Nonetheless, Rutter observed that causal hypotheses regarding psychiatric illness can be tested using high-risk samples. Furthermore, Rutter explained that an epidemiologic study does not have to be a population study. Rather, what is distinctive about an epidemiologic study is a distribution of disorders in a defined population together with examination of the factors associated with variations in the distribution. Insofar as the literature suggests that a sample of children with speech/language disorders may be at high risk for psychiatric disorders, such a sample could provide insights into the risk factors associated with the development of psychiatric disorder.

Assessment and Diagnosis Problems

The diagnostic process in child psychiatry can be conceptualized as the determination of answers to a series of questions (Cantwell 1980). These questions include the following:

- Is there a disorder present?
- If so, what disorder is present?
- What are the possible etiological factors?
- What forces may be maintaining the problem?
- What strengths (e.g., within the family, school, or psychosocial environment) may offset the effects of the child's disorder?

Making these determinations is a difficult task requiring that a large amount of information be obtained and analyzed. For each child, specific information must be obtained both on problems or symptoms (e.g., developmental lags, situational and qualitative variations in behavior) and on competencies or strengths (e.g., within the family, at school, and with peers) (Achenbach 1986). Furthermore, a longitudinal approach is necessary in order to differentiate between problems that are severe or persistent and the minor or transient difficulties that may normally occur in children. Thus, information is needed regarding 1) the duration of the child's behavioral disturbance, 2) the type of problem and its frequency, 3) the intensity of the problem (or the degree of abnormality in comparison to age and sex norms), 4) the presence of other associated abnormalities, and 5) the circumstances in which the behavior occurs.

Assessment and diagnosis in the field of child psychiatry has been hampered by a lack of reliable and valid assessment tools for collecting the information necessary to the diagnostic process. Projective assessment procedures are of particularly dubious reliability and validity (Gittelman 1980). In addition to problems with assessment instruments, there are problems with the psychiatric diagnostic classification systems themselves.

Similarly, in the field of speech/language pathology, assessment and diagnosis problems are common. As in child psychiatry, there is a lack of standardized assessment instruments that cover the full range of behaviors and that are diagnostically relevant. Thus, tests using standardized administration and scoring procedures are needed for many areas of speech and language development. The literature reveals that instead of such tools, subjective evaluations of speech and language have frequently been used, producing results of questionable reliability. In speech-language pathology, as in child psychiatry, there has been limited development of classification systems for disorders based on operational definitions of the various disorders.

With regard to the classification of child and adolescent psychopathology, rapid changes in the field have resulted in the availability of only limited amounts of empirical data by which to assess the reliability and validity of many diagnoses. In other areas of medicine, conversely, symptom patterns have been validated by data demonstrating shared prognoses, responses to treatment, and/or etiologies. In the case of childhood psychiatric diagnostic categories, however, there is a lack of knowledge of etiology, the existing knowledge of prognosis is fragmentary, and little is known of the differential response to treatment (Cantwell 1979). As a result, the external validity of most child psychiatric diagnostic categories is less than optimal.

Another problem with the psychiatric diagnostic classifications is that until recently there has been limited use of operational definitions for the various categories. This was especially true for DSM-I (American Psychiatric Association 1952) and DSM-II (American Psychiatric

Association 1968), which provided no specific criteria for the diagnosis of any types of psychiatric disorders. Furthermore, both DSM-I and DSM-II dealt primarily with adult psychopathology: DSM-I had no real classification of childhood and adolescent disorders, and DSM-II provided only one overall category of disorders with six subtypes described in very brief clinical notes.

The present study was able to benefit from DSM-III (American Psychiatric Association 1980), which provided the first detailed diagnostic breakdown of childhood and adolescent psychopathology along with clearly stated diagnostic criteria for each category. However, since our study was completed, DSM-III was revised and reissued as DSM-III-R (American Psychiatric Association 1987). This revision entailed a number of changes in the classification of childhood and adolescent psychiatric disorders that are discussed elsewhere by the present authors (Cantwell and Baker 1988). The diagnostic criteria for many of the childhood and adolescent disorders did not change significantly in DSM-III-R. However, some of the definitions of specific disorders in DSM-III-R are rather different from those of DSM-III, and, consequently, some of the results of the present study would have been different had DSM-III-R been used. It is unlikely that the overall prevalence rate for psychiatric illness would have been affected. The specific diagnoses most likely affected (e.g., infantile autism, attention-deficit disorder without hyperactivity) are discussed in more detail in Chapter 3.

As the present manuscript was being written, we were involved with the formation of DSM-IV, which will supplant DSM-III-R in early 1993. Many issues are being addressed (Shaffer et al. 1989), including compatibility with the 10th revision of the *International Classification of Diseases* (ICD-10), multiaxial decisions, and specific diagnoses such as subthreshold and adjustment disorders. The significance of such possible changes for DSM-IV with regard to the findings of the present study is discussed in Chapter 3.

Finally, it should be mentioned that all of the DSM diagnostic systems are categorical systems having specific diagnostic criteria based on phenomenology. Another approach to the diagnosis and classification of psychopathology is the dimensional system of classification (e.g., Achenbach and Edelbrock 1978, 1989; Achenbach and McConaughty 1987; Jenkins 1966; Lessing et al. 1976; Quay 1966, 1972; Rescorla 1986; Wolff 1971). Dimensional classification systems may be viewed as complementary to the categorical classification systems. For example, a child with the categorical diagnosis of attention-deficit disorder may also have underlying symptoms in other areas that do not meet the full criteria for another diagnosis. In the present study, data from parent and teacher rating scales provided a dimensional measure to the classification of psychopathology. Thus, in addition to having the categorical diagnosis, it could be seen to what degree an individual child manifested symptoms of other disorders such as hyperactivity and depression. It remains for future research to ultimately determine which set of diagnostic criteria are "correct" in the sense of being able to better predict outcome without treatment, treatment response, and biological and psychosocial correlates of illness.

Data-Analysis Problems

The most common data-analysis error found in the studies of speech/language–disordered children has to do with ignoring or "confounding" of variables. Because there are a large number of factors that may contribute to speech/language disorders or psychiatric disorders, these factors need to be considered separately in data analysis. Such factors include the following:

- Age of the child
- Age of onset of the speech/language problem
- Severity of the speech/language problem
- Medical and audiologic status of the child
- Educational status of the child
- Intellectual status of the child
- Socioeconomic class of the child
- Demographic and family background of the child

Methodology of the Present Study

The present study was a clinical diagnostic study examining the prevalence, type, and correlates of psychopathology in a sample of children with speech/language disorders. Although the sample was drawn from a speech/language clinic, it was not a clinical sample in the sense of the children having been referred because of psychopathology. Rather, the children were selected because of having a handicap in one other particular area, namely communication skills. It was hypothesized that because of this handicap, the children as a group were at high risk for psychopathology; consequently, the study of this sample of children may provide insights into the mechanisms by which psychopathology develops.

The methodology of the present study was generally modeled after that of the Isle of Wight studies (Rutter et al. 1970a, 1970b,

1976b). As in the Isle of Wight studies, the methodology for the present study employed 1) an operational definition of psychiatric disorder, 2) multiple standardized assessment instruments (e.g., parent and child interviews, parent and teacher rating scales), and 3) psychiatric diagnoses following a specified diagnostic classification scheme. Thus, the methodology in this study was an advance over previous studies in the area that had used terms such as "emotionally maladjusted," "disturbed," or other broad terms that are not revealing about the nature of the psychopathology.

The present study was also unique for its use of strict definitions of speech/language disorders, comprehensive multifaceted assessments of both psychopathology and speech/language functioning, and rigorous assessments of ancillary areas (e.g., academic functioning, neurological status, parental psychopathology, and aspects of parent-child interaction). The details of the sample selection, speech/language assessment and diagnosis, psychiatric assessment and diagnosis, and other evaluations (e.g., neurological status, hearing, family assessment) used in the present study are described below.

Sample Selection

A sample size of 600 was chosen in order, first, to provide a sufficiently large number of children to exemplify the wide range of diagnoses, severity levels, and ages of children who have speech/language disorders and, second, to measure differences between subgroups. In order to feasibly obtain such a large number of speech/language–disordered children, the sample was drawn from incoming new patients presenting to a large community speech-and-hearing clinic in the greater Los Angeles area. This clinic served as a referral source for agencies (including MediCal, Regional Center, the State Department of Rehabilitation, the Cleft Palate Society, and the Easter Seal Agency), as well as for a large number of private physicians such as pediatricians, ear-nose-throat specialists, and neurologists. For this reason, the sample pool lacked a socioeconomic-class bias.

To prevent "contamination" of the subjects by therapy or treatment programs, the subjects were selected from the new incoming cases that presented to the clinic for their first speech/language evaluation. The research study was described to patients as providing an additional free evaluation covering psychological, linguistic, educational, and psychiatric functioning. As a result, there was a low refusal rate (2%).

Speech/Language Evaluation

Two different approaches to speech/language evaluation were used in the present study: formal (standardized) tests and informal naturalistic observational ratings. The standardized tests were used in order to provide a consistent sampling of linguistic skills across children and so that normative scores could be obtained for each child in each of the different areas of linguistic skills. A free-speech analysis was also used for a variety of reasons. At the time the study began, standardized tests were not available for all age levels of children and for all areas of linguistic development. Furthermore, certain types of information (e.g., how a child uses language in a communicative situation) could not be obtained at all through formal testing. Finally, the free-speech analysis was needed for those children who would not cooperate in a formal testing situation.

Thus, in this study, disordered speech and language were defined operationally in terms of both scores on the standardized tests and in terms of observed behaviors. The operational definitions of the various types of speech/language disorders are described below.

Operational Definitions of Speech Disorders

Speech, or the motor production of the sounds of a language, involves several aspects: articulation (accurately pronouncing the sounds), fluency (stringing the sounds together in a smooth rhythm), rate of speech, and voice quality. Hence, four different types of speech disorders were operationally defined in the present study. Children who met the diagnostic criteria for any one of these types of disorders were considered to have a "speech disorder."

Articulation disorder. Articulation disorder is characterized by frequent and recurring mispronunciations of one or more speech sounds as compared with the pronunciation of most people of the same age in the same community (Baker and Cantwell 1985a; Cantwell and Baker 1987b). The presence of articulation disorder was determined in the present study by one of two standardized tests of articulation: the Goldman-Fristoe Test of Articulation (Goldman and Fristoe 1972) or the Denver Articulation Screening Exam (Drumwright 1971). Articulation disorder was operationally defined as a score (on either of these tests) below the 20th percentile for the child's chronological age level.

For the small percentage of children who could not be evaluated with these tests (because of refusal or inability to participate in testing), a sample of each child's speech was elicited, and the occurrences of correct articulations and misarticulations were noted. The child's articulatory inventory was then compared to published articulation norms (Sander 1972; Templin 1957). Articulation disorder was operationally defined as frequent misarticulations of any sounds that at least 75% of same-aged children, according to the norms, would correctly articulate.

Other speech disorders. The diagnosis of other types of speech disorders was made by the independent subjective ratings of the sample of free speech. Subjective ratings were necessary because standardized test procedures did not exist at the time of the study for the diagnoses of stuttering, voice disorder, or rate of speech disorder. For each of these diagnoses, independent ratings were made by three separate raters (i.e., two speech pathologists and a psycholinguist). *Speech dysfluency,* or *stuttering,* was defined as repetitions or prolongations of words or sounds, or as inappropriate silent intervals in speech, occurring throughout a variety of speech situations and being sufficiently marked so as either to impair communication or to cause distress to the child. *Rate of speech disorder* was defined as speech that was so rapid that more than 10% of utterances were rendered unintelligible. *Voice disorder* was defined as abnormal pitch, loudness, nasality, or hoarseness noticeable throughout the majority of a representative sample of speech.

Operational Definitions of Language Disorders

For the purposes of the present study, four major areas of language were evaluated: comprehension, expression, processing, and pragmatics. Definitions of disordered functioning were established for each area using evaluation procedures consisting of either standardized tests or an analysis of a language sample. Children who met the diagnostic criteria for any one of these types of disorders were considered to have a "language disorder."

Language-comprehension disorder. At the time the study was designed, there was no single comprehensive test of language comprehension that was normed for the wide age-range of children involved in the study. Consequently, *language-comprehension disorder* was operationally defined in the study using several different instruments depending upon the age levels of the children. The different standardized instruments used to assess language-comprehension disorder included the Peabody Picture Vocabulary Test (Dunn 1965); the Receptive-Expressive-Emergent Language (REEL) Scale, receptive portion (Bzoch and League 1971); the Test of Auditory Comprehension of Language (Carrow 1973/1978); and the Token Test for Children

Table 2-1. Definition of language-comprehension disorder

Age level	Procedure used	Definition of "disorder"
Below 3 years	Receptive-Expressive-Emergent Language (REEL) Scale, receptive portion (Bzoch and League 1971)	More than 6 months below chronological age
3 to 6 years	Test of Auditory Comprehension of Language (Carrow 1973/1978)	Below 20th percentile for age level
7 to 12.5 years	Token Test for Children (DiSimoni 1978)	Two SDs or more below mean on any subtest
All	Peabody Picture Vocabulary Test (Dunn 1965)	Standard score of 69 or less

Note. SD = standard deviation.

(DiSimoni 1978). The ages of children for which each test was used and the specific cutoff scores that were taken to indicate the presence of a deficit are outlined in Table 2-1.

Expressive language disorder. No single standardized test was available at the time of the study for assessing the expressive language of all the age levels of children in the study. Hence, a variety of tests and subtests were used, including the following: the expressive portion of the REEL Scale (Bzoch and League 1971); the verbal expression and grammatic closure subtests of the Illinois Test of Psycholinguistic Abilities (ITPA) (Kirk et al. 1968); and the Carrow Elicited Language Inventory (Carrow 1974). The age levels of children for each test and the specific cutoff scores that were taken to indicate the presence of a deficit are outlined in Table 2-2.

In addition, because the existing standardized tests elicited only a limited sample of expressive language, an analysis of a spontaneous-language sample was also included as part of the assessment. The spontaneous-language sample was obtained in a clinical setting, with the child seated at a table and having a variety of toys, art supplies, and pictures. The child was permitted to play freely with the materials. If necessary, speech was prompted by means of open-ended questions such as, "Tell me about this," "What are you doing?" and "What's happening now?"

A corpus of 50 utterances was analyzed for each child's speech. Three measures obtained were grammatical complexity (as defined by the Developmental Sentence Scoring method [Lee 1974]), mean utter-

Table 2-2. Definition of expressive language disorder

Age level	Procedure used	Definition of "disorder"
Below 3 years	Receptive-Expressive-Emergent Language (REEL) Scale, expressive portion (Bzoch and League 1971)	Score more than 6 months below chronological age
3 to 10 years	Illinois Test of Psycholinguistic Abilities (ITPA), verbal expression and grammatic closure subtests (Kirk et al. 1968)	Psycholinguistic age 6 months or more below chronological age level
3 to 8 years	Carrow Elicited Language Inventory (Carrow 1974)	Below 20th percentile for age level
All	Spontaneous-language sample analyzed (Brown 1973; Lee 1974) and converted to age levels using norms in literature	Estimated "expressive age" 6 months or more below chronological age
All	Spontaneous-language sample rated for message nonfluency, word-finding difficulty, overgeneralization, and limited output	More than five occurrences of any one of these features in 50-word spontaneous sample

ance length, and "stage" of language development. (The latter two measures were based on the definition of Brown [1973].) Each child's "expressive age level" was determined using these three measures. Any child whose levels were more than 6 months below his or her chronological age level was considered to have an "expressive language disorder." When an adequate spontaneous language sample could not be obtained (e.g., with extremely shy children who were reluctant to vocalize spontaneously), the Carrow Elicited Language Inventory was used to elicit a sample of utterances. This instrument uses an imitation format to elicit utterances of increasing grammatical complexity. The imitation approach has been shown to correlate with the spontaneous speech analysis in measures of grammatical complexity (Connell and Myles-Zitzer 1982; Lahey et al. 1983; Rodd and Braine 1971).

In addition, the presence of features suggestive of expressive language disorder was noted when they occurred in the free-speech sample. Such features included nonfluency of message (numerous pauses of inordinate length before responses, numerous revisions or self-interruptions, and/or false starts); word-finding difficulty (defined by

Nicolosi et al. [1983] as an inability to evoke words corresponding to specific concepts); limited verbal output; and semantic over-generalizations (excessive use of deictic expressions such as "this," "that," or "it," or of generics such as "thing," or "stuff"). Children who showed marked presence of such features were considered to have an expressive language disorder.

Thus, the operational definition of an expressive language disorder used both observational and formal testing criteria. (See Table 2-2 for a more detailed presentation of these criteria.) A child who met *any* of the diagnostic criteria listed in Table 2-2 was considered to have an "expressive language disorder."

Language processing disorder. *Language processing* refers to the act of receiving, perceiving, encoding, and decoding spoken language (Cantwell and Baker 1987b). As discussed in Chapter 1, the skills involved in language processing are not well understood. However, among the many skills that appear to be involved, the following are generally recognized as crucial: auditory attention, auditory discrimination, auditory memory, sound synthesis, sound segmentation, and sequencing.

Language processing was assessed in the present study using standardized tests. As with language expression and comprehension, no single test was applicable to the entire age-range of subjects in the study, so a variety of tests were used. These included the auditory reception, auditory association, auditory sequential memory, auditory closure, and sound blending subtests of the ITPA (Kirk et al. 1968); the Memory for Sentences Test (Spencer 1958); the auditory attention subtests of the Detroit Tests of Learning Aptitude (Baker and Leland 1967); and the Auditory Discrimination Test (Wepman 1958/1973). The specific definitions of "language processing disorder" used in the study (including the age levels of children and the cutoff definitions for each of the tests) are summarized in Table 2-3.

Pragmatic language disorder. The final aspect of language that was evaluated in the study was *pragmatics,* or language usage. At the time the study was designed, no definitions or tests were published for this aspect of language. Hence, subjective ratings were made of the presence of various "features of abnormal usage" in the children's spontaneous speech. The features selected for rating included delayed echolalia, echolalia, egocentric speech, excessive verbal output, inappropriate language usage, neologisms, poor topic maintenance, pronoun reversals, and undergeneralizations. The operational definitions of these features of pragmatic language disorder are given in Table 2-4. Children exhibiting significant presence of two or more

Table 2-3. Definition of language processing disorder

Age level	Procedure used	Definition of "disorder"
3 to 10 years	Auditory reception, association, sequential memory, closure, and sound blending subtests of the Illinois Test of Psycholinguistic Abilities (ITPA) (Kirk et al. 1968)	Psycholinguistic age of 6 months or more below chronological age
3 to 10 years	Memory for Sentences Test (Spencer 1958)	Age-level score 6 months or more below chronological age
3 to 19 years	Detroit Tests of Learning Aptitude (Baker and Leland 1967); auditory attention subtests	Age-level score more than 6 months below chronological age
5 to 8 years	Auditory Discrimination Test (Wepman 1958/1973)	Score below "adequacy" threshold

of these features were considered to have a "pragmatic language disorder."

Assessment of Childhood Psychopathology

As stated above, the assessment of childhood psychopathology begins by obtaining a large amount of data pertaining to the problems or symptoms of the child, their situational and qualitative variations, and the competencies or strengths of the child. Because of the well-documented lack of reliability between different types of informants (Achenbach et al. 1987a, 1987b; Angold et al. 1987; Edelbrock et al. 1986; Gould et al. 1981; Herjanic and Reich 1982; Kashani et al. 1985; Kazdin et al. 1983; Moretti et al. 1985; Stavrakaki et al. 1987; Verhulst et al. 1987; Weissman et al. 1987), it is also necessary that information be collected from multiple sources. Parents, for example, typically provide adequate information about the child's home behavior but may be unaware or unconcerned about other aspects of the child such as learning, concentration in school, peer interactions, or "private" symptomatology (such as hallucinations, delusional thinking, or suicidal ideation). Children provide better information about private symptomatology as well as depressive symptomatology, but may be reluctant to admit to symptoms of overt behavior disorders, and especially conduct disorders.

Table 2-4. Symptoms of pragmatic language disorder

Delayed echolalia	Repetition of utterances heard some time ago
Echolalia	Immediate repetitions of own or other's utterances with no communicative function
Egocentric speech	Self-directed utterances
Excessive verbal output	Many spontaneous utterances and overly rapid speech
Inappropriate usage	Utterances conveying bizarre or inappropriate information
Neologisms	Use of words with idiosyncratic meaning
Poor topic maintenance	Rapid and inappropriate changes of topic with no transitional cues or no turn taking
Pronoun reversals	Switching of the pronouns "I/me" and "you"
Undergeneralization	Use of very narrow word meanings or overly personalized or concrete words or statements

Consequently, the present study tapped parents, teachers, and the children themselves as sources for psychiatric symptomatology information. Data were collected using a variety of methods (enumerated in Table 2-5), including parent interviews, child interviews, and parent and teacher behavior rating scales (see below).

Parent interview. Because the parent interview is considered the single best source of information for psychiatric diagnosis of the child (Rutter et al. 1970a), the present study employed a very detailed parent interview. Aspects of childhood behaviors and psychopathology covered in the parent interview included the chief complaint, the symptom inventory, recent behavior, and temperament and personality characteristics. In addition, past and present medical, developmental, and family histories were explored in interviews with (one or both) parents.

The parent interview consisted of both a structured section and an unstructured section in order to elicit both "factual" information and "feeling" information about major and minor events. The structured section of the interview consisted of the Diagnostic Interview for Children and Adolescents (DICA) (Herjanic and Reich 1982; Welner et al. 1987). This interview was selected for both parents and children because at the time the study was begun it was the most comprehensive standardized interview available. (Subsequently, several other equally comprehensive standard interviews for both parents and children have become available, including the Diagnostic Interview Schedule for Children [DISC] [Costello et al. 1984]; the Kiddie Schedule for

Table 2-5. Assessment of childhood psychopathology

Type of procedure	Name of procedure	Description of procedure
Unstructured parent interview		Probes present and past history in various areas, including general health, behavior, emotions, cognition, and interpersonal relations
Structured parent interview	Diagnostic Interview for Children and Adolescents (DICA; parent version) (Herjanic and Reich 1982)	Covers specific psychopathological symptoms probing severity, frequency, onset, and manifestations
Unstructured child interview		General queries in an informal play setting, with the child being encouraged to relax and verbalize
Structured child interview	DICA (child version) (Herjanic and Reich 1982)	Structured inquiry on specific psychopathological problem areas
Observational ratings (by psychiatrist)	Children's Psychiatric Rating Scale (NIMH 1973)	54 ratings of behaviors and verbal productions based on the psychiatric interview responses
Behavior ratings (by parents)	Conners Parent Rating Scale (Conners 1970)	Consists of approximately 90 symptoms to be rated on a four-point severity scale; scale has been factor-analyzed into eight factors
Behavior ratings (by parents)	Rutter parent questionnaire (Rutter et al. 1970a, 1970b)	Consists of approximately 30 symptoms to be rated on a three-point scale; "antisocial" and "neurotic" factor scores may be derived
Behavior ratings (by teachers)	Conners Teacher Rating Scale (Conners 1969)	Teacher ratings of symptom severity and academic function with a four-point scale; four factor scores may be derived
Behavior ratings (by teachers)	Rutter teacher questionnaire (Rutter et al. 1970a, 1970b)	Teacher ratings of severity of common symptoms; two factor scores may be derived

Affective Disorders and Schizophrenia [Kiddie-SADS] [Orvaschel et al. 1982]; and the Interview Schedule for Children [ISC] [Kovacs 1978].)

Child interview. Like the parent interview, the child interview used in the study consisted of both structured and unstructured parts. Initially, an unstructured approach was taken, with the child being encouraged to verbalize spontaneously and play in an informal setting. Subsequently, all children whose language capabilities permitted (in general those 6 years of age and above) were given the DICA structured interview to systematically cover all areas of symptomatology.

There was no attempt to make a "speech/language diagnosis" during the child interview. However, attention was paid to the possibility of deficits in language comprehension or expression, conceptual abilities, cognitive status, attention, or memory that could affect a child's responses during the interview. For instance, young children were not expected to recall the time a symptom began, since this requires the ability, not acquired until later in development, to locate events in lapsed time.

There is evidence that children may be better sources of information about mood and depressive symptoms (Herjanic et al. 1975). Thus, one of the focuses of the child interview was this type of information. In order to elicit information from the child about his or her feelings and attitudes, various techniques were used in the informal interview, including direct inquiries, attentive listening, and expressions of sympathy following feeling responses (as suggested by Cox and Rutter 1985).

The children's interview responses were noted in detail during the interview. Following the interview, the psychiatrist completed a rating form summarizing his impressions of the child's verbal responses and nonverbal behaviors.

Rating scales. Although parent and teacher ratings have been shown to be equally effective in their frequency of selection of children with psychiatric disorders, they appear, to a considerable extent, to select different children (Rutter et al. 1970a). Consequently, both parent and teacher behavior rating questionnaires were used in the present study.

These scales also provide a way of quantifying dimensional information about the children's symptomatology. For example, these scales reveal the degree to which a child with a categorical diagnosis (e.g., attention-deficit disorder) also has additional symptoms in other areas (e.g., anxiety, depression) that do not meet the full criteria for a second diagnosis.

The study employed two different sets of rating scales with both the parents and the teachers, one authored by Keith Conners (1969, 1970; Goyette et al. 1978) and one authored by Michael Rutter and colleagues (Rutter et al. 1970b). The Conners scales were selected because at the time of this study, they were the most commonly used scales for rating childhood psychopathology in the United States. The Rutter parent and teacher scales were chosen because of their prior use in epidemiologic studies and in studies of children with various types of handicaps. It must be noted here that the selection of these particular scales for the present study was a relatively simple choice due to the limited number of scales that were in use at the time the study began. Today, however, there are additional "normed" rating scales available that would warrant consideration were the study being redesigned. Two of the more comprehensive scales having both parent and teacher versions are the Behavior Problem Checklist (Quay and Peterson 1979, 1983) and the Child Behavior Checklist (Achenbach and Edelbrock 1983).

The Conners questionnaires each consist of approximately 90 symptoms rated for severity on a four-point scale. The questionnaires have been factor-analyzed, yielding eight factors for the parent report (conduct, anxiety, hyperactivity, learning problem, psychosomaticism, perfectionism, antisociality, and tension) and four factors for the teacher report (conduct, passivity, tension, and hyperactivity). The Rutter scales each consist of fewer items (approximately 30) and have been factor-analyzed into two factors (antisocial behavior and neurosis/emotional disorders).

For ease of use in the present study, the Rutter and Conners questionnaires were reprinted on two single forms: one for the parents and one for the teachers. A number of additional items having to do with mood, anxiety, and speech/language symptomatology were added to both of these forms. Thus, although the Rutter and Conners scales included many items measuring overt behaviors such as attention and motor activity, they actually had few items dealing with mood and anxiety. The items in these areas that were added for the present study were similar to those later delineated by Gittelman (1985). The items reflective of speech/language functioning were added in order to quantify the perceived severity of the children's speech/language disorders in the eyes of the parents and teachers.

Diagnosis of psychopathology. In order to diagnose the presence of psychiatric disorder, the information from the multiple assessment tools was integrated, and any disagreements between sources of information were resolved. For this study, *psychiatric disorder* was operationally defined as a disorder of behavior, emotions, cognition, or relationships sufficiently severe and/or sufficiently prolonged to cause disturbance in the child's adaptive functioning or disruption of his or her immediate environment.

Specific types of psychiatric disorders were diagnosed according to the criteria specified in DSM-III (American Psychiatric Association 1980). The DSM-III criteria were chosen (even though they were still under development at the time the present study was ongoing) because they constituted the most comprehensive classification system of childhood psychopathology available, and the only one with specific diagnostic criteria for the various disorders. As well as using the DSM-III diagnostic criteria for specific diagnoses, the DSM-III multiaxial coding scheme was used for capturing various aspects of each child's functioning. The multiple axes used included clinical psychiatric syndromes (Axis I); developmental disorders (Axis II); medical-biological disorders (Axis III); contributing psychosocial stressors (Axis IV); and overall levels of impairment and adaptive functioning (Axis V).

Certain specific modifications were made to the DSM multiaxial scheme for the present study. For example, contrary to DSM-III, stuttering was not considered an Axis I mental disorder; nor were any of the DSM-III speech/language disorders included as Axis II diagnoses. In the present study, Axis II consisted of the DSM-III specific developmental (learning) disorders and, additionally, mental retardation and coordination disorder (the latter an ICD-9 [World Health Organization 1978] diagnosis not in DSM-III). Types of psychosocial stressors and their severity levels were coded on Axis IV using a list drafted for an early version of DSM-III. On Axis V, the child's highest level of adaptive functioning in the past year was recorded using a seven-point scale, and, in addition, the current level of impairment was recorded also using a seven-point scale. The latter rating is not used in DSM-III.

Subtypes of psychopathology. In addition to the general determination of presence or absence of psychiatric illness and the specific determination of DSM-III diagnosis, an intermediate classification of type of psychiatric disorder was also made. Psychiatric disorders were thus classified into five general subtypes: overt behavioral disorders, emotional disorders, pervasive developmental disorders (PDDs), physical disorders, and all other disorders.

The distinction between disorders involving emotional distress or suffering for the child (emotional disorders) and disorders involving socially disapproved behavior causing disturbance to other people (behavioral disorders) has been recognized in child psychiatry for many decades (Ackerson 1931; Hersov 1985; Hewitt and Jenkins 1946). (See

Chapter 4 for further discussion of the data supporting this distinction in child psychiatry.) For purposes of the present study, *behavioral disorders* consisted of the DSM-III diagnoses of attention-deficit disorder (with or without hyperactivity), conduct disorders (undersocialized aggressive, undersocialized unaggressive, and socialized), and oppositional disorder. *Emotional disorders* consisted of the DSM-III anxiety disorders (i.e., separation-anxiety disorder, avoidant disorder, overanxious disorder, and simple phobia), affective disorders (i.e., cyclothymia, dysthymia, bipolar disorder, and major depression), and adjustment disorders. *Pervasive developmental disorders* consisted of two DSM-III diagnoses: infantile autism and childhood-onset PDD. *Physical disorders* consisted of the stereotyped movement disorders and organic brain syndromes.

Reliability of psychiatric diagnoses. The reliability of the psychiatric diagnoses was tested in two ways. In one test of reliability, the author (D.P.C.) and a resident child psychiatrist each diagnosed 50 children, using the assessment tools described in Table 2-5. Subsequently, each psychiatrist examined the assessment data for the children he had not seen, and made a diagnosis based on those data. Because the second diagnosis was made without actually seeing the child, it was unlikely to be affected by knowledge of the child's speech/language disorder. In this test of reliability, a 96% agreement between diagnosticians was obtained on the presence or absence of any psychiatric disorder, and a 94% agreement was obtained on the specific psychiatric disorder diagnosed.

In a second test of reliability, an additional 50 cases were diagnosed first using only the parent interview and the (Conners and Rutter) parent and teacher rating scales. Then, after interviewing the child, a second diagnosis was made. In no case did these diagnoses differ as to the presence or absence of psychiatric disorder. This finding is in keeping with studies of the diagnostic process in child psychiatry that have shown that the child interview alone is the least valuable instrument for making a psychiatric diagnosis (Rutter et al. 1970a).

Other Evaluations

In addition to the assessments of speech/language and psychiatric status, the children in the study were evaluated in other areas of functioning, including intelligence and learning, neurological development, and hearing. In addition, psychiatric evaluations were done of the children's parents and siblings, and aspects of family interaction were assessed. Descriptions of these assessments follow.

Intelligence. Epidemiologic investigations have shown that psychiatric disorders are more common among children with lower IQ levels (Rutter 1971). Thus, intelligence level was an important variable to measure in the present study. Because extensive language testing was done with all children, the intelligence measures used focused on "nonlanguage" or performance intelligence.

Several different performance intelligence tests were used, depending upon the age of the child being tested. For children below the age of 4 years, the Developmental Activities Screening Inventory (DASI) (DuBose and Langley 1977) was used; for children ages 4.0 to 5.9 years, the Wechsler Pre-School and Primary Scale of Intelligence (WPPSI) (Wechsler 1967) was used; and for children ages 6 years and above, the Wechsler Intelligence Scale for Children, Revised Edition (WISC-R) (Wechsler 1974) was used.

Because of the necessity of limiting the evaluation time, some of the subtests were omitted from the WPPSI or WISC-R for some of the children. Nonetheless, a minimum of three subtests were always done for the WPPSI (picture completion, geometric design, and block design), and a minimum of four subtests were always done for the WISC-R (picture completion, block design, object assembly, and picture arrangement). When a child did not complete all of the performance subtests, then the child's performance intelligence score was calculated using the procedures specified in the test manuals for prorating the scores.

Learning achievement.   School grades are one measure of learning achievement; these were obtained in the present study as part of the teacher questionnaire. However, because the subjects came from a number of different schools, standardized achievement testing was also necessary in order to ensure that comparable standards were being applied to all the children.

Learning achievement testing was attempted for all children over 4 years, 11 months of age. The measures obtained included grade level and standard scores in arithmetic, spelling, and reading (word recognition or decoding) from the Wide Range Achievement Test (WRAT) (Jastak et al. 1976) and oral reading grade level, comprehension rate, and error types from the Gray Oral Reading Tests (Gray 1967).

The diagnosis of specific developmental learning disorders was made using DSM-III criteria. These criteria require performance on standardized tests of achievement that is significantly below the level expected taking into account the child's schooling and chronological and mental age. In addition, the child's performance on academic tasks in school (as specified on the teacher report) must be significantly below his or her intellectual capacity.

DSM-III does not specify a method for determining the discrepancy between expected and actual achievement; nor does it define the amount of discrepancy that is significant. While this is unfortunate for research purposes, it is helpful in the clinical setting in avoiding the problem of excluding from special services children who may need help but who may not meet a predetermined cutoff definition.

There are a number of methods currently available for defining the cutoffs of learning disorder. For example, in a recent literature review, Friedrich et al. (1984) identified 94 empirically derived formulae for assessment of learning disability. Judgments of learning disability using these different methods generally tend to have low rates of agreement (Algozzine et al. 1982; Epps et al. 1982; Forness et al. 1983; Kavale and Forness 1985). Thus far, it is not clear that any one method is the "gold standard." The problems underlying this lack of agreement are too complex to discuss here but have been clearly summarized by Kavale and Forness (1985). They include difficulties in measuring "actual" achievement based on standardized tests, difficulties with definitions of expected achievement, and unreliability in discrepancy formulations due to regression phenomena or due to problems in procedures for determining discrepancy.

In the present study, *learning disorder* was clinically defined based upon 1) a discrepancy between actual and expected achievement based on scores from the WISC-R, Gray Oral Reading Tests, and WRAT; and 2) documented school performance below the levels expected from age and intellectual capacity. It is possible that this method results in an underestimate of the prevalence of learning disorders. This possibility is discussed and some relevant data are presented in Chapter 3.

Neurological assessment. The Isle of Wight studies (Rutter et al. 1970a, 1970b) have provided good evidence that brain damage increases the risk for a wide range of child psychiatric disorders. Thus, an attempt was made in the present study to quantify the presence of definite or suspected organic brain pathology.

"Hard" measures of neurological impairment (X rays, electroencephalographs, evoked responses) were considered to be impractical for the present study. (Nonetheless, a small number of subjects had received these as part of other evaluations, and in those cases the results were coded as "Axis III" diagnoses.)

For all children in the study, the parent(s) or guardian(s) was questioned regarding the presence of possible neuromaturational indicators (e.g., deficits in skill acquisitions, gross or fine motor performance "like a younger child," or tremors). In addition, for all children over the age of 60 months, an attempt was made to assess the presence of "neurological soft signs" using the Peters Neurological Examination (Peters et al. 1975). The Peters Neurological Examination involves simple neuromotor tasks such as hopping, skipping, tapping fingers, eye tracking, and distinguishing right versus left. The exam is intended to detect the presence of subtle or "soft" signs of neurological disorder through symptoms such as clumsiness, sequencing problems, and right-left confusions and associated movements.

This was one of the only tests of neurological soft signs available when the present study was being designed, and its reliability is around 85%. Subsequent to the present study, several other procedures have been developed that may have higher levels of reliability (Szatmari 1985). These include the Revised Physical and Neurological Examination for Subtle Signs (Denckla 1985; Holden et al. 1982), the Pediatric Examination of Educational Readiness (Levine et al. 1980), and the Pediatric Early Elementary Examination (Levine et al. 1983).

Hearing screening.   All children in the study received a hearing assessment consisting of screening at 25 decibels for frequencies of 250, 500, 1,000, 2,000, and 4,000 hertz. A child who failed any of these screening frequencies was subsequently given more extensive audiologic testing including pure tone, speech threshold, and air and bone conduction tests. Any child tested as having a hearing loss greater than 45 decibels was not accepted into the study.

Family mental health assessment.   Each available parent was interviewed separately about his or her own psychiatric status and about the known psychiatric status of other family members. Both immediate family members (i.e., the siblings of the index child) and extended family members (e.g., aunts, uncles, grandparents, cousins) were included in the interview. The first step of the interview procedure was the drawing of a systematic pedigree identifying the proband child and all family members through first, second, and third degree, living or dead. The pedigree indicated the sex, current age (or age at death), and exact biological relationship of each person. Generally, this information was obtained only from one parent—in most cases the mother.

After establishing the pedigree and identifying the family members, the available parent (or parents) was interviewed directly about his or her own mental status using the then-available version of the adult Diagnostic Interview Schedule (DIS) (Robins et al. 1981). This interview permitted the determination of broad psychiatric diagnoses following DSM-III criteria similar to those used in the Epidemiologic Catchment Area (ECA) studies of a number of cities funded by the

National Institute of Mental Health (Myers et al. 1984; Regier et al. 1984; Robins et al. 1984).

The available parent or parents were then interviewed regarding other family members using material from the Family History–Research Diagnostic Criteria (FH-RDC) (Endicott and Spitzer 1978). This interview was developed by Endicott, Andreasen, and Spitzer, with the assistance of other participants in the NIMH Clinical Research Branch Collaboration Program on the Psychobiology of Depression. The procedure itself was based on the family-history method, originally developed by George Winokur and his colleagues. The FH-RDC permitted the diagnoses of a variety of adult psychiatric disorders according to criteria similar to the DSM-III criteria. However, these diagnoses were less rigid, since the information was not obtained directly from each family through interview.

The FH-RDC do not include childhood psychiatric and learning problems. Thus, these criteria were supplemented in the present study by questions tapping into the presence of learning disorders, speech/language disorders, and childhood psychopathology (including attention-deficit, conduct, oppositional, mood, and emotional disorders). Information was also obtained regarding any attempted and completed suicides, hospitalizations for medical and/or psychiatric reasons, and treatments for psychiatric, learning, or speech/language disorders in childhood and in adult life.

Assessment of family interactions. Aspects of family interaction were assessed in an interview consisting of sections of interviews developed by Rutter and Brown (1966) and by Cantwell et al. (1978). The family-interaction interview covered various aspects of parenting such as the relationship between each parent and the index child, the expectations and prohibitions that parents had about the index child, and the presence of disagreements regarding child rearing of the index child.

Finally, global ratings were made by the interviewer of the degree of parental irritability, warmth, hostility, and criticism shown toward the index child. These global measures were based on the interviewer's assessment of various indicators demonstrated throughout the entire interview. For example, the scale for warmth of the parent toward the child was based on the following interview behaviors: tone of voice, expression, and gestures used when speaking about the child; spontaneity when talking about the child; sympathy, concern, and empathy manifested toward the child; and interest shown by the parent in the child as a person. These ratings were previously used by Cantwell et al. (1978) in their study of family interactions with children having infantile autism and children having receptive dysphasia and were shown to have high test-retest and interrater reliabilities.

Missing Data

Cox et al. (1977) observed that it is not at all uncommon in epidemiologic studies for missing data rates to be as high as 25% to 50%. In the present study, persistent efforts were made by the investigators to maintain a very high level of completeness of data. As stated above, a high participation rate (98%) was obtained, most likely because the study was offered at a time when parents were seeking evaluations for their children and the study was described as providing an additional free evaluation.

Once subjects agreed to participate in the study, every effort was made by the investigators to maintain a high level of cooperation. Appointments were scheduled at the parents' convenience, including during the early evening or weekend hours. As a result, all 600 subjects who agreed to participate in the study were seen for evaluation.

The protocol of the study was structured so that the maximum amount of information would be obtained. Data on psychiatric symptomatology were always sought from multiple sources (e.g., parent interview, parent questionnaires, teacher questionnaires, child interview, child observations, testing). Consequently, the presence or absence of psychiatric illness could still be determined, even if one source of information was missing. Similarly, linguistic diagnoses could be made for all children, even though all of the children did not receive all of the speech/language tests. For example, all children were assessed for expressive language, even though the specific measures used were different depending upon each child's age and abilities.

Table 2-6 lists the general types of data that were obtained in the study along with the number of cases for whom those data were obtained. It can be seen that, despite all efforts to avoid incompleteness, there were some missing data. A small number of parents failed to return for second appointments, resulting in parent interview and background history data being incomplete for 1% to 2% of the cases. A somewhat larger number of parents (6%) failed to return the parent questionnaires.

Teacher questionnaire, neurological exam, and educational achievement data were not obtained for a larger number of cases. However, the figures are somewhat misleading in that most of these "missing data" were actually "not applicable" rather than truly "missing." Thus, the teacher questionnaires could only be obtained for those children in school at the time of the evaluations, and the neurological

Table 2-6. Missing data in the present research sample

Type of data	Number of cases with data[a]
Psychiatric diagnosis	600
Speech/language diagnosis	600
Parent interview	592
Background history data	586
Child interview	568
Parent questionnaire	562
Teacher questionnaire	430
Educational achievement data test	297
Neurological examination	254

[a]Sample size of 600.

examination and educational achievement data could be obtained only for those children who had been able to participate in the tests. In general, educational and neurological testing was only attempted with those children 5 years of age and above ($n = 307$), although not all of those children were able to complete the tests.

When data were not available, no attempts were made to extrapolate them. Thus, only the data that were actually collected were used in the analyses for the present study.

Follow-up Data

The present study was designed as a cohort study with the aim of following the 600 speech/language–disordered children over time to investigate the interactions between speech/language and psychiatric disorders. Four years after the initial study, letters of inquiry were sent out to the first 500 cases in this sample asking if they would like to be seen in the follow-up study. Cases were seen for follow-up in order of response, with the follow-up methodology being identical to the initial methodology. Complete analysis of the follow-up data is not yet available. However, some of the follow-up data on the speech/language–disordered children will be reported in the following chapters.

Factors Associated With Speech and Language Disorders

3

IN THIS CHAPTER WE PRESENT the data on the general characteristics of the research sample in the present study. First, the speech/language diagnoses of the children (according to the definitions provided in Chapter 2) are delineated. Then, we present four general categories of other (nonlinguistic) variables: 1) demographic or background factors, 2) developmental or cognitive factors, 3) biological factors, and 4) psychosocial factors. This method of grouping variables is somewhat parallel to the multiaxial groupings used in the DSM-III system (American Psychiatric Association 1980). Thus, in the DSM-III framework, Axis II refers to developmental disorders, Axis III refers to physical disorders and conditions, and Axis IV refers to psychosocial stressors.

As background to the presentation of nonlinguistic data, there is a brief discussion of how these factors have been viewed in the literature on childhood speech/language disorders. Data from the present study are then presented, and comments are made indicating how these data fit in with findings from the literature.

Finally, we present the data on the prevalence of psychiatric disorders in the 600 speech/language–impaired children. These data are relevant to the literature outlined in Chapter 1.

Types of Speech/Language Disorders

A total of 600 children were seen in the present study. These were all new incoming cases presenting for speech/language evaluation during the period between March 1977 and February 1980. By definition, all of the 600 children in the study had some type of speech/language disorder. The prevalence data for the different subtypes of speech and language disorders found in the sample are presented in

Table 3-1. The majority of the sample (555 of the 600 children, or 92.5%) had some type of disorder involving the production of speech. More than half of the sample (397 of the 600, or 66%) had some type of language disorder.

The *speech disorders* found in the sample were (in order of prevalence) articulation disorder, speech dysfluency (or stuttering), voice disorders, and rate-of-speech disorder. In addition, there were six children who were nonverbal or who vocalized insufficiently for a specific speech diagnosis to be made; these individuals were considered to have an undiagnosed speech disorder. The *language disorders* found in the sample of 600 children were (in order of prevalence) expressive language disorder, receptive language disorder, language processing disorder, and pragmatic language disorder (i.e., language-use disorder). The prevalence figure ($n = 154$) for language processing disorder was low, in part, because 129 of the 600 children were "untestable" in this area for various reasons (e.g., young age, low level of linguistic functioning, lack of cooperation).

As the figures in Table 3-1 reveal, there was some overlap between speech disorders and language disorders. For purposes of data analysis in the study, it was desirable to divide the large sample into major linguistic diagnostic subgroupings that did not overlap. Following the intuition that the speech/language distinction would prove to be clinically valid, the sample was divided into three major mutually exclusive subgroupings: 1) pure speech disorder, 2) speech/language

Table 3-1. Prevalence of speech/language disorders in the present research sample

Disorder	Number of cases
Speech disorders	
Articulation disorder	510
Speech dysfluency (stuttering)	39
Voice disorder	19
Undiagnosed speech disorder	6
Rate-of-speech disorder	2
Any speech disorder	555
Language disorders	
Expressive language disorder	363
Receptive language disorder	237
Language processing disorder	154
Pragmatic (language) disorder	63
Any language disorder	397

disorder, and 3) pure language disorder. The *pure speech disorder group* consisted of children with impairments in speech production but with no impairments in language comprehension, expression, usage, or processing. *The speech/language disorder group* consisted of children with impairments in both speech and language functioning. The *pure language disorder group* consisted of children with normal speech production but with impairments in some aspect of language functioning. A comparison of these three linguistic subgroups is presented in Chapter 6.

Factors Associated With Childhood Speech/Language Disorders: A Review of the Literature

Impairments in the acquisition of speech and language may be the direct result of other problems such as mental retardation, hearing impairment, overt brain damage, physical abnormalities of the speech mechanism, or severe environmental deprivation. However, by far, the majority of speech/language disorders are "developmental" or without obvious cause.

Much has been written concerning possible causes or risk factors for both developmental language disorder and developmental articulation disorder. (For reviews, see Baker and Cantwell 1985a, 1985b; Bernthal and Bankson 1988; Bishop 1987; Cantwell and Baker 1987b; Pennington and Smith 1983; Rapin and Allen 1988.) The risk factors that have been postulated generally fall into one of four main areas: 1) demographic or background factors (e.g., sex, socioeconomic class, family size, birth order); 2) developmental-cognitive factors (e.g., "neurodevelopmental immaturity"); 3) biological factors (e.g., otitis media–intermittent hearing impairment, pregnancy or birth complications, genetic influences); and 4) psychosocial factors (e.g., specific auditory-verbal deprivation).

The present study was not specifically concerned with the etiology of speech/language disorders. However, because of the large number of children examined in the study, there is a large amount of data regarding the possible risk factors involved in speech/language disorders. In order that the significance of these data can be fully appreciated, we will summarize here some of the factors postulated in the literature as being associated with childhood speech/language disorders.

Demographic and Background Factors

Age and sex. An association between age and sex and the presence of speech/language disorders has been documented in numerous epidemiologic studies. These studies have found the prevalence rates of both speech (especially articulation) disorders and language disorders to be elevated in young males. Thus, speech/language disorders are more prevalent in boys than in girls (Beitchman et al. 1986a, 1986b; Blanton 1916; Calnan and Richardson 1976; Drillien and Drummond 1983; Gillespie and Cooper 1973; Mills and Streit 1942; Randall et al. 1974). Similarly, speech/language disorders are more prevalent in younger children than in older children (Carhart 1939; Dickson 1971; Elliott 1978; Hull et al. 1971; Milisen 1971; Mills and Streit 1942). The sex data have been interpreted as being indicative of a genetic component to speech/language disorders (Kidd et al. 1978), but they could also reflect an effect of sex steroids upon intrauterine maturation (Rapin and Allen 1988). The age data are more likely to be artifacts of the developmental nature of the disorders (i.e., that children outgrow the disorders) than to be indicative of a critical age risk.

Socioeconomic status. Several studies have reported that speech/language disorders are more common among children from lower–socioeconomic-class families than among children from upper–socioeconomic-class families (Adler 1973; Beitchman et al. 1988; Bendel et al. 1989; Butler et al. 1973; Calnan and Richardson 1976; Klackenberg 1980; Lassman et al. 1980; Randall et al. 1974). Similarly, studies of normal children have indicated superior rates of acquisition for certain aspects of language in the higher socioeconomic classes (Jay et al. 1980). However, at least one study reported that severe language disorders are more likely to occur in children from higher socioeconomic classes (Byrne et al. 1974), and other studies have found only weak or limited correlations between lower socioeconomic status and the presence of language disorders (DiSimoni and Mucha 1983).

There is also apparently a trend for speech/language disorders to be more common in children from larger families and among later-born children (Beitchman 1985; Beitchman et al. 1988; Bendel et al. 1989; Butler et al. 1973; Calnan and Richardson 1976). Twins are also at more risk for speech/language problems than are singletons (Hay et al. 1987). This latter finding could reflect either the increased perinatal problems of twins (Schubert et al. 1983) or the different parental expectations occurring with twins (Alin-Akerman 1987). In addition, low socioeconomic class and large family size have themselves been associated with decreased parent-child interactions. (The possible significance of this finding is discussed below in "Psychosocial Factors.")

Developmental and Cognitive Factors

Delays. Children with specific speech/language disorders are usually within "normal limits" for achieving nonlinguistic developmental milestones. However, several studies have reported that these children have a somewhat elevated prevalence of delays in at least one motor milestone (Butler et al. 1973; Crookes and Greene 1963; Rosenbek and Wertz 1972; Sommers and Kane 1975; Stark et al. 1983).

Specific disorders. Motor clumsiness and poor fine motor coordination in particular are often reported in children with speech/language disorders (Amorosa et al. 1986; Bishop 1984; Bishop and Edmundson 1987b; Cermak et al. 1986; Hermansen et al. 1985; Shriberg et al. 1986). Also, speech/language problems have frequently been reported in children with motor coordination disorder (Abbie et al. 1978; Henderson and Hall 1982).

These findings support a "neurodevelopmental immaturity" model in which speech/language and motor delays are viewed as reflections of neurological immaturity rather than of true brain damage. The neurodevelopmental-immaturity model has difficulty, however, accounting for the failure of many of these children to "catch up."

Biological Factors

Perinatal factors and brain damage. Follow-up studies of premature infants of low birth weight indicate that these children are at risk for speech/language delays (Bee et al. 1982; de Hirsch et al. 1964; Fitzhardinge and Ramsay 1973; Largo et al. 1986; Lassman et al. 1980; Michelsson and Noronen 1983; Siegel et al. 1982; Wright et al. 1983). In addition, various specific complications (including respiratory distress syndrome, low birth weight, birth asphyxia, and pregnancy complications) have been found to correlate negatively with language development. Generally, however, perinatal measures are very weak predictors of later language development.

Subtle, localized brain damage was often postulated in early works as an underlying factor in developmental speech/language disorders (Baker and Cantwell 1985b; Bishop 1987). As support for this hypothesis, somewhat elevated rates of atypical lateralization or dominance and left-hemisphere electroencephalographic abnormalities have been cited (Caceres 1971; Eisenson 1972; Ingram 1959; Morley 1965; Sato and Dreifuss 1973). However, both the data and their interpretations are controversial (Goodman 1987; Kinsbourne and Hiscock 1983).

Hearing loss and middle-ear infections.   An early history of recurrent middle-ear infections has also been reported as a common risk factor for subsequent disorders of language development (Brandes and Ehinger 1981; Brookhouser et al. 1979; Eimas and Kavanagh 1986; Gottlieb et al. 1979; Paradise 1981). However, not all studies have found this association (Allen and Robinson 1984; Fischler et al. 1985; Roberts et al. 1986), and there is some thought that the association may be the result of interactions with other factors such as neurological impairment, genetic disposition, or poor environment (Bishop and Edmundson 1986; Rapin 1979).

Other physical factors.   Certain studies of children with articulation disorders have reported that these children are more likely to have subtle abnormalities of the speech mechanism such as oral motor weakness, tongue thrust, history of feeding problems, or poor dentition (Eisenson 1972; Shriberg et al. 1986; Snow 1961; Yoss and Darley 1974). The data, however, are not robust.

The tendency for speech/language disorders to run in families has also been reported, but systematic studies are limited (DeFries and Plomin 1983; Neils and Aram 1986; Shriberg et al. 1986; Tallal et al. 1989b). Nonetheless, the existing data suggest the possibility of an inherited predisposition toward these disorders.

Psychosocial Factors

Children who have suffered maltreatment and/or extreme environmental deprivation inevitably manifest delayed development in speech and language (Blager and Martin 1976; Cicchetti and Beeghly 1987; Fox et al. 1988; Hughes and DiBrezzo 1987; McCauley and Swisher 1987). Studies of the linguistic input and verbal interactions that are received by these children indicate a number of significant differences from the input and interactions that are received by children who were treated normally (Allen and Wasserman 1985; Wasserman et al. 1983).

Similarly, studies of children in other deprived environments (e.g., later-born children, children from noisy or overcrowded homes, children from lower–socioeconomic-class backgrounds) have shown that these children also tend to receive less verbal interaction than do children in normal environments (Davie et al. 1984; Gottfried and Gottfried 1984; Ninio 1980). Conversely, with nonspeech/language–disordered children, superior speech/language development has been associated with certain types of positive mother-child interactions (Barnes et al. 1983; Walsh and Greenough 1976). However, no consistent differences have been established regarding verbal interactions

of speech/language–disordered children versus nonspeech/language–disordered children (Conti-Ramsden 1985; Lasky and Klopp 1982).
  Other psychosocial factors (e.g., broken homes, family discord, parental mental illness) have not been systematically studied with regard to their association with speech/language disorders. Nonetheless, clinicians often note the presence of these factors in children with speech/language disorders (Caceres 1971). In fact, the Canadian epidemiologic study of 5-year-olds (Beitchman et al. 1986b) found elevated rates of psychosocial stressors among children with speech/language disorders as compared with children with normal speech/language development. Of the speech/language–disordered children, 26% had moderate to severe stressors, compared to only 6% of the nonspeech/language–disordered control subjects.
  In conclusion, as with the other types of factors associated with speech/language disorders, no causative link has been clearly established for psychosocial factors. However, there is limited agreement across such studies, and within single studies, of a weak association between speech/language development and psychosocial factors. The evidence for any particular factor, however, is generally weak.

Description of the Research Sample in the Present Study

Demographic and Background Factors

Age and sex distribution.   Over a 3-year period, 600 children were evaluated in this study. Of the 600, 413 (69%) were males and 187 (31%) were females. The children ranged in age from 1 year, 8 months to 15 years, 11 months, with the group mean age being 5 years, 7 months. The majority of the children in the study were in the preschool age-range (see Table 3-2); in fact, one-half of the sample was below the age of 5 years, and the median age of children in the study was 4 years, 11 months.
  These age and sex distributions of the sample appear to be representative of the general population of speech/language–disordered children. Thus, the literature indicates that boys are more likely to have speech/language disorders than are girls and that younger children are more likely to have speech/language disorders than are older children. Fitting this description, the sample of the present study consisted predominantly of young males.
  Family background.   Data on the family backgrounds of research subjects were obtained during interviews with the parents. The

Table 3-2. Age distribution of the present research sample

Age level	Number of cases	Percentage of sample
Below 2 years, 0 months	6	1
2-year-olds	57	9
3-year-olds	126	21
4-year-olds	118	20
5-year-olds	79	13
6-year-olds	52	9
7-year-olds	46	7
8-year-olds	38	6
9-year-olds	20	3
10-year-olds	10	2
11-year-olds	13	2
12-year-olds	10	2
13-year-olds	5	1
14-year-olds	10	2
15-year-olds	6	1
16-year-olds	4	1

socioeconomic background data on the children, including data on parental occupation, education, and ethnicity, are presented in Table 3-3.

Socioeconomic-class membership was calculated based on parental occupational and educational data using Hollingshead's (1957) method. Thirteen percent of the children were "upper" class, 13% were "upper middle" class, 42% were "middle" class, 26% were "lower middle" class, and 6% were "lower" class.

The socioeconomic-class distribution of the sample was representative of the general population of the greater Los Angeles area at the time of the study. This is due to the referral sources for the clinic patients, which included both agencies serving lower–socioeconomic-class families (e.g., MediCal, Regional Center, the State Department of Rehabilitation, the Easter Seal Agency) and private medical practitioners (i.e., pediatricians, ear-nose-throat specialists, neurologists) serving upper–socioeconomic-class families.

The family size and family structure data for the subjects of the study are also presented in Table 3-3. Contrary to the literature (which suggests that speech/language disorders are more common in larger families and in later-born children), the children in this study tended to come from smaller families and to be first-borns. The majority of

Table 3-3. Family background of the present research sample

	Fathers (%)	Mothers (%)
Highest level of education		
Graduate work	16	4
College degree	28	27
High school graduation	47	63
No high school graduation	9	6
Occupation		
Professional, managerial, administrative	45	11
Clerical, sales, or technician	33	16
Skilled or unskilled labor	18	7
Student or unemployed	4	66
Ethnic background		
White	92	92
Black	2	1
Hispanic	4	4
Asian	1	2
Other	1	1
Health		
Good	95	94
Fair	3	5
Poor	2	1

	Percentage of sample
Family structure	
Two-parent family	84
Biological mother and father	70
Family size	
One child	19
Two children	47
Three children	23
Four or more children	11
Birth order	
First-born	43
Second-born	37
Third-born	13
Later-born	7

the children lived in intact two-parent families consisting of the biological mother and father.

The fathers of children in the study ranged in age from 21 to 64 years (mean age = 35 years), and mothers ranged in age from 18 to 52 years (mean age = 32 years). The mean ages of the mothers and fathers at the time of the target child's birth were 26.2 and 29.8 years, respectively. In general, the parents were predominantly white high school graduates, with the fathers working in clerical or higher positions and the mothers being homemakers. The vast majority of parents of both sexes were in good health.

Developmental-Cognitive Factors

Developmental delays. Developmental histories were obtained for the children in the study by means of parent interviews. These interviews covered the ages of attaining all basic motor milestones and self-help skills (e.g., sitting, crawling, standing, walking, self-feeding, self-dressing).

The majority of children in the study had unremarkable developmental histories. Although 28% of the parents indicated that they considered their children to have been somewhat "slow" in reaching some (nonspeech/language) developmental milestones, few of these children were significantly delayed. Significant delay was defined using the cutoff age definitions of "late" for each milestone specified in the Isle of Wight study (Rutter et al. 1970a, 1970b). Following these definitions, fewer than 10% of the sample qualified as being "late developers" in *any* nonlanguage milestone. For most milestones, fewer than 5% of the children in the sample were "late."

Table 3-4 presents the developmental data for the sample, including the group mean ages of reaching developmental milestones and the prevalence of "late" development for various milestones. It can be seen that the group mean ages for achieving all nonlanguage developmental milestones were within normal limits, and few children met the definitions of being "late" in achieving developmental milestones.

Specific developmental disorders. In the current investigation, mental retardation, the various developmental learning disorders, enuresis, encopresis, and coordination disorder were all grouped together as "Axis II developmental disorders." It was hypothesized that these Axis II developmental disorders as a group would be relatively common among the children in the sample. The data on the prevalence and types of Axis II developmental disorder diagnoses are presented in Table 3-4. (The specific DSM-III developmental speech/language disorders are not included in the table, because, by definition, all the children in this study had some type of speech/language disorder.)

Of the 600 children, 79% (n = 473) had no Axis II diagnosis, whereas 21% had some Axis II diagnosis. Excluding mental retardation, approximately 15% of the children were diagnosed as having

Table 3-4. Developmental data for the present research sample

Ages at attaining developmental milestones

Milestone	Mean age (months)	SD
Sitting	7.0	3.1
Eating solids	6.8	5.9
Crawling	8.1	3.9
Standing	11.7	6.4
Walking alone	14.6	6.3
Self-feeding	16.2	8.1
Self-dressing	33.1	13.9

Frequency of late development

Milestone	Defined "late" age (months)	Percentage late
Sitting	13	3
Crawling	14	3
Standing	16	8
Walking alone	25	3

Prevalence of DSM-III developmental disorders

Axis II diagnosis	Percentage of cases
No Axis II diagnosis	79
Any Axis II diagnosis	21
Enuresis	6
Encopresis	1
Developmental reading disorder	2
Developmental arithmetic disorder	<1
Mixed specific developmental disorder	4
Atypical specific developmental disorder	<1
Developmental coordination disorder	5
Mental retardation	6

Prevalence of (variously defined) learning disorders

Area of functioning	Prevalence (%) of learning disorders according to:		
	Teacher report	McLeod formula[a]	DSM-III
Reading	26	21–37[b]	7
Arithmetic	18	25	1
Spelling	18	31	1
Any learning	26	52	15
Mixed learning	23	31	8

Note. SD = standard deviation.
[a]See McLeod 1979.
[b]Depending upon test score used: 21% for Wide Range Achievement Test word recognition; 30% for Gray Oral Reading Tests grade-level score; 37% for Gray Oral Reading Tests score adjusted for comprehension.

some nonlanguage developmental disorder. Enuresis was found in 6% (n = 34) of the children; developmental coordination disorder in 5% (n = 32); encopresis in 1% (n = 8); and mental retardation in 6% (n = 34). Some type of developmental learning disorder was present in 42 children (7% of the sample). The most common type of learning disorder was mixed specific developmental disorder.

Mental retardation.   Six percent of the sample received a diagnosis of mental retardation according to the DSM-III definition, which requires subaverage intellectual functioning (defined as a score below 70 on an individually administered IQ test), and concurrent deficiencies in adaptive behavior—both occurring before 18 years of age. Although 6% of the children met this criteria, it should be mentioned that a total of 9% of the children scored below 70 on performance intelligence testing. However, not all of these children were judged clinically to be mentally retarded. Of the children who were considered to be mentally retarded (n = 34), 17 were mildly retarded, 10 were moderately retarded, 1 was severely retarded, and 6 had unspecifiable degrees of retardation.

Because general mental retardation is known to be associated with deficits in speech and language development (Baker 1988; Carrow-Woolfolk and Lynch 1982; Lillywhite and Bradley 1969; Schiefelbusch 1972), it was hypothesized that there would be a relatively high prevalence of general mental retardation among children in this sample. The prevalence rate found in the study (6%) was indeed higher than the 3% estimated for the general population (Grossman et al. 1983). However, in view of the fact that mental retardation may be the single largest cause of delayed language development (Rutter and Martin 1972), this prevalence rate might be considered low for a speech-clinic sample.

It appears that the above finding is, in fact, a referral artifact. California has a well-developed network of regional centers established for children with general mental retardation. Apparently, physicians and agencies refer the majority of mentally retarded children to these centers rather than to a speech clinic. Those mentally retarded children who were referred to the speech clinic were the ones whose speech/language development was delayed additionally beyond the delays in nonlanguage skills. Indeed, closer examination of the children in our sample who received the diagnosis of general mental retardation revealed language functioning far below the levels of their psychomotor, cognitive, and academic functioning (although these too were at a retarded level in comparison to chronological age). It remains unclear whether the limiting of referrals of mentally retarded children to speech/language clinics is purely a California phenomenon or whether it is more widespread.

Enuresis, encopresis, and coordination disorder. DSM-III-R states that the prevalence of functional enuresis is 7% for males and 3% for females at age 5 years; 3% for males and 2% for females at age 10; and 1% for males and almost nonexistent for females at age 18. DSM-III estimates the prevalence of encopresis to be approximately 1% for 5-year-olds.

In our sample, the prevalence rates found were 6% for enuresis and 1% for encopresis. These prevalence rates were calculated for the entire sample of children, who ranged in age from 1.9 to 16.0 years. It is important to remember, however, that approximately half of the children in our sample were under the age of 5 years (and thus ineligible, according to DSM-III criteria, to receive the diagnosis of enuresis). Similarly, approximately 30% of the children in our sample were under the age of 4 years (and thus ineligible to receive the diagnosis of encopresis). Consequently, if only those children eligible because of age to receive the enuresis or encopresis diagnoses were to have been considered, the prevalence figures would have been almost double those reported in Table 3-4.

Several authors have suggested that there is an association between developmental coordination disorder and speech/language disorders in children (Amorosa et al. 1986; Bishop 1984; Cermak et al. 1986; Henderson and Hall 1982; Hulme and Lord 1986). The prevalence rate for coordination disorder among children has not been studied in detail, although it may be as high as 6% among children aged 5 to 11 years (American Psychiatric Association 1987; Johnston et al. 1987). If so, then the 5% prevalence rate obtained in the present study would not be considered elevated.

Learning disorders. In our sample, 42 children had some type of developmental learning disorder according to the clinical (DSM-III) diagnosis based upon a discrepancy between actual and expected achievement (determined by scores from the Wechsler Intelligence Scale for Children [WISC], Gray Oral Reading Tests, and the Wide Range Achievement Test) and documented school performance below expected levels. Of the 42 learning-disordered children, 13 had specific developmental reading disorder, 1 had specific developmental arithmetic disorder, 26 had mixed specific developmental disorder, and 2 had atypical specific developmental disorder, according to DSM-III definitions.

The rates of developmental learning disorder found must be considered to be a minimum estimate, because the majority of children

(60%) were of preschool age and thus ineligible to receive the diagnosis. Furthermore, of the 40% of the sample who could possibly have received the diagnosis, a large number were just beginning school. Thus, it is to be expected that many of these children will develop a learning disorder as they get older. In fact, based on the preliminary results of data from these children 4 years after they were seen in the present study (Baker and Cantwell 1987), the prevalence of learning disorders was found to be significantly higher.

Furthermore, as suggested in Chapter 2, it is possible that the clinical definition of learning disorder used in the present study resulted in an overly low prevalence estimate. In order to examine this possibility, learning achievement data, teacher-report information, and clinical DSM-III diagnoses were compared for 172 of the children in the study (see Table 3-4). The prevalence of learning disorders among the 172 children varied considerably according to the method used for determining the presence of the disorders. For example, with regard to reading disorder, teachers identified 26% of the children as reading below the level expected based on age and IQ. Using a regression-formula equation developed by McLeod (1979), from 21% to 37% of the children were identified as having a reading disorder, depending on which achievement test score was used. In comparison to these rather high prevalence figures, the DSM-III clinical diagnosis identified only 7% of the children as having a specific reading disorder.

Generally, the teachers' estimates of learning disorder were closer to the estimates from the statistical formulation of McLeod than were the DSM-III diagnoses. This is most likely because the DSM-III diagnoses were based primarily upon information derived from the parents and the child. Because the parent and child interviews did not concentrate on academic performance, this area tended to be explored in detail only if the child was having significant problems. The teachers, on the other hand, identified children based primarily upon actual performance in the classroom. The statistical-formula approach identified even higher numbers of learning-disabled children because it picked up children from classrooms where the mean level of functioning was low. Such children were considered by parents and teachers to be functioning "adequately," but on standardized testing they were functioning below expected levels. These data show that no one method of identifying learning-disabled children is fully adequate.

Biological Factors

Regarding medical and biological conditions (see Table 3-5), 42% of the 600 children were without any significant medical-biological problems at any time, 35% suffered from some medical-biological condition at the time of the study, and 23% had recovered at the time of the study from some previous medical-biological condition.

Table 3-5. Medical, biological, and neurological data for the present research sample

Types of medical problems

CNS abnormalities	13%
Ear disorders	24%
Respiratory disorders	30%
Perinatal and pregnancy complications	12%
Congenital anomalies	10%
Speech mechanism disorders	5%

Performance on neurological examination items

	Normal (%)	Mild-to-moderate problem (%)	Moderate-to-severe problem (%)
Hop on one foot	64	22	14
Skip	59	25	16
Fingers to thumb	52	32	16
Alternating hand movements	54	33	13
Tapping	67	25	8
Associated movements			
Symmetrical	68	25	7
Nonsymmetrical	75	21	4
Eye tracking			
Does not hold head fixed	81	14	5
Poor eye tracking	83	12	5
Right-left confusion during:			
Hand on ear or knee	77	15	8
Point to examiner's knee	64	25	11
Stand and turn	74	17	9
Uses fixed base	75	14	11
Only a part of the body turns	78	12	10
Writing to dictation			
Reversals and inversions	84	12	4
Confused letter attack	88	8	4
Labored writing	62	29	9
Spelling difficulties	96	2	2
Reckless speed	85	14	1

The most common types of medical conditions afflicting the children in the sample were respiratory disorders (30%) and ear disorders (24%). The most common respiratory disorders were chronic respiratory infections (afflicting 28% of the sample), and, as the literature suggests, the most common ear disorder was otitis media (afflicting 21% of the sample).

Central nervous system (CNS) abnormalities (including seizure disorder, febrile seizures, cerebral palsy, skull injuries, neoplasms, meningitis, and congenital abnormalities) occurred in 13% of the sample according to parent interview information. Miscellaneous congenital anomalies were present in 10% of the children, and speech mechanism or oral disorders were present in 5% of the children. Pregnancy complications (including use of drugs or medications, Rh factor, maternal illnesses, and toxemia) and perinatal complications (including cesarean section, induced labor, forceps, premature delivery, and breech presentation) posed significant problems for 12% of the children.

Although documented history of brain damage and/or frank CNS abnormalities were present in only a relatively small portion of the sample (13%), there was evidence of "neurological soft signs" in more of the children. The neurological examination data (available for 254 children—those 5 years of age and above who were capable of participating in the examination) are presented in Table 3-5. Approximately 75% of the children tested performed all of the various neurological exam items correctly. The remaining children manifested difficulties including gross motor dyscoordination, associated motor movements, right-left confusions, eye-tracking problems, and fine motor incoordination. When difficulties were present in performing the exam items, these difficulties tended to be in the mild-to-moderate range.

Psychosocial Factors

The data on psychosocial stressors are presented in Table 3-6. Stressors that occurred in fewer than 1% of the sample have been omitted from this table. These rarely occurring stressors included remarriage of a parent, death of a family member, child abuse, hospitalization of the child, illness of a close friend, physical illness of the child, in-law problems, parental uncertainty about child raising, change in family composition, arrest, social isolation, parental employment changes, specific types of financial problems, overcrowding, legal problems, and disasters. It is of interest that abuse of the child was only detected in 4 of the 600 cases.

Some type of psychosocial stress was present in 66% of the cases.

The major sources of psychosocial stress (in order of frequency) were discordant family relations (affecting 39% of the sample); illnesses in family members (27%); family changes (such as divorce, remarriage, or death) (15%); significant events (such as frequent moves, hospitalization, or physical illness of child) (12%); personal difficulties for the child (including peer problems, school difficulties, or physical handicap) (9%); parental financial problems (7%); parental employment problems (5%); environmental deprivation (2%); and miscellaneous other parental worries (2%).

The results of the mental status examinations for the parents are also reported in Table 3-6. A surprising number of parents, approximately one-third of the entire group, had psychiatric disorders. Behavioral spectrum disorders and substance abuse disorders were most common among the fathers, and emotional and affective disorders were most common among the mothers.

Finally, at the end of Table 3-6, some data are presented regarding the interpersonal relations and life-styles of the children. The majority of the children (according to parental interview) had average or better relationships with their parents and siblings. Furthermore, the majority of the children had a special friend and had well-developed skills in both creative and imaginative play. However, approximately 10% of the children suffered from lack of parental or sibling warmth, approximately 25% had limited play development, and nearly 40% lacked a special friend. Surprisingly (considering that the majority of children had some type of speech disorder), only 30% of the children had been teased by their peers about their speech.

Psychiatric Symptoms in the Present Research Sample

Data on the psychiatric symptomatology of the children were available from three different sources: the child's parents, the child himself or herself, and the teacher (if the child was in school). The data from all of these sources were considered in establishing the psychiatric diagnoses of the children.

Parent Questionnaire Symptom Data

The data on the psychiatric symptomatology of the children that were reported in the parent questionnaires are presented in Table 3-7. This table lists (in order of their frequency of occurrence in the sample)

Table 3-6. Psychosocial stressors in the present research sample

Types of psychosocial stressors	n	Percentage of sample
Illness in family (any)	164	27
Major physical illness of parent	30	5
Major mental illness of parent	102	17
Illness of close relative (sibling)	12	2
Illness of other relative	20	3
Family discordant relations (any)	235	39
Parental fighting	76	13
Lack of warmth from parents	17	3
Parental overinvolvement	25	4
Inadequate parental control	74	12
Inadequate intrafamily communication	6	1
Discordant relations with family	33	5
Family changes (any)	92	15
Parental separation	34	6
Parental divorce	44	7
Death of parent	6	1
Environmental deprivation (any)	14	2
Inadequate stimulation	8	1
Significant events (any)	71	12
Separation from parents	10	2
Frequent moves in residence	12	2
Change in residence	26	4
Frequent change of caregiver	10	2
Personal problems of children (any)	51	9
Problems with peer group	14	2
Problems in school setting	31	5
Parental employment problems (any)	33	5
Heavy workload	23	4
Parental financial problems (any)	40	7
Miscellaneous other parental worries	13	2
Parental mental health ($n = 573$)		
Both parents psychiatrically well	281	49
Either parent psychiatrically ill	200	35
Both parents psychiatrically ill	92	16

Psychiatric diagnoses	Fathers (%)	Mothers (%)
Psychiatrically well	69	67
Psychiatrically ill	31	33
Behavioral disorders	14	5
Emotional disorders	10	19
Schizophrenia	1	1
Substance abuse disorders	13	5
Affective disorders	4	10
Other disorders	4	3
Psychiatric treatment	9	12

Table 3-6 *(continued)*

	Fathers (%)	Mothers (%)	Siblings (%)
Attitude toward child			
Very warm	39	40	15
Average warmth	47	53	73
Less warm than average	14	7	12
Child's life		Percentage of sample	
Has limited creative play		28	
Has limited imaginative play		24	
Prefers to play alone		18	
Has a special friend		60	
Plays well with sibling (*n* = 469)		88	
Plays well with father		74	
Has been teased about speech		30	

Note. Stressors occurring in fewer than 1% of the sample have been omitted from this table.

those symptoms rated by parents as being "pretty much" or "very much" present in the children. These symptoms include those from the Rutter questionnaire and the Conners questionnaire, as well as the mood and speech/language items added for the study. Low-frequency symptoms (i.e., those occurring in fewer than 5% of the children) have been omitted from the table in order to conserve space. These rarely occurring symptoms were primarily in the areas of conduct disturbance (e.g., fighting, destroying property, truancy from school, stealing, setting fires) and somatic disorder (e.g., aches and pains, headaches, muscular tension, tics, health worries).

The most commonly occurring symptoms according to the parent reports were as follows:

1. Speech/language symptoms (e.g., being difficult to understand, having limited language)
2. Attention-deficit/hyperactivity symptoms (e.g., easily frustrated, short attention span, restless, excitable, squirmy, always climbing)
3. Developmental immaturity symptoms (e.g., sucking thumb, wetting)
4. Anxiety symptoms (e.g., feelings easily hurt, shyness, afraid of new situations, solitary behavior)

Table 3-7. Symptomatology of the present research sample based on parent questionnaires

Symptom	Percentage of sample with symptom
Difficult to understand	41
Limited language	37
Feelings easily hurt	34
Easily frustrated	32
Short attention span	30
Restless	27
Excitable	25
Sucks thumb	21
Immature	21
Wets	19
Angry, irritable	19
Disobeys often	19
Shy	18
Picky eater	17
Fights with sibling	17
Solitary	17
Squirmy	17
Afraid of new situations	16
Always climbing	16
Tantrums	15
Inappropriate speech rhythm	15
Drastic mood changes	14
Problems getting to sleep	12
Perfectionist	12
Insists on sameness	11
Soils	10
Clings, separation anxiety	10
Overasserts self	10
Is bullied	10
Acts as if driven by motor	10
Difficulty understanding others	10
Uses language inappropriately	9
Nightmares	9
Fears not being liked	9
Sibling rivalry	9
Lies	9
Blames others for his or her mistakes	9
Inappropriate intonation: flat or odd	9
Daydreams	8
Quarrelsome	8
Unhappy	8
Stomachaches	7
Does not learn	7
Stutters	7
Asthma	6

Table 3-7 *(continued)*

Symptom	Percentage of sample with symptom
Keeps anger to self	6
Often worries	6
Overweight	5
Not liked	5
Dislikes school	5

Note. Symptoms occurring in fewer than 5% of the sample have been omitted from this table.

Although the more serious conduct symptoms (such as stealing, fire setting, and school truancy) occurred rarely, less serious conduct symptomatology (such as anger, irritability, frequent disobedience, sibling fights, and tantrums) was somewhat common.

Unfortunately, there are no data in the literature that are directly comparable with the prevalence rates reported by the parents of the speech/language–disordered children in this study. This is because the other studies in the literature that have reported on parent ratings have not examined similar age or sex distributions of children and have not used the same questionnaires for obtaining their data. For example, the most comprehensive parent and teacher questionnaire symptom data that have been published to date (Achenbach and Edelbrock 1981) reported the data separately for the different sexes and age levels (e.g., 4–5 years, 6–7 years, 8–9 years, 10–11 years, etc.). For many symptoms, there was a vast range in frequency across the age and sex levels. For example, concentration problems ranged from 13% among 16-year-old girls to 38% among 14- to 15-year-old boys.

However, a few studies have examined parent-reported symptomatology in groups of children of ages roughly similar to those of the children in the present study. Such reports include Agras et al.'s (1969) work on the full age-range of children; Cullen and Boundy's (1966) work on 3- to 16-year-olds; Lapouse and Monk's (1958) work on 6- to 12-year-olds; MacFarlane et al.'s (1954) work following children from ages 21 months through 14 years; and Verhulst et al.'s (1985) work on 4- to 16-year-olds. These works suggest that symptomatology may be somewhat elevated in the speech/language–disordered children in the present study. For example, Cullen and Boundy (1966) found shyness reported for 4% of their sample (vs. 18% of the present sample), and MacFarlane and colleagues (1954) found thumb sucking reported in approximately 10% of their sample (vs. 21% of the present sample).

However, there were differences in both the age and sex distributions of these samples as well as differences in the way the data were collected. Therefore, the apparent differences in frequency of symptoms may not have any clinical significance.

Teacher Questionnaire Symptom Data

The teacher questionnaire data on the psychiatric symptomatology of those children in the present research sample attending some type of school are presented in Table 3-8. As in Table 3-7, Table 3-8 includes those symptoms that were rated as being "pretty much" or "very much" present in the children. The symptoms are listed in order of their frequency in the sample, and those rarer symptoms occurring in fewer than 5% of the children are not listed. The rarely occurring symptoms (according to the teachers) included complaining of aches or pains, telling lies, being absent for trivial reasons, being tearful upon arrival at school, being truant, and stealing. These are among the same symptoms that were rarely reported by the parents.

Similarly, the symptoms reported by the teachers as being of high frequency were among the same ones reported by the parents as being of high frequency. The symptoms most commonly reported by the teachers tended to fall into three general types:

1. Speech/language symptoms (e.g., difficult to understand, limited language, inappropriate intonation, inappropriate language usage)
2. Attention-deficit/hyperactivity symptoms (e.g., short attention span, constant fidgeting, restlessness, overactivity, impulsivity, easily frustrated, attention-demanding, disturbing other children, daydreaming)
3. Anxiety symptoms (solitary, lacking leadership qualities, submissiveness, shyness, being bullied, worrying)

Poor coordination was the only developmental immaturity symptom reported commonly by the teachers. Milder conduct disorder and oppositional disorder symptoms (e.g., stubbornness, resentment, defiance, disobedience, fighting) were reported by teachers with approximately the same frequency as they were reported by parents (i.e., in about 15% of the children).

As with the parent questionnaire data, the teacher questionnaire data obtained in this study cannot be directly compared with similar data from other studies because of differences in the methodology of other studies. Studies reporting teacher questionnaire data on children in approximately the same age-ranges as the present study include

Table 3-8. Symptomatology of the present research sample based on teacher questionnaires

Symptom	Prevalence (%)
Difficult to understand	42
Short attention span	41
Limited language	34
Lacks leadership	30
Constantly fidgets	25
Restless, overactive	24
Solitary	23
Poor coordination	21
Impulsive	21
Stubborn	20
Disturbs other children	20
Submissive	20
Shy	19
Easily frustrated	19
Demands attention	18
Inappropriate intonation	18
Daydreams	16
Is bullied	15
Worries	15
Uses language inappropriately	15
Resentful when corrected	14
Defiant	14
Disobedient	13
Unresponsive	13
Difficulty understanding others	13
Inappropriate speech rhythm	13
Fights	12
Stutters	11
Is not liked	10
No fair play	10
Unhappy	10
Overly sensitive	10
Hums	9
Quick, drastic mood changes	9
Bullies, teases	9
Does not get along with same sex	9
Sullen	9
Fearful	9
Tics	8
Tantrums	8
Sucks thumb	7
Does not get along with opposite sex	7
Cries often and easily	6
Destroys property	5

Note. Symptoms occurring in fewer than 5% of the sample have been omitted from this table.

Chawla et al.'s (1981) study of 6- to 12-year-olds; Trites et al.'s (1979) study of Canadian schoolchildren; and Rutter et al.'s (1970a, 1970b) Isle of Wight study of 10- to 12-year-olds. Of these, the Isle of Wight study is perhaps most relevant to the present work, because the teacher questionnaire it used was among those employed in the present study. Unfortunately, direct comparisons are not possible because of the age differences of the samples and the fact that the Isle of Wight data set was reported separately for boys and girls. Nonetheless, the Isle of Wight data seem to show several interesting trends with regard to the present data.

First, in the Isle of Wight study, attention-deficit and hyperactivity symptoms were less common than in the present study. For example, restlessness was identified by Isle of Wight teachers for 15.7% of boys and 6.5% of girls (vs. 24% of the present sample), and fidgetiness was identified for 20% of boys and 9.8% of girls (vs. 25% of the present sample).

Similarly, symptoms of conduct and oppositional disorders appeared to be less common in the Isle of Wight sample than in the speech/language–disordered children studied here. Destructiveness was reported by Isle of Wight teachers for 1.5% of boys and 0.4% of girls (vs. 5% of the present sample); disobedience for 10.6% of boys and 3.6% of girls (vs. 13% of the present sample); lying for 6.9% of boys and 2% of girls (vs. 3% of the present sample); and fighting for 11% of boys and 3.7% of girls (vs. 12% of the present sample).

Emotional symptomatology was sometimes more common among the speech/language–disordered children in the present study and sometimes more common among the Isle of Wight students. For example, the Isle of Wight teachers reported solitary behavior in 17% of boys and 10% of girls (vs. 23% of the present sample); worrying in 23.5% of boys and 22.2% of girls (vs. 15% of the present sample); tearful on arrival at school in 0.4% of boys and 0.8% of girls (vs. 2% of the present sample); and fearfulness in 17.6% of boys and 6% of girls (vs. 9% of the present sample).

Child Psychiatric Interview Symptom Data

Table 3-9 presents the data from the psychiatric interviews of the children in the research sample. Both symptom data (according to the children's self-reports) and psychiatric ratings based upon behaviors and affect manifested during the interview are included. The symptom data have been grouped according to subject matter and the types of symptoms, and individual symptoms are reported in order of frequency of occurrence. Symptoms present in fewer than 5% of the sample (e.g., auditory, visual, tactile, olfactory, or gustatory hallucinations; delusions; and ideas of reference or persecutory ideas) were omitted from the table.

Learning difficulties were the single most common problem reported by the children. These occurred in 41% of the children interviewed. Interestingly, other school problems (including relationship problems with the teacher and school behavior problems) were far less common, affecting 12% to 16% of the children.

The next most common types of problems were relationship or antisocial problems and worries, anxieties, or fears. Approximately one-quarter to one-third of the sample admitted to having poor relationships with siblings, with one or both parents, or with peers. Fighting was common with siblings (38%) and peers (21%) but not common with parents (7%). Almost one-third of the children reported having some fear or phobia, and a similar number (23%) reported generally worrying a lot. Somatic problems were the most common type of worry; these bothered 29% of the sample. Fear of being alone was expressed by 21% of the children and fear of meeting new people, by 16%. Other specific fears or worries occurred in fewer than 15% of the children.

In addition to the children's self-reports of anxious feelings, the psychiatrists' ratings of observed affect were also suggestive of anxiety in the children. The psychiatrist rated between 25% and 50% of the children interviewed as having anxious, apprehensive, or constricted affect. Other abnormal affects (i.e., sad, depressed, elated, histrionic, angry) were manifested in approximately 10% of the children.

The children reported more symptoms of depression than the psychiatrists' ratings of affect would have led one to expect. Approximately 31% of the children interviewed reported being "sad most of the time," 24% reported nightmares, and 18% reported trouble sleeping. Other symptoms of depression, such as poor self-esteem and suicidal ideation, were less common, occurring in 10% or fewer of the children.

Abnormal motor behaviors were also common according to the psychiatric ratings. The majority of the children observed manifested either definite overactivity or definite underactivity. Other symptoms of ADDH were also common: almost one-half the children in the sample were fidgety during the interview, one-third had a short attention span, and one-quarter were distractible.

Finally, the psychiatrists' ratings of overall degree of impairment and of highest level of adaptive functioning were suggestive of significant problems. The psychiatrists found some degree of overall impairment in 80% of the children, 39% of whom were moderately to severely

Table 3-9. Child psychiatric interview data in the present research sample

Symptomatology	Percentage reporting significant problems
School and learning difficulties	
Learning difficulties	41
School behavior	16
Poor relationship with teacher	12
Fighting and relationship problems	
Poor relationship with siblings	38
Fights with siblings	38
Temper outbursts	33
Poor relationship with peers	25
Poor relationship with mother	23
Poor relationship with father	22
Lack of peer interaction	21
Fights with peers	21
Fights with parents	7
Fears and anxieties	
Any phobias or fears	32
Somatic worries	29
Overall worrying, ruminations	23
Specific anxiety about being alone	21
Specific anxiety about meeting new people	16
Specific anxiety about animals	13
Specific anxiety about school	7
Compulsions	6
Generalized anxiety	5
Obsessive thoughts	5
Mood (affective) symptoms	
Sad most of time	31
Nightmares	24
Trouble sleeping	18
Believes others dislike him or her	14
Wishes he or she was dead	10
Dislikes self	7
Suicidal thoughts	5
Psychiatrist's ratings: observed affect	
Apprehensive	50
Anxious expression	48
Apprehensive about separation	43
Constricted affect	24
Elated affect	13
Sad expression	9
Depressed affect	8
Histrionic behavior	7
Angry affect	7

Table 3-9 *(continued)*

Symptomatology	Percentage reporting significant problems
Thought disorder symptoms	
Peculiar fantasies	5
Psychiatrist's ratings: motor behavior	
Activity level (over- or underactive)	82
Fidgety	45
Short attention span	32
Distractible	24
Disinhibited	14
Irritable	9
Habitual mannerisms	6
Psychiatrist's ratings: speech/language	
Abnormal amount of conversation	32
Abnormal comprehension	28
Abnormal volume of conversation	17
Abnormal speech rhythm	12
Abnormal intonation	7
Abnormal voice	7
Psychiatrist's ratings: relationship with examiner	
Stranger anxiety	46
Limited eye contact	29
Egocentric attitude	23
Negative attitude	10
Suspicious	6
Psychiatrists' ratings: degree of overall impairment	
None	20
Mild	41
Moderate	34
Severe	5
Psychiatrists' ratings: highest level of adaptive functioning	
Superior	2
Very good	11
Good	33
Fair	37
Poor	14
Very poor	1
Grossly impaired	2

Note. Symptoms occurring in fewer than 5% of the sample have been omitted from the table.

impaired. Adaptive functioning was somewhat better: 46% of the children had good to superior adaptive functioning, 37% had fair adaptive functioning, and 17% had poor to grossly impaired functioning.

Psychiatric Disorders in the Present Research Sample

Prevalence of Psychiatric Disorders

Table 3-10 presents the data on the prevalence and types of psychiatric disorders found in the sample. Of the 600 children with speech/language disorders, 298 (nearly 50%) were found to have no psychiatric diagnosis and 302 (again, 50%) were judged to be psychiatrically ill. The great majority of the psychiatrically "ill" children (n = 272) had only one psychiatric diagnosis. However, 30 children were found to have two concurrent psychiatric diagnoses.

These results confirm the hypothesis that children with speech/language disorders are "at risk" for psychiatric illness. The prevalence rate for psychiatric illness of 50% among these children is alarmingly high. And, even though there is no control group for this study, it seems safe to infer that this rate is significantly greater than could be found in a random sample of the general population.

One source of comparison is the study conducted by the President's Commission on Mental Health of Children (1980). Based upon somewhat similar methodology to that used in the present study, the Commission estimated that from 10% to 15% of children in the general population suffer from a clinically significant psychiatric disorder. That is, children with speech/language disorders have from three to five times more risk for psychiatric illness.

Types of Psychiatric Disorders

As can be seen in Table 3-10, the speech/language–disordered children manifested a variety of types of psychiatric disorders. The most common types of disorders were, first, behavioral disorders (affecting 26% of the children) and, then, emotional disorders (affecting 20% of the children). Physical disorders and PDDs were each present in only 1% of the children, and miscellaneous other disorders were present in a total of 7% of the children.

Few of the psychiatric studies of speech/language–disordered children have examined the prevalence of general types of psychiatric disorders. However, there is some confirmation of the present findings in a Canadian epidemiologic study of 5-year-old children (Beitchman et al. 1986b). In this study, behavioral disturbance was, by far, the most common type of psychiatric disorder found among speech/language–disordered children.

The specific disorders diagnosed in the present study are dis-

Table 3-10. Prevalence and type of psychiatric disorders in the present research sample

Types of psychiatric disorders	Prevalence (%)
General	
No mental illness	50
Behavioral disorders	26
Emotional disorders	20
Pervasive developmental disorders	1
Physical disorders	1
Other disorders	7
Specific	
Attention-deficit disorder	19
Anxiety disorders	10
Oppositional disorder or conduct disorder	7
Adjustment disorders	5
Affective disorders	4
Parent-child problem	4
Unspecified mental disorders	3
Infantile autism	1

Note. Specific diagnoses occurring in fewer than 1% of the sample have been omitted from this table. These included organic personality syndrome, organic brain syndrome, atypical stereotyped movement disorder, childhood-onset pervasive developmental disorder, elective mutism, schizoid disorder, gender identity disorder, child abuse, and other interpersonal problem.

cussed below. As Table 3-10 shows, no particular psychiatric diagnosis was uniquely associated with speech/language disorders. This finding is consistent with studies of children with other types of handicaps that have reported increased rates for all types of psychiatric disorders (Rutter et al. 1970a, 1970b). For example, children with brain damage, epilepsy, chronic physical disorders, or low IQ have elevated rates of psychiatric disorder but no unique associated diagnoses. Thus, the risk seems to be for psychopathology in general and not for any particular type of psychopathology.

Attention-deficit disorder. The most common psychiatric disorder found among the speech/language–disordered children was attention-deficit disorder (ADD). This disorder affected 19% of the sample. ADD, which had previously been called hyperkinetic reaction of childhood, hyperactive child syndrome, and minimal brain dysfunction, is one of the best studied childhood psychiatric disorders. It is characterized by features such as a developmentally inappropriate short attention span, poor concentration, impulsivity (cognitive and behavioral), and inappropriately high levels of motor activity. There is some suggestion that the quality of the motor activity is also different from that of other children in being more globally restless and less goal directed (Barkley and Ullman 1975). The quality of cognitive functioning may also be different for children with ADD (Ackerman et al. 1986; Campbell et al. 1971; Cotugno 1987; Radosh and Gittelman 1981; Stoner and Glynn 1987; Tarnowski et al. 1986).

Attention-deficit disorder is the most common childhood psychiatric disorder found in child-guidance clinics (President's Commission 1980). The prevalence of the disorder is generally estimated to be around 5% in boys (Cantwell 1978; Chawla et al. 1981; Miller et al. 1973). Thus, the prevalence rate found in the present study is considerably higher than the population estimates.

DSM-III identified two primary subtypes of ADD: attention-deficit disorder with hyperactivity (ADDH) and attention-deficit disorder without hyperactivity (ADDW) (first defined in DSM-III), the two subtypes being distinguished by the presence or absence of motor activity disturbances. The majority of the children in the present speech/language study (n = 106) received the ADDH diagnosis. A small number of the speech/language–disordered children (n = 9) received the ADDW diagnosis. A third subtype of attention-deficit disorder—attention-deficit disorder, residual type (ADDR)—was also described in DSM-III. However, this subtype was not found in any of the speech/language–disordered children in the present study, most likely due to the young age of the sample.

Studies comparing ADDH with ADDW have provided some evidence that the nonhyperactive variety of the disorder may be substantially different in terms of both behavioral manifestations and learning-cognition (Berry et al. 1985; Carlson 1986; Carlson et al. 1987; King and Young 1982; Lahey et al. 1987). In fact, the ADDH children in the present study gave the clinical impression of being quite different from the ADDW children. This prompted the hypothesis that the two groups would have differential outcomes at follow-up. The 4-year follow-up data available for 35 "pure" ADDH children and 5 "pure" ADDW children did indeed reveal very different psychiatric outcomes for the two groups of children. Unfortunately, the number of ADDW children followed was so small that statistical comparison was not possible.

Nevertheless, the distinction between ADDH and ADDW was not maintained in DSM-III-R (American Psychiatric Association 1987). DSM-III-R viewed attention-deficit hyperactivity disorder (ADHD) as having heterogeneous manifestations involving various aspects of hyperactivity, attention deficit, and/or impulsivity. The DSM-III-R category of "undifferentiated attention-deficit disorder" (p. 95) was a residual diagnosis to be used when signs of impulsivity and hyperactivity were not present.

Recent data have indicated that children diagnosed as having ADDH under the DSM-III system almost always satisfy the diagnostic criteria for ADHD under DSM-III-R (Newcorn et al. 1989). Thus, it is likely that the children in the present study with ADDH would have qualified for the ADHD diagnosis had DSM-III-R been used for diagnosis. Reexamination of the charts for those children with ADDW diagnoses under DSM-III indicated that under DSM-IV, all would qualify for the ADHD diagnosis. None of the patients in the speech/language study met the DSM-III-R criteria for undifferentiated ADD, because all manifested impulsivity.

The very high rate of ADD among the speech/language–disordered children in the present study gives support to the hypothesis that some type of verbal or linguistic deficit may underlie at least some cases of ADD. It is of interest that in Beitchman et al.'s (1986b) study of speech/language–disordered 5-year-olds in Canada, the most commonly found psychiatric diagnosis was also ADD. It has also been found that preschool-age children presenting for psychiatric evaluation with ADHD have a high rate (67%) of speech/language disorder (Love and Thompson 1988). Linguistic deficits involving word retrieval or semantic-feature clustering have been postulated (August 1987; Felton et al. 1987; Tarver 1981; Weingartner et al. 1980), as well as verbal interactional deficits (Hamlett et al. 1987; Landau and Milich 1988; Tarver-Behring et al. 1985).

Conduct and oppositional disorders. Other behavioral disorders (aside from ADD) were found in 41 (or 7%) of the speech/language–disordered children in the present research sample. Of these 41 behaviorally disordered children, 29 (or 5% of the sample) had oppositional disorder and 12 (or 2% of the sample) had conduct disorder. These rates appear slightly elevated in comparison to available population estimates. For example, the Isle of Wight study found a prevalence rate of 4% for conduct disorder at ages 10 to 11 years (Rutter et al. 1970a, 1970b) and 2% at ages 14 to 15 years (Graham and Rutter 1973), and the New Zealand epidemiologic study (Silva et al. 1984) found a 3.4% prevalence rate for conduct disorder.

Conduct disorder is characterized by repetitive and persistent patterns of antisocial behavior that violate the rights of others and go beyond ordinary childhood mischief and pranks. Some form of conduct disorder has been recognized for almost a century (Koch 1891; Kraepelin 1909), and the disorder has played an important part in the history of child psychiatry in the United States (Cantwell 1989).

Oppositional disorder is characterized by 1) pervasive opposition to all in authority regardless of self-interest, 2) continuous argumentativeness, and 3) unwillingness to respond to reasonable persuasion. It is not clear that conduct disorder and oppositional disorder indeed constitute separate disorders, although they are so viewed in DSM-III and DSM-III-R. It is possible that oppositional disorder is an early stage or a milder form of conduct disorder (Rey et al. 1988).

Because the DSM-III diagnostic criteria for conduct disorder require a long pattern of antisocial behaviors, it is unlikely that a preschool-age child or a young grade school–age child would satisfy the criteria. This may explain the fact that relatively few of the children in the present study (only n = 12) qualified for a conduct disorder diagnosis, whereas considerably more (n = 29) received the oppositional disorder diagnosis. Two-thirds of the speech/language–clinic sample were of preschool age, and many others were young grade school–age children.

Four-year follow-up data were available for 15 of the children with oppositional disorder. Oppositional disorder showed a poor prognosis but did not directly lead to conduct disorder. Thus, at follow-up, four of the oppositional children had a conduct disorder diagnosis and another six had ADD.

The subtyping of conduct disorder is a controversial issue. DSM-III specified four subtypes of conduct disorder: undersocialized aggressive, undersocialized nonaggressive, socialized aggressive, and socialized nonaggressive. The socialization dimension refers to the existence of some social attachment, bonding, and/or empathy with others; the aggression dimension refers to the presence of aggressive behavior violating the rights of others.

DSM-III-R, on the other hand, specified only three subtypes of conduct disorder: solitary aggressive, group, and undifferentiated. The solitary aggressive subtype is characterized by physical and verbal aggressive behavior toward adults and peers, not occurring in a group situation. The group subtype is characterized by conduct symptomatology that occurs mainly in the company of friends with similar problems and with whom the patient is loyal. Whether these subtypes differ in meaningful ways, such as outcome and response to treatment, is presently not established.

Among the speech/language–disordered children who received the conduct disorder diagnosis, 10 children had the (DSM-III) undersocialized aggressive subtype, one child had the undersocialized un-aggressive subtype, and one child had socialized nonaggressive conduct disorder. The numbers of children with the different subtypes of the disorders were too small for any meaningful conclusions to be drawn with regard to differential prognoses.

Anxiety disorders. The second most common type of psychiatric disorder (and the most common type of emotional disorder) occurring in the speech/language–disordered children was anxiety disorder. Sixty-one children (10% of the sample) had some type of anxiety disorder. The subtypes of anxiety disorders found were avoidant disorder ($n = 29$), separation anxiety disorder ($n = 19$), overanxious disorder ($n = 12$), and simple phobia ($n = 1$).

Both DSM-III and DSM-III-R have identified the same subtypes of anxiety disorders, which are distinguished by the focus of the anxiety. In separation anxiety disorder, avoidant disorder, and simple phobia, the anxiety is focused on specific situations or objects. In overanxious disorder, the anxiety is generalized to a variety of situations.

Avoidant disorder was the most common type of anxiety disorder in the research sample, affecting 5% of the speech/language–disordered children. The disorder was described for the first time in DSM-III. The essential feature is persistent and excessive shrinking from contact with strangers that interferes with the child's social functioning in peer relationships. At the same time, the child has a clear desire for affection and acceptance, and experiences warm and satisfying relationships with family members and other familiar figures. Children with avoidant disorder may cling to their caregivers and may seem inarticulate or even mute when their social anxiety is very severe. These children may become fearful and inhibited when confronted with even minor demands for contact with strangers. Although this disorder is described as "uncommon" in DSM-III, there are few epidemiologic studies to support that statement.

Separation anxiety disorder is a condition that has been recognized and well studied in child psychiatric populations. The essential feature is extreme anxiety manifested by the child when placed in a situation likely to lead to separation from major attachment figures, from home, or from other familiar surroundings. When such separation does occur, the child may experience extreme anxiety to the point of panic. Common symptoms of separation anxiety disorder include unrealistic worry that parents or other major attachment figures will somehow be harmed, will be kidnapped, or will leave and not return to the child. This worry is coupled with repeated nightmares involving separation themes. There are often associated physical complaints, particularly on school days, such as stomachaches, headaches, nausea, and vomiting. There may be persistent refusal or reluctance to go to school because of a desire to remain at home with the major attachment figure (usually the mother). The child may follow the attachment figure around the home, and, if separation is anticipated or actually occurs, there may be signs of excessive distress including temper tantrums, crying, pleading with parents not to leave, social withdrawal, apathy, sadness, and difficulty in concentration.

Three percent of the sample (n = 19) had separation anxiety disorder. Many of these children also manifested some school refusal, but this was generally of a mild-to-moderate degree, with no children totally refusing school.

Twelve children (or 2% of the sample) were diagnosed as having overanxious disorder. The essential features of this disorder are generalized and persistent anxieties and worries not related to specific situations. Typical manifestations are unrealistic worries about the future (what will happen to the child or the parents); preoccupation with events that have occurred in the past; overconcern about the child's own competence in the sense that the child feels he or she is inferior to peers in, for example, sports, academic performance, and dress; excessive need for reassurance from the parents; self-consciousness; a tendency to be embarrassed or humiliated; and marked feelings of tension or inability to relax. Somatic complaints, particularly headaches or stomachaches, are often prominent, but generally no physical basis can be established. The occurrence of somatic complaints in overanxious disorder tends to be consistent and not situation-specific, which is in contrast to separation anxiety disorder, in which the somatic symptoms generally occur only with anticipated or actual separation.

It is thought that this disorder is more common in children from small families, from higher–socioeconomic-class families, and in families where there is higher concern about the child's performance. Because speech/language disorders often impair performance in several areas, it seems reasonable that they may be a precipitating factor for overanxious disorder.

One child in the sample was given a diagnosis of simple phobia. This was an animal phobia, of the type that typically occurs in childhood. No children received a diagnosis of social phobia, a disorder characterized by persistent, irrational fear of situations involving exposure to possible scrutiny by others and avoidance of social situations. However, a number of the children who were diagnosed as having avoidant disorder showed some elements of this problem. DSM-III does not allow the diagnosis of social phobia when avoidant disorder is present, with the implication being that avoidant disorder is more pervasive and basic. It was clear that a number of the children who had pervasive anxiety symptoms also had specific fears of situations such as reading out loud in school, where their speech/language disorder (particularly articulation problems and stuttering) might lead to ridicule and embarrassment.

Adjustment disorders.   Five percent of the children (n = 31) in the research sample were diagnosed as having an adjustment disorder. Adjustment disorder is characterized by a symptom pattern that is a maladaptive reaction to a clearly identifiable psychosocial stressor that occurred within 3 months of the onset of the symptomatology. The maladaptive nature of the symptomatic reaction to the stressor can be indicated by significant impairment in social functioning or in functioning in school, or by a symptom pattern that is in excess of a normal reaction to the stressor. There is an assumption that the symptomatic disturbance on the part of the child will remit if the stress is removed. The stressors that are involved in adjustment disorder may be single, multiple, recurrent, or continuous.

The symptomatology of adjustment disorder can mimic that of other psychiatric disorders, especially anxiety disorders and affective disorders. However, the diagnosis of an adjustment disorder cannot be used if the child meets the criteria for another disorder. Adjustment disorder is subtyped according to the predominant symptomatology. Among the speech/language–disordered children in the present research sample, the various subtypes of adjustment disorder (in order of frequency) were as follows:

1. With mixed emotional features (n = 11)
2. With disturbance of emotions and conduct (n = 9)
3. With disturbance of conduct (n = 4)
4. With withdrawal (n = 2)
5. With anxious mood (n = 2)
6. With atypical features (n = 1)
7. With depressed mood (n = 2)

Thus, only 4 of the children had predominantly pure conduct symptomatology; the remaining 27 children had various combinations of anxiety, affective, and mixed symptomatology. The adjustment-disordered children with conduct symptomatology are hypothesized to be different from children with conduct disorder or oppositional disorder in that their disorder is more likely to remit.

The adjustment disorder category is one area that is currently under discussion by the child work group for DSM-IV. Adjustment disorder in DSM-III and DSM-III-R is diagnosed when there is a real stress in the environment and the patient reacts to that stress with symptoms that do not meet the full clinical criteria for another disorder. There is some concern that the adjustment disorder diagnosis is used by clinicians disproportionately more often with children and adolescents than with adults. It may be that there are some children who do not meet specific criteria for a specific childhood disorder and who are therefore given an adjustment disorder diagnosis, when indeed what they have is a subthreshold version of a childhood psychiatric disorder. If this is the case, the subthreshold disorder will become more clear with time.

Follow-up data to the present study were available for 19 of the children with adjustment disorders. The data indicated a surprisingly low recovery rate; only 26% of the children who had adjustment disorders were psychiatrically well at 4-year follow-up. The types of psychiatric diagnoses that these children had at follow-up were not related to the general types of symptoms they had initially. That is, children having initial adjustment disorders with emotional symptoms did not tend to have emotional diagnoses at follow-up, and children having initial adjustment disorders with conduct symptoms did not tend to have behavioral disorders at follow-up. Generally, the adjustment-disordered children were most likely to have follow-up diagnoses of behavioral disorders or anxiety disorders, regardless of their specific initial type of adjustment disorder.

Affective disorders.   Twenty-two children (4% of the sample) had a diagnosis of some type of affective disorder. The affective disorders fell into four different subtypes: major depression, single episode ($n = 9$), cyclothymic disorder ($n = 7$), dysthymic disorder ($n = 5$), and bipolar disorder, manic episode ($n = 1$).

According to DSM-III, a major depressive episode is characterized by dysphoric mood or anhedonia plus other vegetative, cognitive, and psychomotor symptoms. A manic episode is characterized by elevated, expansive, or irritable mood plus other symptoms in the psychomotor and cognitive areas. Major depression consists of a major depressive episode without manic episodes. Dysthymic disorder is a more chronic disorder characterized by depressive symptomatology of at least 1 year's duration that is not of sufficient severity to meet the criteria for a major depressive episode. Manic symptomatology is not present in dysthymic disorder. Cyclothymic disorder consists of multiple periods over the course of years in which symptoms characteristic of both depressive syndromes and manic syndromes occur but are not of sufficient severity and duration to meet criteria for a major depressive episode or a manic episode. The diagnosis of bipolar disorder, manic episode, requires a current manic episode. The speech/language–disordered child who received this diagnosis in the present study had a classic picture of mania with both elevated and irritable mood for several weeks' duration, associated with flight of ideas, increased activity level, push of speech, decreased need for sleep, and distractibility.

Although the diagnostic criteria for the various subtypes of depressive disorders changed somewhat for DSM-III-R, it is likely that the children diagnosed as having major depression under DSM-III would have received the same diagnosis under DSM-III-R. However, the prevalence of the other subtypes of affective disorders might have been different had DSM-III-R been used.

The prevalence of depressive disorders among children appears to be relatively low. For example, in the New Zealand epidemiologic study (Anderson et al. 1987), the prevalence of depression and dysthymic disorder among 11-year-olds was 1.8%. The duration requirement in the DSM-III diagnostic criteria may be one reason why so few youngsters receive the diagnosis. Although the duration requirement for children and adolescents is shorter than for adults, it still represents a substantial amount of time in the life of the youngster.

Parent-child problem. The next most common diagnosis among the speech/language–disordered children in the present research sample was parent-child problem. Twenty-one children (4% of the sample) received this diagnosis. The parent-child problem diagnosis is not considered a true psychiatric disorder. Rather, it is a "V code" diagnosis in DSM-III and indicates a disturbance in the relationship between the parent and the child, rather than a primary psychiatric problem in the child.

Of the 21 children with the parent-child problem diagnosis, 15 were seen for follow-up. The prognosis for these children was as poor or poorer than that of the children with true psychiatric disorders. Only three of the children with parent-child problem (20%) were found to be psychiatrically well at follow-up. Of the remaining 12 children, 10 had some type of behavioral disorder at follow-up. Multiple psychiatric diagnoses were very common among these children at follow-up, with one-third of the group having more than one psychiatric illness.

Pervasive developmental disorder and infantile autism. Eight children in the research sample had a diagnosis of one of the PDDs: six had classical infantile autism and two had childhood-onset PDD. Childhood-onset PDD is a DSM-III category for children who do not meet the classical symptomatology of infantile autism (Kanner

1943) or the criteria for schizophrenia, but who nevertheless fall into the overall rubric of the PDDs. The relationship of childhood-onset PDD to classical infantile autism is unknown at the present time.

The diagnostic criteria for autistic disorder in DSM-III-R are considerably broader than those in DSM-III. Thus, it is very likely that some of the children classified as having atypical PDD by DSM-III criteria would have been diagnosed as being autistic under DSM-III-R.

The prevalence in the general population of infantile autism is about 5 per 10,000 (Lotter 1967). The prevalence of childhood-onset PDD is unknown and may be greater or smaller than that of infantile autism. Nevertheless, it appears that the prevalence rate for infantile autism and childhood-onset PDD found among the speech/language–disordered children is considerably elevated. Because a serious disturbance of language is one of the core criteria for the diagnosis of infantile autism, it is not surprising that in a group of children selected on the basis of having a speech/language disorder, there would be an elevated prevalence rate for infantile autism.

Nonetheless, the prevalence rates of autism and childhood-onset PDD among the speech/language–clinic patients are lower than among psychiatric-clinic patients. In a study at the UCLA Neuropsychiatric Institute examining children with primary speech/language symptomatology, we (Cantwell and Baker 1980) found a very high prevalence of infantile autism. This finding was replicated almost 10 years later by Baltaxe and Simmons (1988). Apparently, autistic children are most often referred to a psychiatric clinic because of their behavioral abnormalities.

Physical disorders.   Five children (less than 1% of the sample) had physical disorders. Of these, three children had organic personality syndrome, one child had unspecified organic brain syndrome, and one child had atypical stereotyped movement disorder.

Elective mutism.   Two of the children from the speech/language clinic received a diagnosis of elective mutism. Both of these children had the rather classic symptomatology of speaking in the home setting and to family members but not speaking in settings outside the home, especially at school. Both children had relatively mild speech/language problems that were not severe enough to account for the mutism or even for a significant reduction in speech output. In fact, one of the children came from a bilingual home and talked quite fluently at home in both Spanish and English but did not usually talk to people outside the home.

The prevalence of elective mutism is consistently estimated to be less than 1% (Bradley and Sloman 1975; Brown and Lloyd 1975;

Fundudis et al. 1979; Haenel and Werder 1977). Because the symptomatology for elective mutism mimics to some degree that of a speech/language disorder, it is not unexpected that these children would present to a speech/language clinic. However, both of the children with elective mutism also had true speech/language disorders involving both speech articulation and expressive and receptive language.

Unspecified mental disorder. Nineteen children (just over 3% of the sample) had a diagnosis of unspecified mental disorder. This diagnosis was used to indicate the presence of a psychiatric disorder that did not meet the criteria for any specific DSM-III diagnosis. In many cases, these children had a potpourri of symptoms that defied any specific categorization.

Miscellaneous diagnoses. Two other true psychiatric diagnoses and two "V code" (DSM-III) diagnoses were found among the speech/language–disordered children. The true psychiatric disorders were schizoid disorder and gender identity disorder. One child received each of these diagnoses. The "V code" diagnoses were "other interpersonal problem" and child abuse. Two children received the "other interpersonal problem" diagnosis, and one child received the child abuse diagnosis.

Discussion of the Findings

The findings from the present study clearly show that children with speech/language disorders have high rates of psychiatric illness. Although a control group was not used, general population studies using similar methods suggest that the prevalence of psychiatric illness in the general population of children is around 10%. Thus, the rate of 50% in the present study could indicate as much as a fivefold increase in risk for psychiatric illness for children with speech/language disorders.

The psychiatric diagnoses of the speech/language–disordered children in the research sample fell into two main categories. The most common type of diagnosis was some type of externalizing (overt behavior or disruptive behavior) disorder. The next most common type of diagnosis was internalizing (or emotional) disorder. These two large clusters of disorders are the major types of disorders that turn up in epidemiologic studies and also among clinically referred children.

It has been observed (Kraemer et al. 1987) that the diagnostic system used in a study has a major effect on the results obtained. Thus, a concern is that the diagnoses made in this study according to DSM-III criteria would have been different under the newer diagnostic systems. Nonetheless, it is unlikely that children who were found to be psychiatrically ill by DSM-III criteria would not have been found ill by DSM-III-R criteria. Similarly, it is also unlikely that these children would not have been found ill by DSM-IV criteria. Thus, the prevalence rate of overall psychiatric disorder obtained in the present study would most likely have remained the same under DSM-III-R (and ultimately DSM-IV) criteria.

However, it is probable that the prevalence rates for some specific types of psychiatric diagnoses would have been different under the revised diagnostic systems. The specific diagnoses most likely to have been affected and the most likely effects are discussed above. It remains for future research to determine which set of diagnostic criteria are "correct" in the sense of being able to better predict outcome without treatment, treatment response, and biological and other correlates of the illness.

Because the children in the present study were relatively young (being seen, as they were, for their first speech/language evaluations), the data may even underestimate the incidence and risk of psychiatric disorders among these children. It is likely that older children who have had speech/language disorders for some time would have higher rates of psychiatric illness. In fact, data analysis of 4-year follow-ups for 300 of the children in the present study revealed a psychiatric illness rate of 60%, a significant ($P < .0001$) increase over the initial level.

The high rate of psychiatric illness in these children has direct clinical implications, especially for pediatricians. Any child manifesting speech/language difficulties should be closely followed with the possibilities of both psychiatric and developmental (learning) disorders in mind. Speech/language therapists also need to be aware that a failure to make adequate progress in speech/language therapy may be directly related to the presence of a psychiatric disorder. Closer examination of the children in this study who were psychiatrically ill may help to identify the risk factors of psychiatric illness. This, in turn, could lead to the development of the most appropriate preventive or early treatment approaches.

The literature review at the beginning of this chapter indicated that there were certain antecedent factors associated with the presence of speech/language disorders. Such factors included male sex, lower socioeconomic status, presence of other developmental delays, perinatal and neuropsychological problems, otitis media, oral abnormalities, environmental deprivation, and maltreatment. The majority of the children in the present study were males, and substantial numbers of children had other developmental disorders and middle-ear infections. However, the remainder of the reported risk factors occurred only rarely among the 600 children in the study. In Chapter 4 we examine these and other factors in the psychiatric literature in order to identify specific risk factors that may be associated with the presence of psychiatric disorders in these children.

Correlates and Classification of Childhood Psychiatric Disorders

4

IN THIS CHAPTER WE DISCUSS the correlates and classification of childhood psychiatric disorders. The chapter is organized into two sections: one dealing with the correlates of childhood psychiatric disorders in general, and the other dealing with the classification of two major subtypes of childhood psychiatric disorders. In each of these two sections we begin with a discussion of the relevant findings from the literature and then present data from the speech/language–disordered children in the present study.

Correlates of Childhood Psychiatric Disorders

Review of the Literature

In the field of epidemiology, the term *risk factor* is used to refer to some variable or factor that is statistically associated with a higher incidence of disease. (The term *correlate* has been used here in the same sense.) Following this usage, it appears that childhood speech/language disorder is a risk factor for psychopathology. Thus, the results presented in Chapter 3 indicate that children with speech/language disorders have a prevalence of psychiatric disorder that is many times higher than that of the general population of children.

In epidemiology, risk factors refer to statistical associations that are not necessarily etiological associations. Thus, although we know that speech/language disorders are associated with psychiatric disorders, it has not been established that speech/language disorders cause psychiatric disorders.

Garmezy (1984) distinguishes between "vulnerability factors" and "risk factors." Vulnerability factors are factors identifiable prior to the onset of disease that heighten an individual's susceptibility to the disease. They are necessary but not sufficient for the development of the disease. Risk factors, on the other hand, are factors that express increased statistical probability of the disease. They are neither necessary nor sufficient for the development of the disease.

The majority of risk-factor research in psychiatry has dealt with psychopathology in adults. The earliest work focused on schizophrenia, examining possible genetic and environmental stress factors (Bleuler 1978; Kraepelin 1909; Meyer 1919). More recent work, however, has concerned itself with a number of the childhood psychiatric disorders. Possible risk factors identified for the various child and adolescent psychiatric disorders include demographic and background factors, developmental and cognitive factors, biological factors, and psychosocial (stress) factors.

Additionally, observations of children at risk for psychopathology have identified the existence of the positive counterpart of risk factors (Garmezy and Rutter 1985; Rutter 1979, 1987a; Rutter and Hersov 1977). These "protective factors" include both individual and environmental characteristics. The various types of risk factors and protective factors that may be significant with regard to childhood or adolescent psychopathology are discussed briefly below.

Demographic and background factors.   Lower levels of parental socioeconomic class have been shown to be strongly associated with lower levels of education, increased learning disorder, and higher rates of mental retardation in children (Alberman 1973; Offord et al. 1987; Rutter and Madge 1976; Rutter et al. 1970b). Among infants exposed to perinatal risk factors, low family socioeconomic status (SES) has been shown to be a powerful predictor of "neuropsychiatric disability" (including reading disability, hyperactivity, behavioral disorders, and general child psychopathology) (Broman et al. 1985; Pasamanick and Knobloch 1960; Sameroff and Chandler 1975; Werner and Smith 1982). In the "children of Kauai" study (Werner and Smith 1982), the adverse effects of lower SES occurred despite the availability of good medical care for all the children, indicating that the adverse outcomes were not due to greater perinatal problems.

The type of family in which a child lives is also associated with his or her behavioral outcome. Data on a nationally representative cohort of British children revealed a significant association between behavioral deviance and family type, even after allowing for correlated social and biological factors (Wadsworth et al. 1985).

Demographic and background factors are most predictive of conduct disorder (i.e., delinquency). Studies of delinquent boys have shown that lower SES, large family size, parental unemployment, geographic overcrowding, broken homes, and inadequate school situations are significantly associated with the development and maintenance of delinquency (Fergusson et al. 1986; Hetherington 1979; Rutter 1981; Rutter and Giller 1984; Rutter et al. 1979; Tittle et al. 1978; Tonge et al. 1975; West and Farrington 1973).

However, even for conduct disorder, the association between psychiatric illness and lower family SES is inconsistent across studies. For example, a recent study (Kashani et al. 1987) found that adolescents with the DSM-III diagnosis of conduct disorder did not differ significantly from the remainder of a community sample in race, socioeconomic class, or family structure.

Further, when SES is examined independently of other associated variables, it is often revealed to be a weak predictor of illness in comparison to family variables such as discord (Robins and Ratcliff 1978–1979; Rutter and Giller 1984). Thus, it appears that the association between delinquency and SES is, at least in part, an indirect one reflecting critical underlying differences such as family discord, disruption and separation, weak relationships with parents, poor supervision of children, and cruel or neglectful attitudes. These factors are discussed further below.

Similarly, the British studies (Gath et al. 1977; Power et al. 1972; Rutter and Quinton 1977; Rutter et al. 1979) have shown that the associations between geographic area and childhood mental illness and between school and childhood mental illness most likely reflect other factors. Rutter and Quinton (1977) found that when family adversities were controlled, the difference in rates of psychiatric illness between rural and inner-city areas became nonsignificant. Also, the analysis of secondary schools and their effects on children by Rutter and his colleagues (1979) revealed that the most important factors were characteristics of the schools (such as social organizations and child-management philosophies). Thus, demographic and background factors in and of themselves do not seem to be highly predictive of childhood or adolescent mental illness.

Developmental-cognitive factors. Innumerable studies have reported an association between developmental learning disorders and psychiatric disorder. The various forms of psychiatric problems that appear to be most strongly associated with learning disorder include attention-deficit hyperactivity disorder (ADHD) (Holborow and Berry 1986), conduct disorder (and/or juvenile delinquency) (Lewis et al. 1980; Rutter et al. 1970a), affective disorder (Brumback and Staton 1983), anxiety disorder (Dudek et al. 1987), and impaired interpersonal relationships (Bruininks 1978; Bryan 1978; Deshler and Schumaker 1983).

The literature documenting these associations has been discussed elsewhere (Baker and Cantwell 1990). A review of the literature indicates that the mechanisms of the association between learning disorder and psychiatric disorders may be various and multiple. It is possible, for example, that the learning disorder produces the psychiatric disorder either directly (e.g., through certain cognitive characteristics) or indirectly (e.g., as a result of school failure and sociodynamic processes). It is also possible that mutual etiological processes may be involved (e.g., lower SES and associated family adversity).

In addition to learning disorders, three other developmental disorders are developmental coordination disorder, enuresis, and encopresis. There has been only limited research on developmental coordination disorder. However, a few studies have reported an association between hyperactivity and other behavior problems, and developmental coordination disorder (Abbie et al. 1978; Ayres 1972; Bradley 1980; Gillberg and Gillberg 1988).

Enuresis has been reported to be associated with elevated rates of behavior problems, anxiety, and other psychiatric symptoms (Essen and Peckham 1976; Gross and Dornbusch 1983; Kales et al. 1987; Lowe 1985; Rutter et al. 1970b). As Shaffer (1988) points out, however, there are several possible reasons for this association, including 1) the enuresis is a stressor leading to psychiatric illness, 2) the enuresis is a symptom of psychopathology, and/or 3) common antecedents (e.g., neurological abnormalities) have produced the enuresis and the psychiatric symptomatology.

Encopresis was first believed to be a manifestation of personal and family psychopathology (Bellman 1966; Bemporad et al. 1971; Hoag et al. 1971; Olatawura 1973). However, more recent work has questioned whether an association between encopresis and psychiatric disorder truly exists (Friman et al. 1988; Gabel et al. 1986, 1988).

Epidemiologic investigations have shown that psychiatric disabilities are more frequent in children of lower IQ than in those of higher IQ (Rutter 1971; Rutter et al. 1970a). This trend is found throughout the IQ distribution, but possibly is greatest in the lowest IQ groups. Furthermore, follow-up studies of children with psychiatric disorders show that IQ level is a good predictor of long-term adaptation (Shapiro and Sherman 1983). For the most part, however, low IQ shows no unique connection with specific psychiatric syndromes.

Finally, there is limited evidence of an association between certain types of abnormal cognitive functioning and certain types of childhood psychiatric disorders (Rutter and Gould 1985). The disorders involved include acute confusional states, infantile autism, disintegrative psychosis, and, to a lesser degree, ADHD. However, as Rutter and Gould (1985) point out, for the first three of these disorders, there is good evidence of underlying organic brain pathology. The association between organic brain pathology and psychiatric disorder is discussed below.

Biological factors. The Isle of Wight studies show that known brain damage is a strong predictor of childhood psychiatric disorder. Analysis of these and other related data (Rutter 1989b) suggests that this association is not entirely due to other associated variables such as mental retardation or physical crippling. Various other studies (summarized in Szatmari 1985) have also reported on an association between psychiatric disorder and various indicators of brain dysfunction. Generally, it appears that (with the exception of the four disorders mentioned above) the presence of brain damage is not associated with any particular clinical psychiatric syndrome (Kindlon et al. 1988; Rutter et al. 1970a; Shaffer et al. 1975).

Other physical or biological factors that may be associated with psychiatric disorder in children include physical handicap, genetic predisposition, and "reproductive risks" (e.g., prematurity, pregnancy, delivery complications). Although physical handicap has been shown to be associated with increased risk for psychiatric disorder, this risk is relatively small unless cerebral pathology is present (Seidel et al. 1975).

Reproductive risks are perhaps the best studied of childhood risk factors. Several prospective long-term studies have followed children suffering from these reproductive risks, and various aspects of child development were considered as outcome variables (Broman et al. 1985; Kopp 1983; Pasamanick and Knobloch 1960; Sameroff and Chandler 1975; Werner and Smith 1982). These studies demonstrate, for the most part, that pre-, peri-, and postnatal risk factors are all associated with increased risk of subsequent neuropsychiatric disability. However, in the absence of other risk factors, the biological factors do not always lead to a poor outcome. The data are difficult to sort out because risk and outcome are often complicated by multiple risk factors that are not readily separated or treated (Masten and Garmezy 1985).

The factor of genetic risk has recently been examined, particularly with regard to the affective disorders. Evidence from twin studies, family history studies, and adoption studies strongly implicates a familial factor in affective disorders (Beardslee et al. 1983; Cantwell

1983; Dwyer and Delong 1987; Gershon et al. 1977; Livingston et al. 1985; Mendlewicz and Rainer 1977; Puig-Antich and Weston 1983; Weissman et al. 1984; Wierzbicki 1987). However, the majority of the evidence is from family history studies and is amenable to both genetic and psychosocial explanations. Specifically, it has been suggested that the psychosocial stresses of having a depressed parent (i.e., inadequate caregiving, psychological unavailability, lack of social interactions) may induce vulnerability in the child (Cicchetti and Aber 1986; Cox et al. 1987; Jaenicke et al. 1987; Orvaschel 1983).

Psychosocial (stress) factors. There is a relatively large literature indicating an association between life stress and psychiatric disorder in adults (Brown et al. 1973; Jacobs et al. 1974; Myers et al. 1975). Until recently, however, there has been limited interest in the possible roles of various childhood stressors. Furthermore, although adolescence is a time of life that has generally been seen as one of stress and turmoil, surprisingly little is known about the impact of life stress on adolescents (Rutter 1980; Rutter et al. 1976a).

The recent renewed interest in the effects of psychosocial stress has resulted in articles dealing with such diverse stressors as divorce, bereavement, sexual abuse, child abuse, poverty, the holocaust experience, disasters, war, and other forms of trauma. Unfortunately, however, most of the studies are descriptive and not longitudinal in design (Masten and Garmezy 1985). Nonetheless, the literature indicates that stressful life events are often associated with depressive (Kashani et al. 1986) and/or antisocial (Fergusson et al. 1986) symptoms in children. The relevant stressors include family background or demographic factors such as lower SES, large family size, parental unemployment, geographic overcrowding, broken homes, and inadequate school situations. As mentioned above, it appears that the associations between these factors and delinquency are often related to inadequate family and social support mechanisms. For example, specific aspects of parental care such as lack of supervision; inappropriate role modeling; hostility, negative interactions, and lack of warmth; and coercive or punitive parental interactions, have been linked to childhood behavior problems (Campbell et al. 1986; Dadds 1987; Johnson and O'Leary 1987; McCord 1988; Patterson 1982; Patterson et al. 1989). Loeber and Dishion's (1983) literature review of predictors of delinquency concluded that, across all studies, the best predictors of delinquency were composite measures of parental family-management techniques.

Although the literature indicates that there is a relationship between stressful life events and psychiatric illness in children and adolescents, the evidence for a direct etiological role is weak (Compas 1987). The association is further complicated by the existence of certain other factors that seem to protect against the psychosocial risk factors for psychopathology (Daniels et al. 1987; Garmezy 1984; Rutter 1979; Rutter et al. 1979; Werner and Smith 1982). For example, Rutter and his colleagues (1979) found that children living in disadvantaged environments were less vulnerable to psychopathology if they had certain individual personality dispositions, a supportive family milieu, and an outside support system encouraging their efforts to cope with adversity. Werner and Smith's (1982) study of children exposed to perinatal stress, poverty, and family problems reaffirmed the protective importance of these variables.

Correlates of Psychiatric Disorder in the Present Research Sample

In the preceding section we outlined some of the possible risk and protective factors associated with childhood psychopathology according to the literature. In this section we examine the data from the speech/language–disordered children in the present study in order to determine the factors associated with their psychiatric disorder. The factors examined include demographic and background factors, developmental and cognitive factors, speech and language factors, biological factors, and psychosocial (stress) factors.

The methodology involves comparing those children who had at least one Axis I psychiatric diagnosis with those children who had no Axis I psychiatric diagnosis. Thus, the 302 children with a psychiatric diagnosis (referred to as the "psychiatrically ill" group) were compared to the 298 children with no psychiatric diagnosis (referred to as the "psychiatrically well" group).

Demographic and background factors.   The psychiatrically well and psychiatrically ill groups of speech/language–disordered children were compared on the following demographic and background variables:

- Age
- Sex
- Birth order
- Family size
- Family structure (two biological parents, mother and stepfather, mother alone, etc.)
- Religious background
- Language background (bilingual, monolingual, or linguisti-

cally deprived)
- Ethnicity
- Maternal education, occupation, and age
- Paternal education, occupation, and age

Very few of these comparisons showed any significant differences between the two groups. Furthermore, of the significant comparisons, the majority were not highly significant.

The psychiatrically ill and well groups had no significant differences in sex distribution; family size; birth order; religious background; maternal or paternal education, occupation, and age; or bilingual or deprived language background. In both groups, approximately 70% of the children were males; approximately 50% of the children were from families with two offspring; and approximately 80% of the children were first- or second-borns.

There were significant differences between the psychiatrically ill children and the psychiatrically well children with regard to age, ethnicity, and current family structure. The psychiatrically well group had a mean age of 5 years, 6 months (SD = 2.8), whereas the psychiatrically ill group had a slightly older mean age of 6 years, 0 months (SD = 2.9). This difference was significant (t test; $P < .02$).

The ethnic distribution of the sample was as follows: 96% of the psychiatrically well group were Caucasian compared with 88% Caucasians in the psychiatrically ill group. This difference was significant (by chi-square test) at the $P < .01$ level. Comparisons of the different types of non-Caucasian races were not significantly different because of the relatively small numbers involved.

The background factor that most significantly distinguished the psychiatrically well children from the psychiatrically ill children was current family structure. Specifically, 83% of the well group lived with currently married parents as opposed to only 68% of the ill group. This difference was significant (by chi-square test) at the $P < .0001$ level. Comparisons of other types of family structures (e.g., both biological parents, one biological parent alone, one biological parent and one stepparent, etc.), however, showed no significant differences between the well and ill groups. Also, it should be noted that the frequency of intact marriages in the psychiatrically ill group was still rather high in comparison to the then current general population data.

The data from the present study suggest that demographic and background factors are not strongly predictive of the presence of psychiatric disorder in speech/language–disordered children. The only background factor that was strongly associated with psychiatric illness was the child living currently in a "broken home," and this could be considered a psychosocial stress factor rather than a demographic or background factor per se. These findings are in keeping with those of Beitchman and colleagues (1988), who found that while SES, marital status, and maternal education levels distinguished psychiatrically well versus psychiatrically ill children who were not speech/language–disordered, they did not distinguish psychiatric status among speech/language–disordered children.

Developmental-cognitive factors. The psychiatrically well and ill children were compared on a number of (nonlinguistic) developmental-cognitive variables including (from the developmental history interview) ages at attaining motor and developmental milestones, (from the DSM-III diagnoses) presence of specific developmental disorders, and (from cognitive testing) intelligence quotients.

As was the case with the demographic and background factors, many of the developmental-cognitive factors showed no significant differences between the two groups. For example, the two groups did not significantly differ in ages at sitting, eating solids, crawling, standing, walking, self-feeding, or self-dressing.

The overall prevalence of DSM-III Axis II developmental (non-linguistic) disorders was greater in the psychiatrically ill group than in the psychiatrically well group. Approximately one-quarter (27%) of the ill group had an Axis II diagnosis (i.e., learning disorder, enuresis, encopresis, or developmental coordination disorder), as opposed to only 16% of the well group. This difference was significant (by chi-square test) at the $P < .001$ level.

The prevalence rates of the different subtypes of Axis II diagnoses, except for learning disorders, were not significantly different between the two groups. It will be remembered that there was some suggestion in the literature of an association between psychiatric disorder and specific subtypes of developmental disorders, including developmental coordination disorder and enuresis. However, in the present study, such an association was not found.

In the present study, learning disorders were significantly (by chi-square test; $P < .001$) more common in the psychiatrically ill group than in the psychiatrically well group. Ten percent of the ill children were diagnosed as having a learning disorder, versus only 4% of the well group. The literature indicated that learning disorders were associated with higher rates of psychiatric disorder in the general population, and that there was a particularly strong association between developmental reading disorder and conduct disorder. The association between learning disorder and psychiatric disorder was found in the present study. However, the numbers of children with different subtypes of learning disorders were too small to reveal any significant differences between the psychiatrically ill and psychiatrically well children with regard to subtypes of learning disorders or subtypes of psychiatric disorders.

The learning-disabled children in the present study are described in more detail in Chapter 6. For the present discussion, it is important to note that the psychiatrically ill children were also slightly older than the psychiatrically well children, and that insofar as there were more psychiatrically ill children in the school age-range, this age difference may explain some of the increased rate of learning disorders.

The estimated verbal intelligence (derived from the Peabody Picture Vocabulary Test) was significantly lower (by t test; $P < .004$) in the psychiatrically ill group. However, the group mean score was still within normal limits for the ill children (mean score = 92.1; SD = 21.7), as it was for the well children (mean score = 99.5; SD = 21.1).

Performance intelligence (as measured by the performance subtests of the Wechsler Pre-School and Primary Scale of Intelligence [WPPSI] or the Wechsler Intelligence Scale for Children, Revised [WISC-R] tests) was also significantly lower ($P < .001$) in the psychiatrically ill group. However, the group mean intelligence scores again were in the normal range for both groups. The mean performance IQ score for the psychiatrically ill group was 101.9 (SD = 25.2) and for the psychiatrically well group, 108.2 (SD = 24.6). Thus, while the psychiatrically ill group had significantly lower measures of verbal and performance intelligence, these were not in the mentally retarded range.

Interestingly, there was no significant difference in the prevalence of mental retardation even though mental retardation is associated with psychiatric illness in the general population. Nearly identical numbers of psychiatrically well children and psychiatrically ill children (5% and 6%, respectively) were mentally retarded.

Speech/language factors.   The most striking differences between the psychiatrically well and the psychiatrically ill children were in the area of linguistic functioning. The psychiatrically well and psychiatrically ill groups of children were significantly different in virtually all areas of speech/language functioning. Generally, the psychiatrically well children tended to have fewer disorders involving language and more pure speech impairments. Conversely, the psychiatrically ill children tended to have more disorders involving language and fewer pure speech disorders.

It will be remembered that the data on ages at achieving developmental (nonlanguage) milestones (e.g., standing, sitting, walking) showed no significant differences between the psychiatrically ill and psychiatrically well groups. In contrast, the ages at attaining linguistic milestones were significantly different between the two groups, with the psychiatrically ill group being older than the psychiatrically well group. The mean age at the first spoken word was 16.8 months (SD = 8.8) for the psychiatrically well children versus 19.5 months (SD = 10.0) for the psychiatrically ill children. Similarly, the mean age at the first sentence was 26.8 months (SD = 10.6) for the psychiatrically well children versus 30.8 months (SD = 12.8) for the psychiatrically ill children. These differences were significantly different (by t test) at the $P < .003$ and $P < .001$ levels, respectively.

Furthermore, when the average amount of delay between chronological age level and linguistic age level was calculated for various speech/language skills, significant differences were again found between the psychiatrically ill and psychiatrically well groups. The psychiatrically well children had an average delay in expressive language skills of 0.8 years (SD = 1.5), whereas the psychiatrically ill children had an average delay of 1.4 years (SD = 1.7). In language-comprehension skills, the psychiatrically well children had an average delay of 0.3 years (SD = 1.5), whereas the psychiatrically ill children had an average delay of 0.9 years (SD = 1.6). Both of these comparisons were significantly different (by t test) at the $P < .0001$ level. In speech articulation, the amount of delay was less marked between groups but still approached significance (t test; $P < .03$). The psychiatrically well children had an average delay of 1.4 years (SD = 1.5), whereas the psychiatrically ill children had an average delay of 1.8 years (SD = 1.7).

Similarly, there were significant differences between the psychiatrically ill and psychiatrically well groups for all areas of current speech/language functioning. The psychiatrically ill children had significantly more disorders in language comprehension, expression, and processing, and the psychiatrically well children had significantly more disorders in speech production.

Language-comprehension disorders were present in 50% of the psychiatrically ill children versus 28% of the psychiatrically well children. Language-expression disorders were present in 72% of the psychiatrically ill children versus 49% of the psychiatrically well children. Language processing disorders were present in 48% of the psychiatrically ill children versus 19% of the psychiatrically well children. All of these rates of speech/language disorders were significantly different (by chi-square test) between the two groups at the $P < .0001$ level. Speech-production problems were also present at significantly different rates ($P < .001$) in the two groups, but with the difference being in the opposite direction. Thus, speech-production disorders were present in 89% of the psychiatrically ill children versus 96% of the psychiatrically well children.

Finally, the linguistic diagnoses of the two groups showed significantly different distributions. The psychiatrically well group had approximately equal amounts of pure speech disorder (47%) and combined speech/language disorder (49%), with a small amount of pure language disorder (4%). In contrast, the psychiatrically ill group predominantly had combined speech/language disorder (68%), a smaller amount of pure speech disorder (21%), and somewhat more pure language disorder (11%). The distributions of these three types of linguistic diagnoses were significantly different (by chi-square test) between the two groups at the $P < .0001$ level.

These data give empirical support to the suggestion that psychiatric disorder is associated with speech/language disorder. In particular, the data suggest that psychiatric disorder may be most strongly associated with some type of language impairment. These associations between psychiatric disorder and different subtypes of speech/language disorders are explored in more detail in Chapter 6.

Biological factors.   The biological factors examined in the two groups of children in the present study included both information obtained during interviews with the parents (e.g., pregnancy, perinatal, and postnatal medical histories; ICD-9 diagnoses; birth weights, etc.) and information derived from an assessment of the children using the Peters Neurological Examination.

The two groups of children did not differ significantly on many of these biological measures. The overall amount of medical (ICD-9) disorders was not significantly different between the two groups, nor was the amount of CNS disorders, ear and hearing disorders, perinatal and pregnancy problems, congenital anomalies, or speech-mechanism abnormalities. Overall, some type of medical-biological disorder was found in 66% of the psychiatrically well children and 73% of the psychiatrically ill children. Birth weights were also not significantly different between the two groups, although 13% of the well children and 18% of the ill children had birth weights under 6 pounds.

The only significant differences between the two groups with regard to biological factors were in the prevalence of respiratory disorders and in the amount of neurological exam abnormalities. There was a trend (chi-square test; $P < .02$) for the psychiatrically ill children to have more respiratory disorders and, in particular, more chronic respiratory disorders. Thirty-three percent of the psychiatrically ill children had respiratory disorders and 32% had chronic respiratory disorders; only 25% of the psychiatrically well children had respiratory disorders.

On the neurological exam, significantly more (chi square test; $P < .001$) abnormalities were found among the psychiatrically ill children. Over half (51%) of the psychiatrically ill children tested were found to have more than four neurological abnormalities, and another 31% had between one and three abnormalities. Only 18% of the psychiatrically ill children tested had no abnormalities on the neurological exam. In contrast, 31% of the psychiatrically well children tested had more than four abnormalities, 37% had between one and three abnormalities, and 32% had no abnormalities.

With regard to specific neurological exam items, the psychiatrically ill children tended toward more abnormalities. However, the only item that was significantly different between the two groups was the "fingers to thumb movement" task, at which 39% of the psychiatrically well group had problems compared with 56% of the psychiatrically ill group. This difference was significant (by chi-square test) at the $P < .01$ level.

As noted above, there is evidence in the literature that children with chronic medical and neurological disorders (especially those involving CNS functioning) have higher rates of psychiatric disorder than do children in the general population. Here, however, only the number of abnormal items on the neurological exam and the presence of chronic respiratory disorder significantly distinguished the psychiatrically ill from the psychiatrically well children, and these differences were not highly significant.

Psychosocial factors.   The presence of psychosocial stress in the lives of the children was determined through parent and child interviews. Overall number of stressors, severity levels of stress, and types of stressors (e.g., family discord, family changes, physical or mental illnesses in the family, environmental deprivation, stressful changes and events, personal problems for the child, parental employment, financial or other problems) were calculated for all children in the study.

Highly significant differences were found between the psychiatrically ill and psychiatrically well groups with regard to several aspects of psychosocial stress. First, the psychiatrically ill children had significantly more ($P < .0001$) psychosocial stress than did the psychiatrically well children. Seventy-nine percent of the psychiatrically ill children suffered from at least one stressor in their lives compared with 50% of psychiatrically well children.

Second, the number of psychosocial stressors was significantly greater ($P < .0001$) in the psychiatrically ill group. Among the psychiatrically ill children, 27% had one stressor, 29% had two stressors, and 23% had three or more stressors. For psychiatrically well children, 29% had one stressor, while only 15% had two stressors, and 6% had three or more stressors.

Third, the mean severity level of stressors (rated on a seven-point scale, with 1 indicating "no apparent stress," 4 indicating "moderate stress," and 7 indicating "catastrophic stress") was also significantly greater in the psychiatrically ill group. These children had a mean severity rating of 2.9 (SD = 1.0), whereas the psychiatrically well children had a mean rating of 1.9 (SD = 1.3). The comparison (by t test) was also significantly different at the $P < .0001$ level.

Certain specific types of psychosocial stressors showed significant differences in frequency of occurrence between the two groups, whereas other types of stressors showed no significant differences. Four general categories of psychosocial stressors showed significant differences in frequency of occurrence between the psychiatrically ill and psychiatrically well groups. Three types of stressors—family illness, family discord, and parental problems (e.g., legal difficulties, housing worries)—were all significantly more common in the psychiatrically ill group. The rates of occurrence of these stressors were 31% for family illnesses, 46% for family discord, and 3% for parental problems in the psychiatrically ill group, and 16% for family illnesses, 19% for family discord, and 0% for parental problems in the psychiatrically well group. These differences were significant (by chi-square test) at the $P < .0001$ level for the first two stressors and at the $P < .001$ level for the last stressor.

The fourth type of stressor—personal problems—refers to personal problems of the children themselves, such as having a physical handicap, having difficulty with a peer group, or having school problems. This stressor was significantly ($P < .0001$) more common in the psychiatrically well group. This finding of a higher prevalence of such problems among the well group could, however, have been an artifact of the coding procedure. Because peer problems are part of many psychiatric disorders, they may not have been coded separately as a psychosocial stressor for the psychiatrically ill children. In such cases it is difficult to separate stressors that occur independently of a psychiatric disorder from stressors that are an integral part of the psychiatric disorder.

The types of psychosocial stressors that were not significantly different in frequency of occurrence between the psychiatrically ill children and the psychiatrically well children were parental employment problems, parental financial problems, family changes, and environmental deprivation. These types of stressors were generally not very common in either group of children.

The parental mental health and family interaction measures comparing the psychiatrically ill and psychiatrically well children are presented in Table 4-1. In general, there tended to be more psychiatric illness among the parents of the psychiatrically ill children, but the figures did not reach statistical significance. Behavioral spectrum disorders, however, were significantly more common in the fathers of psychiatrically ill children than in the fathers of psychiatrically well children. Also, the particular diagnosis of substance abuse disorder was also significantly more common in the fathers of psychiatrically ill children.

Warmth of family members toward the children was also significantly different between the psychiatrically ill and psychiatrically well children. Significantly greater levels of warmth were present from mothers, fathers, and siblings toward the psychiatrically well children. However, the play patterns among the target children, surprisingly, showed little difference between the psychiatrically well and ill groups. Thus, the numbers of children having a special friend, playing well with their father, and being teased about their speech were similar between the two groups. The majority of children in both groups played well with their siblings. However, there were significantly more sibling play problems in the psychiatrically ill group.

Overall, the psychosocial stressor data from the present study confirm the reports in the literature that stressful life events are associated with psychiatric disorder in children. In the present study, psychiatric illness was strongly associated not only with the general presence of stressors, but also with higher severity levels of stress and with stressors that affect family functioning, such as family discord, family illnesses, and personal problems of parents. Parental mental illness and lack of warmth in family interactions were also associated with psychiatric illness among the speech/language–disordered children.

Symptomatic Correlates of Psychiatric Illness

Symptoms associated with psychiatric illness according to parental reports.   The symptoms reported by parents for the psychiatrically ill and psychiatrically well groups of children are presented in Table 4-2. The symptoms are listed in order of the frequency with which parents reported their presence among the psychiatrically ill

Table 4-1. Psychosocial and family correlates of psychiatric illness in the present research sample

	Significance[a]	Well group (%)	Ill group (%)
Parental mental health			
Both parents psychiatrically well		43	28
Either parent psychiatrically ill		44	53
Both parents psychiatrically ill		13	19
Maternal mental status			
Psychiatrically ill		29	37
Behavioral disorders		4	6
Emotional disorders		17	21
Schizophrenia		0.3	0.7
Substance abuse disorders		4	6
Affective disorders		9	12
Other disorders		2	4
Paternal mental status			
Psychiatrically ill		27	34
Behavioral disorders	*	9	19
Emotional disorders		11	8
Schizophrenia		0.3	0.7
Substance abuse disorders	*	9	18
Affective disorders		4	3
Other disorders		4	5
Paternal attitude toward child	*		
Very warm		45	33
Average warmth		46	49
Less warm than average		9	18
Maternal attitude toward child	**		
Very warm		46	34
Average warmth		52	54
Less warm than average		2	12
Sibling attitude toward child (_n_ = 469)	**		
Very warm		17	11
Average warmth		77	70
Less warm than average		6	19
Child's life			
Has a special friend		59	62
Plays well with siblings (_n_ = 489)	*	93	83
Plays well with father		76	72
Teased about speech		28	32

[a]Chi-square comparisons of psychiatrically well and psychiatrically ill groups: *$P < .01$; **$P < .0001$.

children. Behavioral symptoms (e.g., short attention span, frustration, excitability, disobedience, restlessness) were reported in one-third to one-half of the children. Emotional symptoms were less frequent, but some of these (e.g., shyness, fear of new situations, mood changes) occurred in as many as one-quarter of the children.

Most of the symptoms on the parent questionnaires were reported with significantly different rates between the psychiatrically well and psychiatrically ill groups. Those symptoms that did not show any significant differences in frequency of occurrence between the psychiatrically well and ill groups have been omitted from the table. These were headaches, asthma, wetting, soiling, being overweight, thumb sucking, having aches and pains, school truancy, disobedience at school, having somatic worries, fire setting, stealing, police problems, stuttering, speech that is difficult to understand, and inappropriate language. Items reflective of conduct disorder (e.g., fire setting, being in trouble with the police, school truancy, stealing) all had low frequencies of occurrence in both groups, presumably due to the young age of the children.

Table 4-2. Symptoms reported by parents of psychiatrically well and psychiatrically ill children in the present research sample

Symptom	Significance[a]	Well group (%)	Ill group (%)
Easily frustrated	***	18	48
Short attention span	***	14	48
Limited language	**	31	44
Restless	***	12	43
Feelings easily hurt	***	26	42
Excitable	***	12	40
Disobeys often	***	7	32
Angry, irritable	***	8	31
Immature	***	13	29
Squirmy	***	5	29
Sibling problems: fights	***	10	25
Shy	***	11	25
Fears new situations	***	9	24
Solitary	***	10	24
Drastic mood changes	***	4	24
Tantrums	***	7	23
Picky eater	*	13	22
Always climbing	**	11	22
Inappropriate speech rhythm	**	9	21
Seems driven by motor	***	2	18

(continued)

Table 4-2 *(continued)*

Symptom	Significance[a]	Well group (%)	Ill group (%)
Sleep problems	***	6	18
Perfectionist	**	8	17
Sibling problems: rivalry	***	3	16
Clings, fears separation	***	5	15
Overasserts self	***	5	15
Is bullied	**	6	15
Unhappy	***	3	15
Insists on sameness	**	7	15
Lies	***	4	14
Blames others	**	5	14
Fears not being liked	***	4	14
Not learning	***	1	14
Daydreams	***	3	13
Quarrelsome	***	3	13
Has difficulty understanding others	*	6	13
Inappropriate intonation	*	5	12
Nightmares	*	5	12
Dislikes school	***	1	10
Stomachaches	*	4	10
Often worries	**	3	10
Keeps anger to self	*	4	9
Not liked by peers	***	1	9
Is mean, fights	***	0	6
Destroys property	**	0	5
Muscular tension	*	1	4
Tics	*	0	4

Note. Those symptoms that did not show any significant differences in frequency of occurrence between the psychiatrically well and ill groups have been omitted from the table. These were headaches, asthma, wetting, soiling, being overweight, thumb sucking, having aches and pains, school truancy, disobedience at school, having somatic worries, fire setting, stealing, police problems, stuttering, speech that is difficult to understand, and inappropriate language.
[a]Chi-square comparisons of psychiatrically well and psychiatrically ill groups: $*P < .01$; $**P < .001$; $***P < .0001$.

A large number of behavioral symptoms significantly distinguished the psychiatrically well from the psychiatrically ill group. Frustration, short attention span, restlessness, excitability, disobedience, squirming, fighting with siblings, tantrums, sibling rivalry, overassertion, telling lies, quarreling, and fighting were all significantly (chi-square test; $P < .0001$) more common among the psychiatrically ill children. Shyness, fearing new situations, mood changes, sleep problems, clinging, and unhappiness were also much more common ($P < .0001$) among the psychiatrically ill children. Other emotional symptoms such as stomachaches, nightmares, picky eating, muscular tension, and tics were more common but at lower significance levels ($P < .01$) among the psychiatrically ill children.

Some similar data are available from the British epidemiologic study of 3-year-olds in London (Richman et al. 1975). This study dealt with fewer symptoms (approximately 20) but did provide data comparing parent-reported frequencies in a normal group (corresponding to the psychiatrically well group in the present study) and in a "problem" group (corresponding to the psychiatrically ill group in the present study). The British data found fewer significant differences between groups. In particular, a number of symptoms that significantly distinguished the two groups in the present study were not significantly different in the British study. These symptoms included peer relationship problems, sibling relationship problems, eating problems, sleep problems, poor concentration, and unhappy mood. Overactivity and fears were the only two symptoms that significantly distinguished the two groups of children in both the British study and the present study.

In the Isle of Wight study (Rutter et al. 1970a, 1970b), parent-report data were also presented for two groups of children: those with high symptom scores (i.e., 13 or more) on the parental scale, and those with low symptom scores on the parental rating scale. The findings in the Isle of Wight study more closely resemble those of the present study. For all items on the parental rating scale in the Isle of Wight study, there was a strong association with the presence of a high total score. Also, as in the present study, this significant association was less strong with physical symptoms such as headaches and stomachaches. A further finding from the Isle of Wight study was that poor peer relations and inattention-overactivity stood out as behaviors with an especially strong association with psychiatric disorder (Rutter 1989b). These associations were also found in the present study, although they were by no means unique.

Of recent interest are the so-called "neurodevelopmental" symptoms such as concentration problems, confusion, and clumsiness. While recognizing the elevated rates of these symptoms in children with specific speech/language disorders, Tallal and colleagues (1989) have suggested that they are not necessarily indicative of emotional disturbance in these children. Thus, it is important to note that in the present study, these symptoms were strongly associated with psychiatric disorder. Furthermore, psychiatric disorder in the present study was diagnosed by multiple independent measures including clinical observations, teacher reports, and interviews.

Symptoms associated with psychiatric illness according to teachers' reports. Table 4-3 presents those symptoms significantly distinguishing the psychiatrically well children from the psychiatrically ill children according to teacher reports. As was the case with the parent reports, a large number of symptoms from the teacher reports significantly distinguished the psychiatrically ill and psychiatrically well groups. The symptoms that were not significantly different in occurrence between the two groups were chiefly items that occurred relatively infrequently (in less than 3% of the cases) in both groups (e.g., truancy, being absent at school for trivial reasons, stealing).

In the present study, many emotional and behavioral symptoms were reported significantly more frequently by teachers of the psychiatrically ill children than by teachers of the psychiatrically well children. As with the parent report, teachers found behavioral symptoms to be common among the psychiatrically ill children. Short attention span, fidgeting, overactivity, disturbing others, impulsivity, stubbornness, frustration, demanding attention, defiance, and disobedience occurred in about 20% to 60% of the psychiatrically ill children (as compared to 10% to 20% of the psychiatrically well children). These comparisons were highly significant (chi-square test; $P < .0001$).

Emotional symptoms were reported less frequently by teachers of both groups of children. Among those that significantly distinguished the psychiatrically ill and well groups were submissiveness, shyness, worrying, mood changes, sensitivity, fears, and unhappiness.

The teachers also reported differences in rates of speech/language symptoms between the two groups, with the levels of significance tending to be somewhat higher than those from the parent-report data. Although both the psychiatrically well and the psychiatrically ill children had been referred for speech/language problems, limited language was twice as common in the ill group (45% vs. 22%). Inappropriate language usage was more than twice as common (21% vs. 9%) and inappropriate speech rhythm and trouble understanding others were both five times more common in the ill group than in the well group. However stuttering (which occurred in 9% of psychiatrically well and 13% of psychiatrically ill children) did not significantly distinguish the groups.

Factor scores from parent and teacher questionnaires. The group mean factor analysis scores for the Conners and Rutter questionnaire factors are reported in Table 4-4. The factor data show significant differences between psychiatrically well and psychiatrically ill children on virtually all factors from both of the parent questionnaires. These findings correspond to those from the factor analysis of

Table 4-3. Symptoms reported by teachers of psychiatrically well and psychiatrically ill children in the present research sample

Symptom	Significance[a]	Well group (%)	Ill group (%)
Short attention span	***	19	59
Difficult to understand	*	33	49
Limited language	***	22	45
Lacks leadership	***	16	43
Constantly fidgets	***	7	40
Restless, overactive	***	9	38
Disturbs other children	***	4	34
Impulsive	***	7	34
Solitary	***	12	32
Stubborn	***	9	30
Easily frustrated	***	8	30
Poor coordination	***	13	29
Submissive	**	13	27
Demands attention	***	7	27
Shy	*	13	25
Daydreams	***	6	24
Inappropriate intonation	*	12	24
Defiant	***	3	23
Worries	***	7	22
Is bullied	***	6	22
Disobedient	***	2	22
Inappropriate speech rhythm	***	4	21
Uses language inappropriately	**	9	21
Unresponsive	***	4	21
Resentful when corrected	***	5	21
Fights	***	4	20
Difficulty understanding others	***	4	20
Unhappy	***	3	17
Overly sensitive	***	4	16
Quick, drastic mood changes	***	2	16
Not liked	***	3	16
Bullies, teases	***	3	15
Hums	***	3	15
Fearful	***	3	15
Cannot get along with the same sex	**	4	14
No fair play	*	5	14
Tantrums	***	2	14
Tics	***	2	14
Sullen	*	4	13
Cannot get along with the opposite sex	**	2	11
Cries often and easily	*	3	10
Sucks thumb	*	3	10
Destroys property	**	1	9
Tells lies	**	0	6
Aches, pains	*	1	6

[a]Chi-square comparisons of psychiatrically well and psychiatrically ill groups: *$P < .01$; **$P < .001$; ***$P < .0001$.

Table 4-4. Factor scores from parent and teacher questionnaires for children in the present research sample

Factor	Significance[a]	Well group		Ill group	
		Mean	SD	Mean	SD
Conners parent questionnaire					
Conduct factor	***	0.27	0.34	0.57	0.59
Anxiety factor	***	0.40	0.40	0.65	0.58
Hyperactivity factor	***	0.41	0.42	0.96	0.72
Learning factor	***	0.10	0.21	0.41	0.53
Psychosomatic factor	***	0.32	0.35	0.45	0.47
Perfectionism factor	***	0.34	0.55	0.58	0.71
Antisocial factor	*	0.01	0.06	0.03	0.12
Tension factor	***	0.17	0.27	0.33	0.36
Conners teacher questionnaire					
Conduct factor	***	0.10	0.26	0.42	0.54
Passivity factor	***	0.51	0.52	1.17	0.74
Tension factor	***	0.37	0.42	0.72	0.62
Hyperactivity factor	***	0.32	0.45	0.98	0.79
Rutter parent questionnaire					
Neurotic factor	***	0.33	0.29	0.55	0.42
Antisocial factor	***	0.29	0.25	0.52	0.39
Total score	***	0.36	0.19	0.59	0.25
Rutter teacher questionnaire					
Neurotic factor	***	0.21	0.34	0.48	0.52
Antisocial factor	***	0.15	0.25	0.44	0.47
Total score	***	0.22	0.18	0.59	0.31

Note. SD = standard deviation.
[a] t test comparisons of psychiatrically well and psychiatrically ill groups: $*P < .01$; $***P < .0001$.

the two teacher questionnaires and to the individual symptom data (reported in Tables 4-2 and 4-3). Thus, all factor scores from all four questionnaires showed statistically significant differences between the ill and the well groups, with all factor scores being higher (i.e., more deviant) among the psychiatrically ill children.

All of the factor scores, with the exception of the Conners "antisocial factor," showed highly significant ($P < .0001$) differences between groups. The antisocial factor score did distinguish the two groups, being higher among the psychiatrically ill children, but the level of statistical significance was considerably lower ($P < .01$). This finding most likely reflects the youth of the sample, such that the antisocial symptoms occurred very infrequently.

Symptomatology from the psychiatric interview. Table 4-5 presents the psychiatric interview ratings that significantly distinguished the psychiatrically ill and psychiatrically well groups. These data include the problems self-reported by the children, and the psychiatrists' ratings of affect, motor behaviors, and relationship features manifested during the interview.

Fewer items from the child psychiatric interview significantly differentiated the psychiatrically ill and well groups. The majority of symptoms covered in the child interview, including numerous items having to do with depression, generalized anxiety, and thought disorder, did not have significantly different frequencies of occurrence between the well and ill groups. This finding supports the suggestion based on the Isle of Wight study, that the child interview is a poor single instrument for identifying psychiatrically ill children. Of the four types of diagnostic tools used in this study (i.e., the parent interview, the parental rating scale, the teacher rating scale, and the child interview), the child interview alone appears to provide the least information as to whether or not a psychiatric diagnosis is present. Nonetheless, individual items on the child interview (such as sad expression, tearfulness, and constricted affect) may lead one toward the diagnosis of a particular type of psychiatric disorder.

Classification of Childhood Psychiatric Disorders

The history of child psychiatry has seen many different ways of grouping and classifying disorders. Both categorical systems (e.g., American Psychiatric Association 1952, 1968, 1980, 1987; Freud 1965; Group for the Advancement of Psychiatry 1966, 1974; World Health Organization 1978) and dimensional or factorial systems (e.g., Achenbach and Edelbrock 1983; Hewitt and Jenkins 1946; Jenkins 1964; Lessing et al. 1982; Overall and Pfefferbaum 1982; Quay 1979) have been used.

There is currently no single classification system that is recognized as being the "natural" or "right" system. Furthermore, there is a variety of criteria by which the effectiveness of a particular classification system may be judged (Cantwell 1987a, 1987b; Cantwell and Baker 1988; Rutter et al. 1975b; Spitzer and Williams 1980). One of these criteria for judging a classification system that will concern us in the present work is *external validity*.

Generally speaking, external validity refers to correlates that are uniquely associated with particular psychiatric diagnoses. Thus, in the

Table 4-5. Symptoms of psychiatric illness from child interview data in the present research sample

Symptom	Significance[a]	Well group (%)	Ill group (%)
Stated problems with:			
Phobias and fears	*	25	39
Adequacy of peer relations	***	14	34
Poor relationship with mother	**	15	32
Fighting with peers	***	10	31
Poor relationship with father	*	15	29
Poor peer relationships	***	12	29
School behavior problems	**	7	26
Poor relationship with teacher	**	3	22
Solitary interests	**	7	20
Sullenness	*	4	13
Fighting with parents	**	2	12
Observed affect during interview			
Constricted affect	*	18	30
Elated affect	*	8	17
Sad expression	*	5	13
Angry affect	**		12
Inappropriate affect	***	1	7
Tearfulness	*	2	6
Ratings of motor behavior during interview			
Fidgety	***	34	55
Short attention span	***	21	44
Distractibility	***	16	33
Disinhibition	**	9	19
Irritability	**	4	13
Relationship with examiner			
Eye contact	***	23	36
Egocentricity	***	14	32
Negative attitude	***	4	17
Withdrawal	**	1	7

[a]Chi-square comparisons of psychiatrically well and psychiatrically ill groups: *$P < .01$; **$P < .001$; ***$P < .0001$.

previous chapter we saw that psychiatric disorder in general may be associated with certain specific external characteristics or correlates. The concept of external validity recognizes that just as psychiatric disorder in general may have specific correlates, so each type of psychiatric disorder may have its own specific correlates. Such correlates may include laboratory measures, family aggregation data, follow-up outcomes, treatment responses, psychosocial factors, and epidemiologic data (Cantwell 1975; Feighner et al. 1972; Klerman 1983; Robins and Guze 1970).

Two general categories of psychiatric disorder that have been recognized in the majority of psychiatric diagnostic systems are *emotional disorder* and *behavioral disorder*. Emotional disorders are disorders characterized primarily by emotional distress or suffering for the patient, with symptoms such as fear, anxiety, misery, and/or somatic complaints predominating. Conversely, behavioral disorders are characterized primarily by socially disapproved behaviors causing disturbance to other people. Under the DSM-III-R system, behavioral disorders include the specific diagnoses of ADHD, conduct disorder, and oppositional defiant disorder, and emotional disorders include the categories of anxiety disorder and affective disorder.

These two major categories of disorder are also typically recognized within the dimensional diagnostic systems, although with different labels (Hewitt and Jenkins 1946; Patterson 1964; Peterson 1961; Quay 1964, 1979; Wolff 1971). For example, Achenbach and Edelbrock's extensive analyses (1978, 1981, 1983, 1989) of parent, teacher, and other source data have demonstrated the existence of two "broad-band dimensions" that they label "internalizing syndromes" and "externalizing syndromes." The internalizing syndromes involve overcontrolled behavior and include the factors of anxiety, depression, somatic complaints, and social withdrawal. The externalizing syndromes involve undercontrolled behavior and include the factors of hyperactivity, delinquency, and aggression.

The distinction between emotional disorders and behavioral disorders is based primarily upon the different symptom clustering that the two types of disorders manifest. However, there are also data in the literature supporting the external validity of the distinction. These data include evidence of different correlates with regard to demographic and background factors, developmental-cognitive factors, biological factors, and psychosocial factors.

The following is a brief outline of the correlates of behavioral disorders and of emotional disorders that have been reported in the literature. It is noted when the literature reveals a difference in these correlates that would lend support to the external validity of the distinction between behavioral and emotional disorders. Following this, data are examined from the present study of speech/language–impaired children in order to determine the correlates of behavioral disorders and emotional disorders in these children.

Correlates of Behavioral and Emotional Disorders in the Literature

Demographic and background factors. The demographic-background factor that stands out as different with regard to behavioral versus emotional disorders is sex distribution. (The sex distributions of the various childhood psychiatric disorders are discussed in more detail in Chapter 5.) Briefly, the situation is that, for most childhood psychiatric disorders, the prevalence is greater in boys than in girls (Rutter et al. 1970b). For both attention-deficit hyperactivity and for conduct symptoms and disorders, this is definitely the case (Earls 1980; Holborow et al. 1984; Kastrup 1976; MacFarlane et al. 1954; Miller et al. 1973; Offord et al. 1987; Richman et al. 1975; Rutter et al. 1970a, 1970b, 1975a). However, for emotional disorders, the sex ratio is approximately equal for children in the prepubertal age-range and predominantly female for the older ages (Cohen et al. 1985; Garfinkel et al. 1982; Gove and Herb 1974; Kandel and Davies 1982; Rutter 1986; Rutter et al. 1976a).

A second possible difference between behavioral disorders and emotional disorders may have to do with various socioeconomic-class correlates. As reported in the preceding chapter, there is some evidence of associations between several demographic variables and the presence or persistence of conduct disorder and/or delinquency. The variables involved were lower socioeconomic class, large family size, parental unemployment, geographic overcrowding, broken homes, and inadequate schooling. Across all studies, however, these variables were not always associated with behavioral disorders. There is even less evidence of a consistent association between demographic variables and emotional disorders.

Developmental-cognitive factors. The most compelling developmental correlate of behavioral disorders is, in general, learning disorder and, in particular, reading disorder. The Isle of Wight study (Rutter et al. 1970a) and other studies (Lewis et al. 1980) have provided compelling evidence of an association between reading/learning disorder and conduct disorder. There is also some evidence of an association between learning difficulties and emotional disorders (Brumback and Staton 1983; Dudek et al. 1987). However, this latter evidence is less compelling.

It is also possible that there are specific cognitive correlates of both behavioral disorders and emotional disorders. As described in the preceding chapter, there are suggestions in the literature that ADHD in particular may be associated with certain types of cognitive deficits such as field dependence, poor selective attention, weak automatization, poor sustained attention, lack of self-monitoring skills, and poor social information processing (Ackerman et al. 1986; Brown et al. 1985; Cohen et al. 1972; Cotugno 1987; Douglas 1976; Milich and Dodge 1984; Stoner and Glynn 1987; Tant and Douglas 1982; Tarnowski et al. 1986).

In contrast, these cognitive deficits have not been reported to be associated with emotional disorders. The emotional disorders, however, have been postulated to be associated with cognitive dysfunctions involving, for example, the self system. In particular, deficits such as poor self-concept, lower self-esteem, negative or depressive attributions, negative self-evaluation, lower self-expectations, more stringent criteria for failure, and miscellaneous problem-solving deficits have been reported in children with emotional disorders (Beck and Emery 1985; Hayley et al. 1985; Jaenicke et al. 1987; Kaslow et al. 1984; Nezu 1987; Rutter 1987b).

Biological factors. As noted in the previous chapter, physical handicap and particularly brain damage are associated with increased risk of a wide range of child psychiatric disorders. The possibility of a differential risk for behavioral disorder versus for emotional disorder has not been systematically studied. Behavioral disorders (both ADHD and conduct disorder) are, however, more often linked in the literature with minor physical anomalies and other evidence of organic brain pathology than are emotional disorders (Denckla and Rudel 1978; Frank and Ben-Nun 1988; Kaplan et al. 1987; Lewis et al. 1979; Quinn and Rapoport 1974; Wolff et al. 1982).

There are positive family history data associated with both behavioral disorders and emotional disorders. Thus, children with behavioral disorders are more likely to have relatives with behavioral disorders, and children with emotional disorders are more likely to have relatives with emotional disorders. More specifically, children with ADHD, conduct disorder, or an affective disorder are more likely to have parents with these particular types of illnesses. Nonetheless, genetic links have not yet been established (Carey 1987).

Psychosocial (stress) factors. It appears that psychosocial stress factors are differentially associated with behavioral versus emotional disorders. As described in the previous chapter, behavioral disorder (in particular, conduct disorder) is associated with certain types of psychosocial stress having to do with family disruption, family discord, and/or hostility (Hewitt and Jenkins 1946; Jenkins 1966; Rutter and Giller 1984). However, these family features are not so strongly associated with emotional disturbance in children (Rutter and Gould 1985).

Correlates of Behavioral and Emotional Disorders in the Present Research Sample

In the previous chapter, we saw that in the speech/language–disordered children in the present research sample, the most significant correlates of psychiatric disorder were linguistic factors. Developmental (learning) disorder and psychosocial (stress) factors (amount, severity, and family-type problems) were also strongly associated with psychiatric illness. We now examine the correlates of behavioral disorder and emotional disorder in the speech/language–disordered children in the present study.

The literature indicated that among nonspeech/language–disordered children, behavioral disorder and emotional disorder have different correlates. Our aim here, then, is to determine which factors are associated with behavioral disorder and which factors are associated with emotional disorder (in comparison to psychiatric wellness). It is of interest whether different factors are associated with the two different types of disorders in comparison to psychiatric wellness and also in comparison to each other.

There were 298 psychiatrically well children in the study and 302 psychiatrically ill children. Of the 302 psychiatrically ill children, there were 142 children who had some type of behavioral disorder only (i.e., attention-deficit disorder, conduct disorder, or oppositional disorder) and 92 children who had only an emotional disorder (i.e., anxiety disorders, affective disorders, or adjustment disorders).[1] Eleven children, not considered in the present analysis, had multiple diagnoses including both a behavioral disorder and an emotional disorder. The two major groups of children—the behavioral disorder group and the emotional disorder group—were compared on demographic and background factors, developmental-cognitive factors, linguistic factors, biological factors, and psychosocial factors (stressors).

Demographic and background factors. Table 4-6 presents data comparing the key demographic and background variables for the children with behavioral and emotional psychiatric disorders. The two groups of psychiatrically disordered children were not significantly different in age distribution, birth order, or maternal and paternal occu-

---

[1]These figures are slightly different from the prevalence figures reported in Chapter 3. This is because the data in Chapter 3 referred to numbers of psychiatric diagnoses, whereas the present data refer to numbers of children. Thus, children with more than one behavioral or emotional disorder were counted more than once in Chapter 3 but only once in the present chapter.

Table 4-6. Background and demographic correlates of behavioral
and emotional psychiatric illness in the present
research sample

	Significance[a]	Behavioral disorder group	Emotional disorder group
Age (in years)			
Mean		6.0	6.2
SD		2.6	3.4
Sex (% males)	***	84	50
Birth order (%)			
First-born		51	40
Second-born		32	36
Later-born		17	24
Paternal occupation (%)			
Professional, administrative		41	43
Clerical, technical		37	33
Labor, unemployed		22	24
Maternal occupation (%)			
Professional, administrative		11	11
Clerical, technical		14	22
Labor, unemployed		75	67

Note. SD = standard deviation.
[a] *** indicates significant difference (by chi-square test) between the behavioral disorder and emotional disorder groups at $P < .0001$ level.

pation. Nor were they significantly different with regard to multiple other background variables not listed in the table, including maternal and paternal age, maternal and paternal education, family size, ethnicity, and religion. Furthermore, neither the behavioral disorder group nor the emotional disorder group differed significantly from the psychiatrically well group in any of these factors.

However, the sex distribution data showed highly significant group differences. As can be seen in Table 4-6, males were much more common among the children with behavioral disorders (84% of whom were males) than among the children with emotional disorders (50% of whom were males). This difference was statistically significant (by chi-square test) at the $P < .0001$ level. These data support the prevalence rates reported in the literature indicating a male predominance for behavioral disorders and a higher rate of females for emotional disorders.

Recalling that the majority of the children in this research sample were male, the sex differences between behavioral disorders and emotional disorders are particularly striking. In comparison to the psychiatrically well children (67% males), both the behavioral and the emotional groups showed significantly different sex distributions (at the $P < .01$ and $P < .001$ levels, respectively, for the emotional and behavioral disorder groups).

Developmental-cognitive factors. The comparisons of developmental-cognitive variables between the behavioral disorder and emotional disorder groups are presented in Table 4-7. The behavioral and emotional disorder groups did not differ significantly from each other in the majority of developmental measures. In particular, there

Table 4-7. Developmental and cognitive correlates of behavioral and emotional psychiatric illness in the present research sample

	Significance[a]	Behavioral disorder group		Emotional disorder group	
		Mean	SD	Mean	SD
Age (in months) for milestones					
Sitting		6.4	2.1	7.6	4.5
Eating solids		7.0	5.1	6.9	6.0
Crawling		7.6	4.5	8.1	2.9
Standing		10.7	4.8	12.9	9.1
Walking (unaided)		13.9	5.5	15.0	5.9
Performance IQ score		102.8	27.3	104.0	22.7
		Percentage of group with:			
Any Axis II disorders	**	34		16	
Enuresis		12		5	
Encopresis		3		1	
Specific reading disorder		4		2	
Developmental coordination disorder		6		5	
Mixed specific developmental disorder		8		3	
Atypical specific developmental disorder		1		0	
Mental retardation		6		3	

Note. SD = standard deviation.
[a] ** indicates significant differences (chi-square test; $P < .0001$) between behavioral disorder and emotional disorder groups and between behavioral disorder group and psychiatrically well group.

were no significant differences in (group mean) performance intelligence scores or in the ages at achieving any motor or developmental milestones (i.e., sitting, standing, crawling, walking, eating solid foods). The only significant difference between the behavioral and emotional disorder groups was in the presence of DSM-III Axis II developmental disorders. These disorders were approximately twice as common among the behavioral disorder group, a significant difference (by chi-square test) at the $P < .0001$ level.

The prevalence rates of the various subtypes of developmental disorders (e.g., enuresis, encopresis, developmental coordination disorder, mixed specific developmental disorder, atypical specific developmental disorder, mental retardation) were not significantly different between the two groups. However, the data showed a definite trend for each of the various subtypes of disorder to be more prevalent in the behavioral disorder group.

There were no differences between either the behavioral disorder group or the emotional disorder group, and the psychiatrically well group in ages at achieving motor milestones, types of specific developmental disorders, or performance IQ levels. However, the behavioral disorder group had significantly more (chi-square test; $P < .0001$) Axis II developmental disorders than did the psychiatrically well group. The rate of Axis II developmental disorders was the same (16%) for both the emotional disorder group and the psychiatrically well group. In contrast, 34% of the behavioral disorder group had some type of Axis II disorder.

These data indicate that developmental-cognitive factors were not strong correlates of psychiatric disorder among these speech/language–disordered children. The only factor that was significantly associated with psychiatric illness (in comparison to psychiatric health) was the general presence of some type of developmental disorder. This factor was associated primarily with behavioral disorder and was significantly less common in children with emotional disorder.

Speech/language factors. The above data revealed few developmental-cognitive correlates of psychiatric disorder among children with speech/language disorders. Furthermore, there were few differences between the behavioral disorder group and the emotional disorder group with regard to most developmental-cognitive measures.

The speech/language data, presented in Table 4-8, show a somewhat different picture. There were no significant differences between the behavioral disorder and emotional disorder groups with regard to any of the speech/language measures. Conversely, however, the comparisons between the psychiatrically well group and the two psychi-

Table 4-8. Speech/language correlates of behavioral and emotional psychiatric illness in the present research sample

	Signifi-cance[a]	Behavioral disorder group		Emotional disorder group	
		Mean	SD	Mean	SD
Age (in months) for milestones					
First word	*	19.7	10.0	19.5	10.4
First sentence	*	31.3	11.4	31.1	14.7
Verbal IQ score (mean)	*	91.4	22.1	94.2	21.4
		Percentage of group with:			
Speech/language group	*				
Pure speech disorder		19		29	
Speech/language disorder		70		61	
Pure language disorder		11		10	
Disorder of					
Language expression	*	29		34	
Language comprehension	*	51		54	
Speech production	*	11		11	
Language processing	*	49		61	

Note. SD = standard deviation.
[a] * indicates that the behavioral disorder and emotional disorder groups were significantly different at $P < .001$ from the psychiatrically well group. *There were no significant differences between the behavioral disorder and emotional disorder groups in any of these variables.*

atrically disordered groups revealed significant differences in virtually every measure. Thus, there were significantly more disorders involving language, language comprehension, expressive language, and language processing in the behavioral disorder group than there were in the psychiatrically well group. The children in the behavioral disorder group also had significantly fewer speech disorders, significantly lower verbal intelligence, and significantly later language milestones than did the children in the psychiatrically well group.

The emotionally disordered children were also significantly more likely to have disorders of language, language comprehension, language expression, and language processing than the children in the psychiatrically well group. As with the behaviorally disordered children, the emotionally disordered children were significantly later in achieving language milestones than were the psychiatrically well children.

Biological and psychosocial factors. The data on the biological and psychosocial factors for the behavioral disorder group and the emotional disorder group are presented in Table 4-9. The behavioral

Table 4-9. Biological and psychosocial correlates of behavioral and emotional psychiatric illness in the present research sample

	Significance[a]	Behavioral disorder group	Emotional disorder group
Percentage of group with			
Any ICD-9 diagnosis		56	58
Any neurological abnormalities		69	64
Any psychosocial stressors	*	76	85

Note. ICD-9 = International Classification of Diseases, Ninth Revision.
[a] * indicates that the behavioral disorder and emotional disorder groups were significantly different from the psychiatrically well group (chi-square test; $P < .0001$). *There were no significant differences between the behavioral disorder and emotional disorder groups in any of the above variables.*

disorder and emotional disorder groups did not differ significantly with regard to the presence of medical disorders, abnormalities on the neurological exam, or psychosocial stress. Furthermore, there were no significant differences between these groups and the psychiatrically well group in the presence of medical or neurological disorders. However, both the behavioral disorder and emotional disorder groups had significantly more psychosocial stress than did the psychiatrically well group.

Symptoms of behavioral and emotional disorders. The data on symptoms of behavioral and emotional disorders, in the form of the average factor scores from the Rutter and Conners parent and teacher questionnaires, are presented in Table 4-10. The behavioral disorder and emotional disorder groups differed significantly in a number of factors, including "conduct disorder," "anxiety," "hyperactivity," and "tension" (from the Conners questionnaires); and "antisocial disorder" and total symptom score (from the Rutter questionnaires). Because it was partly based on these measures that the categorical diagnoses were made, these differences are not surprising.

In these comparisons of children with behavioral disorder, emotional disorder, or no psychiatric disorder, several factors distinguished both types of psychiatrically ill children from the psychiatrically well children. Chief among these were various speech/language factors.

In comparing the behavioral disorder group with the emotional disorder group, a different picture emerged. Here, the only significant differences were in sex and in the presence of DSM-III Axis II developmental disorders. (The children with behavioral disorders were more

Table 4-10. Symptomatic correlates of behavioral and emotional
disorders: parent and teacher questionnaire factor
data for the present research sample

Factor	Signifi-cance[a]	Behavioral disorder group		Emotional disorder group	
		Mean	SD	Mean	SD
Conners parent questionnaire					
Conduct factor	**	0.66	0.68	0.43	0.43
Anxiety factor	***	0.49	0.50	0.82	0.59
Hyperactivity factor	***	0.15	0.68	0.64	0.61
Learning factor		0.39	0.44	0.32	0.45
Psychosomatic factor		0.41	0.41	0.49	0.52
Perfectionism factor		0.52	0.68	0.57	0.70
Antisocial factor		0.04	0.13	0.03	0.11
Tension factor		0.30	0.36	0.29	0.32
Conners teacher questionnaire					
Conduct factor	***	0.54	0.54	0.18	0.46
Passivity factor		1.16	0.69	1.09	0.76
Tension factor	***	0.51	0.48	0.94	0.70
Hyperactivity factor	***	1.32	0.72	0.44	0.59
Rutter parent questionnaire					
Neurotic factor		0.48	0.41	0.57	0.41
Antisocial factor	***	0.60	0.42	0.35	0.31
Total score	***	0.64	0.27	0.48	0.20
Rutter teacher questionnaire					
Neurotic factor		0.40	0.45	0.55	0.55
Antisocial factor		0.55	0.45	0.21	0.38
Total score	*	0.63	0.26	0.45	0.33

Note. SD = standard deviation.
[a]Significant differences (by t test) between behavioral disorder and emotional disorder groups:
*$P < .005$; **$P < .001$; ***$P < .0001$.

likely to be males and to have a developmental disorder.) This finding
reflects the situation in the general population where children with
behavioral disorders are likely to be male and to have associated developmental disorders. However, the factors often reported as being
associated with emotional disorders (e.g., divorced families, psychiatrically ill parents, family conflicts, older age, higher SES) were not
found in this sample.

Thus, it appears that in the present speech-clinic sample, the
behavioral disorder and the emotional disorder groups, while having
different symptomatology, are alike with regard to most external correlates. These groups are both most different from the psychiatrically
well children with regard to speech/language factors, but they do not

differ from each other in these factors. This suggests that the linguistic factors may be important in the genesis of both of these types of psychiatric disorders. The roles of various types of speech/language disorders and of developmental (learning) disorders are examined further in Chapter 5.

5 Age and Sex Differences in Psychopathology

IN THIS CHAPTER WE EXAMINE the effects of age and sex upon psychopathology. For both of these variables, the psychiatric literature is first outlined and then the relevant data from the present study of speech/language–disordered children are presented. The effects of both age and sex upon psychopathology are poorly understood, and data are much needed in both areas. It is hoped that the age data presented here will add to our limited stock of information on the age specificity of childhood psychiatric symptoms and disorders. It is also hoped that the sex differences data will be relevant to our limited understanding of the complex issue of how differences between boys and girls may be related to differential rates of psychopathology.

Sex Differences in Psychopathology: A Review of the Literature

Sex Differences in Prevalence and Types of Psychopathology

The majority of epidemiologic studies have reported that childhood psychopathology is more common in prepubertal boys than in girls (Anderson et al. 1987; Gould et al. 1980, 1981; Graham and Rutter 1973; Lavik 1977; Leslie 1974; McGee et al. 1984; Offord et al. 1987; Richman 1985; Rutter et al. 1970b, 1975a). In addition, most psychiatric symptoms and most of the specific subtypes of childhood psychiatric diagnoses are also more common in prepubertal males. For example, a strong male preponderance is found with essentially all of the developmental disorders of childhood (American Psychiatric Association 1987), including intellectual retardation, enuresis, encopresis, motor coordination disorder, speech/language disorders, academic skills disorders, infantile autism, and pervasive developmental disorder (PDD). Gender identity disorders of childhood, tics, and Tourette's syndrome also have a male preponderance (APA 1987).

The disruptive behavior disorders (i.e., attention-deficit hyperactivity disorder [ADHD], conduct disorder, and oppositional defiant disorder) and their symptoms (e.g., overactivity, antisocial behaviors) have been consistently found to be more common in males than in females (Anderson et al. 1987; Chawla et al. 1981; Crowther et al. 1981; Kashani et al. 1989; Kastrup 1976; McGee et al. 1984; Miller et al. 1974; Offord et al. 1987; Trites et al. 1979; Werry and Quay 1971). In fact, in the follow-up of the Isle of Wight cohort (Graham and Rutter 1973), it was found that a high male predominance of conduct disorder was entirely responsible for the overall elevated rate of psychopathology in males. Furthermore, studies of sex differences in the general population have found that aggression is the social behavior that most clearly differentiates boys from girls (Maccoby and Jacklin 1974).

The only behavioral disorder that has not been found to have a greater male preponderance is the DSM-III disorder of attention-deficit disorder without hyperactivity (ADDW). However, this disorder is not common and has not been subjected to widespread epidemiologic studies. Furthermore, it appears that ADDW differs from attention-deficit disorder with hyperactivity (ADDH) in an association with "internalizing" codiagnoses (Lahey et al. 1987) and an association with unique patterns of cognitive functioning (Berry et al. 1985; Carlson et al. 1986). Thus, it is possible that ADDW may not represent a true "behavioral" disorder.

It is interesting that the adult psychotic disorder schizophrenia, which generally has its onset in late adolescence or adult life, has an equal male and female prevalence (APA 1987). However, schizophrenia with an adult-type clinical picture occurring in the prepubertal age-range is more prevalent in males than in females. And, as mentioned above, infantile autism and related forms of PDD are much more common in males. The difference in sex ratios between infantile autism and schizophrenia is one form of evidence for the hypothesis that these two disorders are different conditions. However, this hypothesis does not explain why when adult-type schizophrenia occurs in the prepubertal age-range, it also has a male predominance. Nor does it explain why, for example, Rett syndrome (Rett 1986), which is phenomenologically similar to autism and considered a PDD, only occurs in females.

Emotional disorders do not show a predominately male sex distribution. This was demonstrated in Chapter 4 with evidence from the literature and data from the present study. The literature indicates that among prepubertal children, the male-to-female sex ratio is roughly equal, but that after puberty these disorders become more common in females, and remain so through adult life (Eme 1979; Gove and Herb 1974; Kashani et al. 1989; Rutter 1982, 1985; Rutter et al. 1976a). Thus, the lifetime morbidity risk for an episode of depression is about twice as high in females as it is in males. Furthermore, from age 14 on, measures of depressive mood show higher mean levels of depression in females than in males (Kandel and Davies 1982).

Similarly, the various anxiety disorders (e.g., generalized anxiety disorder, panic disorder, agoraphobia) become more common in females after puberty. Prior to puberty, the rates of anxiety disorders (e.g., separation anxiety disorder, overanxious disorder, simple phobia, social phobia) are roughly equal for males and females (Anderson et al. 1987; Rutter et al. 1970b). Furthermore, there is some evidence that the types of anxiety are different between males and females, with animal phobias and anxiety regarding self-competence being more common in girls (Kashani et al. 1989; Rutter et al. 1970b).

The eating disorders are one group of disorders that seems to be much more predominant in females (Halmi et al. 1981; Healy et al. 1985; Pyle et al. 1983). The usual age of onset for anorexia nervosa and bulimia is in the adolescent age-range, although it can occur both later in life and during the prepubertal age-range. In all reported samples, females seem to predominate, although there is a slight suggestion that the male/female ratio is not as strongly female biased in the prepubertal age-range as it is in the postpubertal age-range. An increase in the incidence of anorexia nervosa, which has been found in recent studies, is being seen in females but not in males (Jones et al. 1980; Russell 1985; Szmukler et al. 1986).

It should be noted that in relation to mood disorders, suicide attempts are more common in females (Garfinkel et al. 1982), but completed suicide is more common in males (Brent 1987). This is true across the age-range from the time that completed suicide becomes relatively common (after puberty in the United States). Furthermore, it appears that there are sex differences in the symptomatology associated with suicidal ideation (Harlow et al. 1986) and attempts (Bettes and Walker 1986; Shaffer 1974).

Sex Differences in Possible Correlates of Psychopathology

The above brief discussion of the literature indicates that there are sex differences in the prevalence of many childhood and adolescent psychiatric disorders. In addition, follow-up studies in the literature support the assumption that various childhood disorders showing sex differences in prevalence rates are precursors of adult disorders with similar sex ratios (Earls 1987).

The reasons for the above-noted sex differences in the prevalence of childhood and adolescent psychopathology are not fully understood. There are, however, a variety of hypotheses encompassing biological, cognitive, and psychosocial areas (Eme 1979). The sex differences data upon which these hypotheses are based will be briefly summarized below.

Biological factors. The differential vulnerability of males versus females to psychiatric disorders may be a result of biological mechanisms such as hormonal and/or chromosomal factors. It is well known, for example, that males are more vulnerable to most physical hazards and that they lag behind females in both physical and intellectual maturation (Garai and Scheinfeld 1968; Ounsted et al. 1986). The biological immaturity of males may place them at a disadvantage in terms of emotional development, possibly (as will be discussed below) by making them more susceptible to psychosocial stressors.

With regard to specific types of psychiatric disorders, it has been hypothesized that males may be biologically predisposed toward gender identity disorders as a result of having to surmount a prenatal hormonal hurdle that females do not (Green 1974). Androgens have also been postulated to play a role in the more aggressive temperament of males, which, in turn, may be linked with their higher incidence of antisocial behaviors and conduct disorders. Additionally, other temperament characteristics of males and their greater physical strength have been postulated to be linked to their greater prevalence of antisocial and conduct disorders. However, other research (Cloninger et al. 1978) has found that females affected with conduct disorders tend to have more affected relatives, suggesting that, for females at least, genetic factors play a more important role. Finally, hormonal changes occurring with puberty and the resulting physical changes may play a role in the changing sex distributions of certain disorders prepubertally versus at adolescence and beyond.

Cognitive factors. Sex differences in cognitive functioning may play a role in the differing rates of certain types of psychopathology, especially the male predominance in learning disabilities. The documented differences in cognitive functioning between males and females consist generally of female superiority in verbal areas versus male strength in visual and mathematical areas (Maccoby and Jacklin 1980; Stevenson and Newman 1986). However, such differences between the sexes are generally small and tend not to be significant before puberty. If truly present, these differences could reflect underlying biological-hormonal-genetic differences between the sexes. However, they could also be a result of sociocultural factors, as will be discussed below.

Psychosocial factors. Differences in psychosocial factors have been cited as possible explanations for sex differences in psychopathology. It is without question that boys and girls are usually raised very differently, being presented with different role models, different types of daily challenges, and different overall behavioral expectations from parents in particular and from society in general. For example, it has long been documented in both longitudinal and observational studies that annoyance thresholds among parents and teachers are lower for male behavioral deviance than for female deviance (Battle and Lacey 1972; Chess and Thomas 1972; Serbin and O'Leary 1975).

"Sex-role theories" focus upon the differing levels of stress that typically occur between the sexes at different points in development. Such theories have been postulated to explain sex prevalence differences in a variety of forms of psychopathology (Gove and Herb 1974). For example, the higher rates of anxiety and mood disorders and of eating disorders among girls at adolescence have been explained as being due to the feminine sex role becoming more stressful in adolescence, when male roles become more favored in our society. Similarly, the greater prevalence of males with gender identity disorders has been explained in the psychoanalytic model on the grounds that the male role is the more difficult one, requiring switching of identification from the mother (Green 1974). In addition, the greater prevalence of learning difficulties in males has been suggested to result from difficulties with the female-dominated educational system in which not only are most teachers female but most reading materials are oriented toward female interests.

It has also been suggested that psychosocial factors, even when they are the same for males and females, may affect the sexes differently. Rutter (1970) is one of the many who have suggested that male children are more susceptible than females to psychological stress (as well as biological stress) and that this is one of the causes of the sex differences in psychopathology. The research on sex differences in vulnerability to psychosocial stressors is contradictory (Goodyer et al. 1986; Rutter 1972). However, there is some evidence that males are more vulnerable to family stress, discord, and separations (Rutter 1970, 1982; Wolkind and Rutter 1973).

Sex Differences in the Present Research Sample

Sex Differences in Possible Correlates of Psychopathology

Biological and psychosocial factors. The speech/language–disordered children in the present research sample consisted of 413 males and 187 females. Comparisons of the males and females on demographic and background factors, biological-medical factors, and psychosocial stressors, revealed no significant differences in these areas.

The ages of the boys and girls in the sample were essentially the same (boys' mean age = 5.7 years, SD = 2.9; girls' mean age = 5.9 years, SD = 2.9). No significant differences were found between the boys and girls in any background or demographic factors, including parental age, occupation, education, health, home environment (e.g., parental warmth), linguistic background (e.g., bilingual), family size, birth order, age, or ethnicity.

The presence of medical disorders was essentially the same for the boys and girls, with 41% of the boys and 44% of the girls having some medical disorder. The presence of psychosocial stressors was also essentially the same (65%) for the two sexes. The prevalence rates of different types of medical disorders and of different types of psychosocial stressors were not significantly different between the boys and girls.

Cognitive factors. The boys and girls were not significantly different in verbal or performance intelligence levels, although there was a nonsignificant trend toward lower IQ levels for the girls. The boys' group mean verbal IQ level was 96.8 (SD = 21) and the girls' was 93.5 (SD = 21). The boys' mean performance IQ level was 106.1 (SD = 23) and the girls' was 102.9 (SD = 27). The other key cognitive and linguistic comparisons between the boys and girls are presented in Table 5-1.

There were significantly ($P < .05$) more Axis II developmental disorders among the girls than among the boys. More than one-quarter of the girls (26%) had some Axis II developmental disorder, as compared with fewer than one-fifth (19%) of the boys. The specific types of developmental disorders were not significantly different for the sexes. However, girls tended (again nonsignificantly) toward more mental retardation and learning disorders. Because, in the general population, males are considered to be at greater risk for both mental retardation and developmental learning disorders, these findings at first glance seem to run counter to expectations. However, there are

Table 5-1. Cognitive, developmental, and linguistic correlates of sex

	Significance[a]	Males (%)	Females (%)
Any developmental disorders	*	19	26
Specific reading disorder		2	2
Other learning disorders		4	6
Mental retardation		4	9
Enuresis		6	5
Encopresis		1	3
Coordination disorder		5	7
Speech and language diagnoses			
Pure speech disorder		33	35
Speech/language disorder		60	56
Pure language disorder		7	9
Disorder in			
Speech production		93	91
Language processing		33	34
Language comprehension		39	41
Language expression		61	58

[a]Significant difference (by chi-square test) between males and females: *$P < .05$.

data to suggest that when females do have a "handicapping condition" that would predispose them to psychopathology, they are just as likely, if not more likely, than males to demonstrate psychopathology. For example, Rutter and colleagues (Cox et al. 1977; Rutter 1989b; Rutter et al. 1970a, 1970b) have shown that brain damage is a predisposing factor to the development of psychopathology in children, as is intellectual retardation. Young girls with either of these conditions are just as likely as boys to develop psychopathology. Another example is exposure to poor-quality institutional care, which has also been demonstrated to be a risk factor for psychopathology (Rutter et al. 1970a, 1970b). Girls receiving such poor-quality care are just as likely as boys to develop psychopathology as a result of such care (Wolkind and Rutter 1973).

One hypothesis is that girls have certain mechanisms that are "protective" for them against the development of psychopathology in childhood, and that the presence of a handicapping condition in a girl overrides the protective effect. However, this is only a hypothesis, and much more research is needed in order to clarify the processes involved.

The girls and boys did not differ significantly in their types of speech/language disturbances. The majority of both boys and girls had combined disorders affecting both speech and language. Approximately one-third of both the boys and the girls had pure speech disorders, and a small minority of both sexes had pure language disorders. The boys and girls also did not differ significantly in the presence of any specific type of speech/language disorder, including specific abnormalities in speech production, language processing, language comprehension, and expressive language.

Sex Differences in Psychopathology

Psychiatric symptomatology. The data on the psychiatric symptomatology in the speech/language–disordered boys and girls (derived from the Conners and Rutter parent and teacher questionnaire factor scores) are presented in Table 5-2. Two factor scores, plus a total score, were derived from each of the Rutter parent and teacher questionnaires. In addition, the Conners teacher questionnaire had four factors and the Conners parent questionnaire had eight factors. Thus, the data in Table 5-2 consist of group means and standard deviations for a total of 18 measures.

The speech/language–disordered boys and girls differed significantly in only three of the 18 factors. For each of these three factors (the hyperactivity factors from the Conners parent and teacher questionnaires and the antisocial factor from the Rutter teacher questionnaire), the boys had significantly higher average scores than the girls. These findings are in keeping with the general population studies that report a higher prevalence in boys than in girls of attention-deficit, hyperactivity, and antisocial symptomatology (Achenbach and Edelbrock 1981; Crowther et al. 1981; Earls 1980; Holborow et al. 1984; MacFarlane et al. 1954; Offord et al. 1987; Werry and Quay 1971).

Mental status. The data comparing the speech/language–disordered males and females in the present study for overall mental status are presented in Table 5-3. The overall levels of impairment, the current levels of adaptive functioning, and the prevalence of any psychiatric illness were not significantly different between the boys and the girls in the present study. Both the sexes manifested predominantly mild-to-moderate overall levels of impairment and predominantly fair-to-good levels of adaptive functioning. Approximately one-half of both the boys and the girls had a psychiatric disorder.

The fact that the prevalence rates for psychiatric disorders did not differ significantly for the sexes was somewhat surprising. As mentioned above, for younger children in the general population, there tends to be more psychiatric illness among males than among females. However, the Canadian study of speech/language–impaired 5-year-olds

Table 5-2. Sex differences (based on average factor scores) in psychiatric symptomatology in the present research sample

Factor	Signifi-cance[a]	Males		Females	
		Mean	SD	Mean	SD
Conners parent questionnaire					
Conduct factor		0.43	0.53	0.38	0.42
Anxiety factor		0.51	0.48	0.56	0.56
Hyperactivity factor	*	0.72	0.67	0.58	0.58
Learning factor		0.26	0.44	0.22	0.39
Psychosomatic factor		0.38	0.41	0.40	0.44
Perfectionism factor		0.45	0.64	0.46	0.65
Antisocial factor		0.02	0.10	0.02	0.08
Tension factor		0.25	0.34	0.23	0.31
Conners teacher questionnaire					
Conduct factor		0.29	0.45	0.21	0.46
Passivity factor		0.82	0.66	0.91	0.84
Tension factor		0.54	0.53	0.58	0.61
Hyperactivity factor	**	0.76	0.73	0.47	0.68
Rutter parent questionnaire					
Neurotic factor		0.43	0.37	0.44	0.39
Antisocial factor		0.42	0.36	0.35	0.32
Total score		0.49	0.26	0.44	0.23
Rutter teacher questionnaire					
Neurotic factor		0.36	0.47	0.33	0.45
Antisocial factor	*	0.35	0.41	0.21	0.38
Total score		0.43	0.30	0.36	0.33

Note. SD = standard deviation.
[a]Significant difference (by *t* test) between males and females: *$P < .01$; **$P < .0001$.

found the opposite result (Beitchman et al. 1986b). In this study, speech/language–impaired girls had significantly higher rates of psychopathology than did speech/language–impaired boys. It should be noted that Beitchman et al.'s study was of an epidemiologically selected sample of children all of whom were 5 years of age, whereas the present study included a speech-clinic sample of children ranging in ages from preschool-age to adolescent. Also, the distribution of various types of speech/language disorders was somewhat different in the two studies. These differences (as well as other factors) may explain the sex differences in psychopathology found in the two studies.

Types of psychiatric diagnoses. The types of psychiatric disorders did, however, distinguish the sexes in the present study. The relevant data are presented in Table 5-4. With regard to general types

Table 5-3. Sex differences in overall mental status in the present research sample

Mental status	Males (%)	Females (%)
Overall level of impairment		
None	19	22
Mild	41	40
Moderate	35	31
Severe	5	7
Current level of adaptive functioning		
Good	45	47
Fair	37	39
Poor	18	14
Presence of any psychiatric		
illness	48	52

of psychiatric disorders, both behavioral disorders and emotional disorders showed significant differences in sex distribution. Behavioral disorders were significantly more common in boys, occurring in more than twice as many boys (28%) as girls (12%). Emotional disorders, on the other hand, occurred in almost three times as many girls (32%) as boys (11%). Other types of psychiatric disorders (including PDDs and physical disorders) occurred rarely in the sample and did not show any significant differences in sex distribution.

Two specific types of Axis I psychiatric diagnoses did show significant differences in sex distribution. ADDH was significantly more common in boys than in girls, affecting 23% of the boys compared with 6% of the girls. This prevalence rate is considerably higher than the estimates given for boys in the general population. There are only limited data on the prevalence of ADDH in girls in the general population. However, the available data would seem to suggest that the prevalence rate of 6% obtained here is unusually high.

The numbers of children in the present sample with other types of behavioral psychiatric disorders (i.e., ADDW, oppositional disorder, conduct disorder) were too small for statistical comparisons of sex. However, the raw data suggest that ADDW was more common in the girls, oppositional disorder was equally common in the boys and the girls, and conduct disorder was more common in the boys.

Anxiety disorders were the only other diagnosis showing a significant difference in sex distribution in the present study. This group of disorders was significantly more common among the girls than among the boys, with 17% of the girls having some type of anxiety

Table 5-4. Sex differences in psychiatric diagnoses in the present research sample

	Significance[a]	Males (%)	Females (%)
General types of psychiatric diagnoses			
No mental illness		52	48
Behavioral disorders	***	28	12
Pervasive developmental disorders		2	1
Emotional disorders	***	11	32
Physical disorders		0	1
Other diagnoses		8	7
Specific DSM-III disorders			
ADDH	***	23	6
ADDW		1	3
Oppositional disorder		5	5
Conduct disorder		3	1
Anxiety disorders	**	7	17
Adjustment disorders		4	4
Affective disorders		4	2

Note. ADDH = attention-deficit disorder with hyperactivity. ADDW = attention-deficit disorder without hyperactivity.
[a]Significant difference (by chi-square test) between males and females: **$P < .0005$; ***$P < .0001$.

disorder compared with only 7% of the boys.

As summarized above, the literature indicates that anxiety disorders are more common in females in the adolescent age-range but are generally equally common among boys and girls in the prepubertal age-range. However, the present sample, being typically in the prepubertal age-range, did not reflect this finding.

Summary of Sex Differences in the Present Research Sample

The speech/language–impaired boys and girls in the present research sample differed in few nonpsychiatric measures. No significant differences were found between the boys and girls in any of the demographic, background, biological-medical, or psychosocial variables measured. The prevalence and types of speech/language impairments found were also not significantly different between the boys and girls. However, the girls did have significantly more (Axis II) developmental disorders.

With regard to psychopathology, there were no significant differences between the boys and girls in the overall prevalence of psychiatric illness, the levels of adaptive functioning, or the degree of overall impairment. As stated above, this finding is somewhat surprising, since in this age-range, boys are thought to be more at risk for the development of psychopathology. However, certain specific diagnoses did have marked differences in prevalence rate between boys and girls. Disruptive behavioral disorders in general (and ADDH in particular) were significantly more common in the boys. Emotional disorders in general (and anxiety disorders in particular) were more common in the girls.

Age Trends in Child Development and Psychopathology

Review of the Literature

The developmental study of behavior problems in both non-psychiatrically disordered children and in children with definable psychiatric disorders has a long tradition. One of the landmark early studies with children from the general population was the Berkeley epidemiologic study of MacFarlane and colleagues (1954). This was the first comprehensive study to document age trends in the prevalence of behavioral and emotional symptoms across the age-range from 1 to 14 years. Since then, a new field of developmental psychopathology has risen, having its own journal of the same name.

Developmental psychopathology, as Rutter and Garmezy (1983) have pointed out, views childhood psychopathology from a developmental perspective. That is, it takes into account continuities and discontinuities between infancy, childhood, and adult life. Such an approach is particularly useful in child psychiatry, because many childhood disorders can only be diagnosed at certain age levels and because many symptoms may be pathological at one age level and normal at another age level.

The present study involved primarily preschool-age children, but there were a substantial number of grade school–age children and a significant minority of children in the adolescent age-range. Thus, it is appropriate to examine the data from the present study separately for these major age groupings. The literature regarding the developmental course of certain symptoms and syndromes provides an appropriate backdrop against which to view the age trends to be reported in this chapter.

Before discussing the available data, some mention is necessary of the methodology that has been used. One of the best approaches, when conducted perfectly, is the *anterospective study*. This is a type of prospective cohort study in which an epidemiologically selected sample of children are identified before birth and then followed at regular intervals throughout their life span, documenting at various age levels the prevalence of specific symptoms or behaviors. The prospective cohort studies that have been attempted (e.g., Chamberlain et al. 1975; Coleman et al. 1977; Crowther et al. 1981; MacFarlane et al. 1954; Miller et al. 1974) have demonstrated that some behaviors are more common in younger children and tend to dissipate with time (e.g., temper tantrums), while other behaviors are rarer in younger children and tend to become more common as the children age. However, the data from this type of study are of limited use in child psychiatry because of methodological problems such as the attrition of subjects over time, the impracticality of studying large groups in a detailed way, and the relatively small numbers of disordered children that are found.

Prospective and retrospective studies of deviant samples of children are other approaches that have provided much information on age trends in psychopathology. The true *prospective study* follows a sample of disordered children as they age. This provides information about the continuities and discontinuities between infancy, childhood, adolescence, and adult life, as well as about the predictive factors associated with the persistence of certain behaviors. The true *retrospective study* starts with older individuals (either adults or possibly adolescents) who have defined problems, and looks backward at prior records to try to determine what childhood behaviors may have presaged the later psychopathology. The *catch-up prospective study* selects its subjects from previous childhood records when the subjects are adults. In this type of study, the sample has already "aged," so that the "real time delay" of a prospective study is avoided. Thus, as long as good records are available for childhood, the study provides reasonable conclusions about continuity and discontinuity between childhood and later life. A classical example of this study design is Robins' *Deviant Children Grown Up* (1966, 1974), one of the landmark studies of developmental psychopathology done in the United States.

What has this variety of studies shown us with regard to the stability, or the lack thereof, of various types of behavior in childhood? Although the developmental literature is contradictory and difficult to interpret because of differences in study designs, samples, measurement techniques, and definitions, there are, nevertheless, some clear trends emerging. These will be summarized below, beginning with the disruptive behaviors and disorders.

Conduct symptomatology and disorders. Generally, there is a decrease in both physical aggression and tantrums from the toddler years through the early school years (Feshbach 1970). Early studies of normal youngsters (Goodenough 1931) have revealed other developmental trends having to do with anger. For example, outbursts of anger and temper are most common during the second year of life; after this, temper outbursts become shorter while sulking, whining, and brooding increase. During the preschool age-range, most outbursts are the result of conflicts with parents; however, at around 4 to 5 years, peer conflicts become more common.

Data suggest that symptoms such as lying, bullying, and destructiveness tend to drop in prevalence between the ages of 5 and 9 years but do not change much between the ages of 10 and 14 years (Achenbach and Edelbrock 1981; Gersten et al. 1976; MacFarlane et al. 1954). Once adolescence is reached, there is an increase in certain types of disruptive behavior (e.g., running away from home, playing hooky from school). Theft and property offenses tend to drop in prevalence during late adolescence, but violent crimes increase during late adolescence, peaking in young adult life.

Thus, it seems that many forms of oppositional negativistic behavior peak in frequency during the preschool years and diminish markedly during the school-age years. However, in an individual child, the existence of a general pattern of angry, defiant, or aggressive behavior may be a relatively stable phenomenon (Coleman et al. 1977; Crowther et al. 1981; Deluty 1985; Gersten et al. 1976; Halverson and Waldrop 1976; Kagan and Moss 1962).

Whether disruptive behavior manifested in the preschool years carries the same meaning as later conduct symptomatology is somewhat of an open question. Clearly, there are oppositional negativistic preschoolers who do not persist with a significant pattern of conduct symptomatology. However, there are also other youngsters in whom early oppositional negativistic behavior is a forerunner of later conduct/antisocial symptomatology or disorder (Griffin 1987; Loeber and Dishion 1983; Moore et al. 1979; Wolff 1961; Zeitlin 1986).

Attention-deficit hyperactivity symptoms and disorder. The individual behavioral symptoms (i.e., hyperactivity, inattention, impulsivity) that make up ADHD have some developmental trends. For example, there is a general tendency for gross motor activity to decrease from preschool age to about 9 years of age and, at the same time, for motor inhibition and sustained attention to increase (Aman 1984; Geffen and Sexton 1978; Murphy and Pelham 1989).

Although there are marked differences among children with regard to activity level, individuals tend to show fairly substantial stability during the grade school age-range (Rutter and Garmezy 1983). This is true of normal children as well as pathological ones (Chess et al. 1967; Fischer et al. 1984; Halverson and Waldrop 1976; Kagan 1971). Thus, clinically defined samples of children with attention, hyperactivity, and impulse control problems tend to show persistence of these difficulties over time (Aman 1984; Borland and Heckman 1976; Gillberg and Gillberg 1988; Gittelman et al. 1985; Hoy et al. 1978). ADHD children may also develop learning difficulties (Cantwell and Satterfield 1978; Charles and Schain 1981; Riddle and Rapoport 1976) and/or conduct symptomatology (Gittelman et al. 1985; Hechtman and Weiss 1986; Mendelson et al. 1971) in adolescence.

Emotional symptoms and disorders. The continuity of emotional-type symptoms (e.g., fears, obsessions, compulsions, anxiety, depressed mood) and disturbances appears to be weaker than the continuity of behavioral disorders and symptoms (Rutter and Garmezy 1983). Correlations for emotional symptomatology are rather modest over middle childhood in both nondisordered and disordered children. Furthermore, several follow-up studies suggest that the continuity of emotional disorder from childhood into adult life is substantially less than that of conduct symptomatology. On the other hand, there is some continuity between emotional personality traits in childhood and corresponding adult disorders (Parnas et al. 1982). Thus, people who were extremely anxious as children are rarely found to have very low anxiety as adults. In addition, children with clearly defined emotional disorders rarely develop conduct-type symptomatology or disorders later in life (Rutter 1980).

Fears, phobias, and anxiety disorders. Epidemiologic studies have shown that childhood fears are very common in young children but tend to decrease with age (Achenbach and Edelbrock 1981; MacFarlane et al. 1954). Several studies have documented that childhood fears may be differentiated on the basis of developmental trends (Agras et al. 1969; Campbell 1986; Kashani et al. 1989; Marks and Gelder 1966; Miller et al. 1974). For example, the normal developmental fears of infancy (e.g., fears of noises, falling, strange objects, and strange persons) reach a peak before 2 years of age and then decline rapidly during the next few years. Fear of animals, the dark, or imaginary creatures is uncommon in infancy but increases during the preschool years and finally drops off during middle childhood.

Other fears that do not show consistent age trends may be more closely associated with psychopathology. For example, fear of meeting people and fear of storms do not show consistent age trends and may be associated with generalized anxiety and avoidant behavior. Agoraphobia first appears in later childhood, adolescence, or adult life, and is not a part of the normal developmental progression. It is often preceded by panic attacks (DSM-III-R).

Stranger anxiety and separation anxiety are part of the normal developmental scheme for all young children. However, marked separation anxiety beginning in the early school years or at the time of junior high school may be a pathological symptom leading to school refusal and concomitant depression.

The anxiety symptomatology having the greatest continuity from childhood through adult life is obsessive-compulsive symptomatology (Zeitlin 1986). The Epidemiologic Catchment Area study (Weissman et al. 1978) found that many adult patients with obsessive-compulsive disorder had anxiety symptomatology in childhood. However, the majority of adults with other anxiety disorders did not have anxiety disorders as children (McDermott 1985). It is not known how many children with anxiety symptoms progress on to an adult anxiety disorder.

Depressive symptomatology and disorders.   Because of the early belief that younger children do not manifest depression (Poznanski and Zrull 1970), little was known until recently about developmental trends and continuities of depressive disorders and symptoms. However, it is now recognized that feelings of unhappiness and dysphoria, as well as depressive disorders themselves, do occur in preadolescent children (Kaplan et al. 1984; Kashani and Simonds 1979; Pearce 1978). Furthermore, depressive symptomatology occurs relatively commonly as a part of other psychiatric disorders, including conduct and disruptive behavior disorders as well as other emotional disorders (Carlson and Cantwell 1980; Werry et al. 1987).

Depressive feelings and disorders are both much more prevalent in adolescents than in prepubertal children (Kaplan et al. 1984; Rutter et al. 1976a; Weissman 1987). There is a sharp increase in prevalence in adolescence for both boys and girls; however, the increase is much sharper for girls.

Thus, there are children who have clear-cut depressive symptomatology analogous to that seen in adults and who can be diagnosed with major depressive episodes using diagnostic criteria similar to those used for adult depression (Cytryn et al. 1980; Weinberg et al. 1973; Weller and Weller 1986). However, there seem to be certain symptomatic differences in depressed individuals of different ages (Carlson and Garber 1986). For example, younger (prepubertal) depressed children appear to differ from depressed adolescents in higher rates of hypersomnia, somatic complaints, and psychomotor agitation, and lower rates of "cognitive" symptoms such as guilt, hopelessness, altered perceptions, and manic behaviors (Carlson and Garber 1986; Mitchell et al. 1988; Pearce 1978; Ryan et al. 1987). There is also some evidence that depressed adolescents differ in some symptoms from depressed adults (Carlson and Strober 1979; Inamdar et al. 1979).

Suicidal ideation, suicide attempts, and completed suicides are all more frequent among adolescents than among prepubertal children (Shaffer and Fisher 1981; Shectman 1970). In addition, it appears that suicidal behavior between childhood, adolescence, and adulthood may be associated with different psychiatric symptomatology (Arieti and Bemporad 1978; Bettes and Walker 1986). In particular, the association of suicide with depression may be stronger in adults than it is in children and adolescents (Miller et al. 1982; Pfeffer et al. 1982; Shaffer 1974). Furthermore, there is evidence that there are gender differences, as well as age differences, in the symptoms associated with suicidal thoughts and acts (Bettes and Walker 1986).

Summary. We now have considerable evidence that the prevalence rates of behavioral and emotional symptoms differ developmentally. Furthermore, the prevalence rates of behavioral and emotional psychiatric disorders, as well as the symptomatology associated with these disorders, differ developmentally. However, we lack understanding as to why these differences occur. As Rutter (1989a) points out, age (like sex) is an "ambiguous variable." Thus, age differences in psychopathology may be the result of a number of external factors including hormonal changes, psychosocial (stressor) changes, cognitive maturation, or the age-dependent expression of a genetic vulnerability. The remainder of this chapter will present data on the age differences found in the speech/language–disordered children in the present study.

Age Trends in the Present Research Sample

The speech/language–disordered children in the present research sample were predominantly preschool-age (i.e., under 6 years of age). Of the 600 children in the sample, there were 386 in this age-range; another 191 children were in the elementary school age-range (6 through 11 years); and 23 children were 12 to 17 years of age. These three age groupings will be referred to as the "preschool" group, the "middle group," and the "older group." The data comparing these three age groups are presented in Tables 5-5 through 5-8.

Age differences in nonpsychiatric measures. Comparisons of the three age groups showed little difference in demographic or background variables, or in overall amount of psychosocial stress. However, the data are suggestive of age differences in the prevalence

Table 5-5. Age differences in developmental, psychosocial, and linguistic variables

	Preschool group (%)	Middle group (%)	Older group (%)
Developmental disorders	12	35	56
Enuresis	3	12	0
Encopresis	1	2	0
Coordination disorder	4	7	4
Reading disorder	0	5	13
Arithmetic disorder	0	1	0
Specific learning disorders	1	9	22
Mental retardation	4	7	17
Psychosocial stressors	63	69	74
Changes	18	18	0
Illness	22	21	41
Events	10	5	12
Discord	34	34	29
Personal problems	2	11	12
Deprivation	2	0	0
Parental employment problems	6	6	0
Parental financial problems	2	0	0
Speech and language diagnoses			
Pure speech disorder	28	45	39
Speech/language disorder	69	41	26
Pure language disorder	3	14	34
Disorder in			
Language expression	71	42	39
Language comprehension	45	31	22
Speech production	97	86	66
Language processing	45	52	57

and types of developmental disorders, in certain types of psychosocial stressors, and in the types of speech/language disorders. The relevant data are presented in Table 5-5.

Because of the great disparity in size between the older group and the other two groups, statistical comparisons across the three groups were rendered invalid. Nonetheless, the raw data clearly suggest certain age trends. For example, there is a clear trend for developmental disorder to be associated with age. Thus, specific developmental disorders were least prevalent (12%) among the preschool group, more prevalent (35%) among the middle group, and most prevalent (56%) among the older group. The different subtypes of developmental disorders also showed differing prevalence rates across the three age groups. Thus, enuresis, encopresis, coordination disorder, and specific arithmetic disorder were the most prevalent in the middle group. On the other hand, specific reading disorder and specific (mixed) learning disorders were most prevalent in the older group. These findings are not unexpected given the nature of developmental disorders. By definition, these disorders cannot be diagnosed in very young children. Also, the nonlearning developmental disorders are often gradually "outgrown," thus becoming less prevalent with increasing age.

The data in Table 5-5 show that the prevalence rates for having any type of psychosocial stressor were very similar across the three age groups. However, there were differences between the three groups with regard to different types of psychosocial stressors. Thus, the older children had considerably less stress due to life changes or parental problems associated with employment. The older children also had considerably more stress arising from (personal and/or family) illnesses. Personal problems were considerably less common among the preschool group.

Finally, the data show age differences in the distribution of types of speech/language disorders. For example, speech disorders were clearly associated with young age; nearly all (97%) of the youngest group had some type of speech disorder. Pure language disorders, on the other hand, were rare in young children but became increasingly common with age. Thus, only 3% of the youngest group had pure language disorders compared with 14% of the middle group and 34% of the oldest group. Disorders of both language expression and language comprehension also seemed to be associated with younger age. Approximately 40% of the middle and older children had expressive language problems, as opposed to 71% of the preschool group. The distribution of language comprehension disorders ranged from a low of 22% in the older group to 31% in the middle group and 45% in the preschool group.

Psychiatric diagnoses in different age groups. The DSM-III diagnoses found in the three age groups are presented in Table 5-6. It can be seen that the rates of psychiatric illness were roughly the same in the three age groups. However, the different types of psychiatric disorders showed different rates of occurrence across the three groups.

Behavioral disorders were most prevalent in the middle group (64%) and least prevalent (27%) in the older group. The preschool group also had a high rate (56%) of behavioral disorder. The most common behavioral disorder in all three groups was attention-deficit disorder (with or without hyperactivity). Indeed, the distribution of

Table 5-6. Psychiatric diagnoses in different age groups of the present research sample

DSM-III Axis I psychiatric diagnoses[a]	Preschool group (%)	Middle group (%)	Older group (%)
No disorder	53	44	48
Behavioral disorder	56	64	27
ADDH/ADDW	15	24	9
Oppositional/conduct disorders	7	5	9
Pervasive developmental disorders	1	2	0
Emotional disorders	44	36	73
Anxiety disorders	11	7	4
Adjustment disorders	5	6	4
Affective disorders	0	8	30
Physical disorders	1	2	0
Other diagnoses	8	6	9

Note. ADDH = attention-deficit disorder with hyperactivity. ADDW = attention-deficit disorder without hyperactivity.
[a]Figures reported combine primary, secondary, and tertiary diagnoses.

this disorder was primarily responsible for the differences reported in the prevalence of behavioral disorders. Thus, 24% of the middle group, 15% of the preschool group, and only 9% of the older group had attention-deficit disorder. Oppositional and conduct disorders were less common and did not show any clear trends across the age groups. The data on these disorders have been combined in Table 5-6.

Emotional disorders followed the opposite pattern of behavioral disorders. Thus, the highest prevalence rate for emotional disorders was found in the older group (73%), and the lowest rate (36%) was found in the middle group. The preschool group had an intermediate rate (44%) of emotional disorders. The different types of emotional disorders followed different patterns with regard to the age groups. Affective disorders were most likely to occur in the older group, but anxiety disorders were most likely to occur in the preschool group. Both of these trends are in keeping with the literature, which reports that affective disorders are more common in older children and that worries and anxiety are more common in younger children. Adjustment disorders had approximately the same prevalence rates across the three groups, as did PDDs and physical disorders.

Psychiatric symptomatology across age groups. Table 5-7 lists the prevalence of the various symptoms reported on the parent questionnaires. The table reveals differences across the age groups in the prevalence of a number of symptoms. Several general trends were found. First, there was a relatively large group of symptoms that showed decreasing prevalence with increased age. Second, there was a smaller group of symptoms that became more prevalent with increasing age. Third, there were several symptoms that showed other significant differences among the three groups. And, finally, there were some symptoms whose prevalence remained quite stable across the age groups.

The symptoms showing a significant decrease in prevalence with increased age were wetting (enuresis), picky eating, clinging and/or fears of separation, tantrums, always climbing, difficult-to-understand speech, inappropriate language use, and limited language development. The same trend was found in a number of other symptoms (e.g., soiling [encopresis], sleep problems and nightmares, immaturity, shyness, fears of new situations, stuttering), although the data for these symptoms did not reach statistical significance. As reviewed above, there is evidence in the literature supporting the decrease in prevalence (or "outgrowing") of these symptoms as children age.

The symptoms that showed significant increases in prevalence associated with increased age were headaches, daydreaming, fighting with siblings, and fears of not being liked. In addition, the data showed a (nonsignificant) trend toward increased prevalence with age for a number of other symptoms. The majority of these were in the behavioral disorder or conduct disorder realm (e.g., not being liked by peers, quarreling, school truancy, anger-irritability, solitary behavior, disobedience, overassertion); but some were indicative of other types of problems (e.g., overweight, motor tics, dislike of school, learning problems, unhappiness, frequent worrying).

Three symptoms showed significant differences between groups that were not associated with age in a linear way. Sibling rivalry and blaming others for one's own mistakes were both significantly less prevalent in the preschool group than in the other two groups. These two symptoms had similar prevalence rates between the older and middle groups. Telling lies was significantly more common in the middle group, least common in the older group, and of intermediate prevalence in the preschool group. This finding contradicts reports in the literature that this symptom tends to decrease in prevalence during the middle years.

Finally, five symptoms showed amazing stability across the three age groups: thumb sucking, short attention span, excitability, stealing, and insistence on sameness. In general, these symptoms would be expected to decrease in prevalence with increased age. One possibility

Table 5-7. Symptoms (based on parent questionnaires) in the three age groups of the present research sample

Symptom	Significance[a]	Preschool group (%)	Middle group (%)	Older group (%)
Headaches	***	18	36	45
Stomachaches		43	51	29
Asthma		10	15	18
Wetting	***	56	28	5
Soiling		27	14	9
Sleep difficulties		41	35	18
Nightmares		39	29	18
Eating: overweight		9	12	32
Eating: picky	*	45	38	14
Muscular tension		9	11	5
Tics		5	9	19
Sucks thumb		41	41	41
Aches and pains		17	33	32
Daydreams	***	25	44	52
Shy		60	59	36
Fears not being liked	***	16	51	55
Not liked		15	29	41
Quarrelsome		40	47	50
Sibling problems: fights	***	48	65	77
Sibling problems: rivalry	***	22	51	50
Dislikes school		13	24	27
Truant from school		2	3	9
Not learning		9	31	59
Mean, fights		17	17	14
Disobedient		13	19	32
Keeps anger to self		12	30	50
Unhappy		39	48	59
Angry, irritable		54	57	82
Solitary		43	47	73
Clings, has separation fears	***	39	21	9
Tantrums	***	59	40	32
Overasserts self		27	34	41
Is bullied		35	46	45
Health worries		8	29	27
Often worried		14	34	41
Immature		50	44	23
Restless		56	58	36
Short attention span		61	67	68
Excitable		56	57	62
Drastic mood changes		31	31	45
Easily frustrated		70	65	59
Fears new situations		50	47	41
Seems driven by motor		20	24	14
Feelings easily hurt		72	78	82
Disobeys often		81	68	73

Table 5-7 *(continued)*

Symptom	Signifi-cance[a]	Preschool group (%)	Middle group (%)	Older group (%)
Lies	**	35	47	14
Sets fires		1	3	0
Destroys property		13	14	9
Trouble with police		0	0	9
Stealing from parents		2	4	5
Stealing from school		1	1	0
Stealing from other places		3	4	0
Blames others	***	31	53	50
Perfectionist		30	33	50
Squirmy		43	47	23
Insists on sameness		32	29	32
Always climbing	***	52	22	14
Stutters		19	14	9
Speech difficult to understand	***	86	60	73
Language-comprehension problem		26	28	50
Inappropriate intonation		17	18	33
Inappropriate speech rhythm		35	28	32
Limited language	***	61	34	41
Language used inappropriately	***	29	14	9

[a]Significant difference (by chi-square test) between groups: *$P < .01$; **$P < .001$; ***$P < .0001$.

(examined further below) is that the stability of these symptoms in this sample may be reflective of psychopathology.

Symptoms of psychiatric illness in preschool-age or elementary school–age children. The preceding section discussed age trends in the prevalence of psychiatric symptoms in speech/language–disordered children. One relevant issue that was not explored there was the association between symptoms and psychopathology at different age levels. This issue is important because of the possibility that a symptom may be pathological at one age level but not at another age level.

Table 5-8 presents the symptomatology data (from the parent questionnaires) broken down to show the prevalence of symptoms in the psychiatrically well versus psychiatrically ill children at different ages. Unfortunately, the older group was too small to be meaningfully subdivided in this way; thus, data are presented only for the preschool and the middle (elementary school) groups.

The majority of symptoms on the parent questionnaires significantly distinguished the psychiatrically well children from the psychi-

Table 5-8. Symptoms of psychiatric illness (based on parent questionnaires) in preschool-age and elementary school–age groups

	Preschool			Elementary school		
	Well (%)	Ill (%)	P	Well (%)	Ill (%)	P
Headaches	15	21		34	39	
Stomachaches	39	48		48	53	
Asthma	8	12		18	13	
Wetting	52	59		31	26	
Soiling	25	29		12	16	
Sleep problems	34	49	**	30	40	
Nightmares	34	44		26	32	
Eating: overweight	9	9		11	12	
Eating: picky	41	49		34	42	
Muscular tension	3	17	***	7	13	
Tics	4	6		6	11	
Sucks thumb	37	45		29	51	
Aches and pains	12	22	*	35	31	
Daydreams	22	28		36	50	
Shy	57	64		59	59	
Fears not being liked	13	20		42	58	
Not liked	8	23	***	17	39	**
Quarrelsome	35	46	*	38	55	*
Sibling problems: fights	47	49		67	64	
Sibling problems: rivalry	18	26		46	55	
Dislikes school	7	20	***	10	37	***
Truant from school	1	2		1	4	
Not learning	3	16	***	13	45	***
Mean, fights	5	32	***	5	28	***
Disobedient	7	20	***	8	29	***
Keeps anger to self	8	16	*	24	35	
Unhappy	32	47	**	37	57	**
Angry, irritable	43	66	***	52	62	
Solitary	39	48		41	53	
Clings, fears separation	27	52	***	14	27	*
Tantrums	48	71	***	28	50	*
Overasserts self	19	36	***	28	39	
Is bullied	30	40		36	54	*
Health worries	7	9		23	34	
Often worried	10	18	*	29	39	
Immature	43	58	**	35	51	*
Restless	46	68	***	43	71	***
Short attention span	52	73	***	47	84	***
Excitable	42	72	***	42	71	***
Drastic mood changes	18	45	***	17	43	***
Easily frustrated	64	77	**	49	79	***
Fears new situations	40	60	***	41	52	
Seems driven by motor	9	34	***	10	36	***

Table 5-8 *(continued)*

	Preschool			Elementary school		
	Well (%)	Ill (%)	P	Well (%)	Ill (%)	P
Feelings easily hurt	67	77	*	75	81	
Disobeys often	77	86	*	58	77	**
Lies	31	40		36	56	**
Sets fires	1	1		1	4	
Destroys property	7	20	***	4	23	***
Trouble with police	1	0		0	0	
Stealing from parents	1	3		1	7	
Stealing from school	1	2		0	1	
Stealing from other places	1	4		4	4	
Blames others	27	36		49	56	
Perfectionist	23	37	*	27	39	
Squirmy	30	58	***	29	62	***
Insists on sameness	27	38	*	22	35	*
Always climbing	44	61	**	22	23	

Note. Significant differences (by chi-square test) between psychiatrically well and
psychiatrically ill groups: *P < .01; **P < .001; ***P < .0001.

atrically ill children. In general, the symptoms associated with psychiatric illness in the preschool-age children were also associated with
psychiatric illness in the elementary school–age children. Similarly,
symptoms not significantly associated with psychiatric illness in the
preschool-age children were also not significantly associated with psychiatric illness in the elementary school–age children. However, a
small number of symptoms were associated with psychopathology in
one age group but not in the other.

Those symptoms that were not significantly associated with psychiatric illness at either age level were primarily somatic symptoms
(e.g., headaches, stomachaches, asthma, wetting [enuresis], soiling [en-
copresis], tics, health worries) or conduct disorder symptoms (e.g.,
fighting with siblings, school truancy, setting fires, being in trouble
with police, stealing, blaming others for one's mistakes).

A number of behavioral symptoms were significantly associated
with psychiatric illness in both the preschool-age group and the elementary school–age children. These symptoms included both attention-deficit disorder symptoms (e.g., restlessness, short attention span,
low frustration tolerance, squirming and fidgeting, excitability, appearing to be driven by a motor) and acting-out (conduct disorder) symptoms (e.g., tantrums, disobedience, quarreling, fighting, destroying
property). Other symptoms that were consistently associated with psy-

chiatric illness were being disliked, immaturity, disliking school, having learning problems, unhappiness, clinging or fears of separation, drastic mood changes, and insistence on sameness.

When a symptom was associated with psychiatric illness in one age group but not the other, the significant association typically occurred in the preschool-age group. Thus, for preschool-age children (but not for elementary school–age children), the following symptoms were significantly associated with psychiatric illness: sleep problems, muscular tension, aches and pains, keeping anger to oneself, anger-irritability, being overly assertive, often worrying, fearing new situations, having feelings easily hurt, being perfectionist, and always climbing. Only two symptoms—being bullied and telling lies—were significantly associated with psychiatric illness in the elementary school–age group but not the preschool-age group.

6

Speech, Language, and Learning Factors in the Development of Psychopathology

A PRIMARY GOAL OF THE PRESENT STUDY was to determine whether speech/language disorders in children constitute a risk factor for the development of psychopathology and/or learning disorders. The data presented in Chapters 3 and 4 clearly suggest that they do. The prevalence data (presented in Chapter 3) demonstrate that children with speech/language disorders have elevated rates of both psychopathology and learning disorders in comparison with the general population.

Furthermore, the data comparing psychiatrically well children to psychiatrically ill children (see Chapter 4) demonstrate that an association exists between the severity and type of speech/language disorders and the presence of both psychopathology and learning disorders. This set of risk factor data indicates that, in effect, children with certain types of speech/language disorders are more at risk for psychopathology than are children with other types of speech/language disorders. In particular, the likelihood of psychiatric illness was significantly higher in children with disorders involving the development of some aspect of language (as opposed to children whose disorders involved only aspects of speech production). In addition, several different measures of language functioning (e.g., expression, comprehension, processing) were each significantly associated with the greater likelihood of a psychiatric illness.

Thus, the risk factor data show that, within the general high-risk group of speech/language–disordered children, those who are most vulnerable to psychopathology are the ones with some degree of language involvement. In this chapter we examine this vulnerability in more detail by comparing the subgroups of children with pure speech disorder, with pure language disorder, and with concurrent speech/language disorders. Such comparisons could provide insights into the etiological mechanisms that have resulted in the development of psychiatric disorders. For example, one possibility to be examined is whether the children with language disorder are distinct with regard to some other factor (such as mental retardation or brain damage) that could underlie the psychopathology.

Speech/Language Factors in the Development of Psychopathology

As in the previous chapters, the factors to be examined in this chapter include demographic and background factors, developmental-cognitive factors, biological-medical factors, and psychosocial (stress) factors. In addition, data will be presented regarding the types of psychiatric symptomatology and diagnoses found in children with different types of speech/language disorders. First, however, some mention will be made of how childhood speech/language disorders have been classified.

Subclassification of Speech/Language Disorders

As discussed in Chapter 1, there is no consensus on the classification of childhood speech/language disorders. In general, the earlier classification systems tended to be based upon etiological concepts, producing subclasses such as motor speech deficits, hearing impairment, mental retardation, and acquired aphasia. However, such systems are hampered by the fact that it is difficult, if not impossible, to establish etiology for the majority of cases of childhood speech/language disorders.

As a result of these difficulties, more recent classification systems have focused more upon linguistic, neuropsychological, and/or clinical-descriptive frameworks, producing categories such as speech perception disruption, semantic comprehension disorder, language integration disorder, and syntactic formulation disorder. A few studies (Aram and Nation 1975; Feagans and Appelbaum 1986; Wilson and Risucci 1986; Wolfus et al. 1980) have used statistical methods such as factor, Q-sort, and cluster analyses to establish groups of children having similar profiles of linguistic and/or neuropsychological deficits. However, the empirical clinical data on such subtypes of disorders are very limited. Thus, the usefulness of these classifications to the clinician, especially in terms of outcome prediction or treatment selection, has not been examined.

Consequently, it was decided that in the present study, very basic clinical methods would be used to subgroup the speech/language disorders. Thus, the classification in the present work consists of three mutually exclusive subgroups: pure speech disorders, combined speech/language disorders, and pure language disorders. This classification is based upon the "speech" versus "language" dichotomy that has long been recognized as basic in both the disciplines of speech/language pathology and of linguistics (Bloomfield 1933; Travis 1957). In fact, there is some recent empirical evidence from follow-up studies that this distinction has predictive validity (Bishop and Edmundson 1987b; Cantwell and Baker 1987a; Hall and Tomblin 1978).

The comparisons in the present chapter may provide further evidence for the validity of the "speech" versus "language" dichotomy. Specifically, they may help to identify the psychiatric and other factors that are associated with these three general types of communication disorders. The groups to be compared are 1) a group of 203 children with pure speech disorder (i.e., impairments in speech production, but without impairments in language comprehension, expression, use, or processing); 2) a group of 352 children with concurrent impairments in both speech and language; and 3) a group of 45 children with pure language disorder (i.e., normal speech production, but with impairments in some aspect of language). Some of the comparisons between these three groups of children are discussed elsewhere (Cantwell and Baker 1987c).

Factors Associated With Different Speech/Language Diagnoses

Background and demographic factors. The majority of the background and demographic variables were not significantly different across the three speech/language disorder groups. These variables included ethnic and religious affiliations, linguistic backgrounds (i.e., bilingual, substandard dialect, limited linguistic stimulation), sex, family size, and birth order. However, the three speech/language disorder groups did differ slightly in their mean ages and in certain demographic variables, most having to do with socioeconomic status (SES).

The three groups of children were significantly different in average age, with the group having concurrent speech and language disorders being the youngest, the group having pure language disorder being the oldest, and the group having pure speech disorder being intermediate. The mean ages were 6.3 years (SD = 2.8) for the pure speech disorder group; 5.0 years (SD = 2.5) for the concurrent speech/language disorder group; and 8.8 years (SD = 3.8) for the pure language disorder group. Each of the three groups was significantly different from each of the other groups (t test comparisons; $P < .0001$).

A likely explanation for these age differences is that children in the group having concurrent speech/language disorders were identified earliest because they had the most global impairments. Children in the pure speech disorder group were referred somewhat later because their impairments were less serious (i.e., less global) but still readily observable. Conversely, children in the pure language disorder group had the most subtle difficulties (restricted to higher levels of language functioning) and were not identified until several years later on the average.

The mean ages of the mothers and fathers of the three groups of children were also significantly different. These data are somewhat reflective of the differences found in the children's ages. Thus, the mothers and fathers of the children with concurrent speech/language disorders were significantly younger ($P < .01$) than the parents in the other two groups.

Parental occupational and educational levels significantly distinguished the pure speech disorder group from the concurrent speech/language disorder group. Thus, on separate measures of maternal and paternal occupational status and educational levels, the concurrent speech/language disorder group manifested significantly ($P < .001$) lower levels than the pure speech disorder group. For example, the concurrent speech/language disorder group had only 38% of its fathers in professional or administrative jobs, compared with 56% in the pure speech disorder group. Paternal unemployment, while rare, was nonetheless approximately three times more common among the children with concurrent speech/language disorders (6%) than among the children with pure speech disorders (2%). Similarly, more than twice as many mothers had professional or administrative positions in the pure speech disorder group (18%) as in the concurrent speech/language disorder group (8%). The occupational and educational levels of parents of the pure language-disordered children were not significantly different from those of either of the two other groups. They tended, however, to resemble more closely those of the pure speech disorder group.

Developmental-cognitive factors.   The   three   diagnostic groups differed in several developmental-cognitive measures, including verbal and performance intelligence levels, and prevalence of developmental disorders. Mean age levels for attaining motor milestones, however, were not different across the three groups.

The concurrent speech/language disorder group had a significantly (t test; $P < .0001$) lower performance intelligence mean score than did the other two groups. (The performance intelligence levels were not significantly different between the pure speech disorder and the pure language disorder groups.) It is important to note, additionally, that all three groups of children had mean scores that were well within the normal range: 95.6 for the concurrent speech/language disorder group; 111.4 for the pure language disorder group; and 118.7 for the pure speech disorder group.

A gross measure of verbal intelligence (derived from the Peabody Picture Vocabulary Test) revealed, not unexpectedly, significant differences across the three groups. The pure speech disorder group scored highest on the average (110.7), and the concurrent speech/language disorder group had the lowest average score (86.7). The average score in the pure language disorder group was 96.2.

The prevalence rates for developmental disorders also differed significantly ($P < .0001$) across the three linguistic groups, with the highest prevalence occurring in the pure language disorder group and the lowest prevalence occurring in the pure speech disorder group. Thus, developmental disorders were found in 9% of the pure speech disorder group, 27% of the concurrent speech/language disorder group, and 31% of the pure language disorder group.

Because of the small number of children with Axis II developmental disorders, the data comparing the three groups on rates of specific subtypes of developmental disorders did not reach significance. However, the raw data showed an elevated rate of learning disorders in the pure language disorder group compared with the other two groups. Learning disorders were thus present in 24% of the pure language disorder group, 3% of the pure speech disorder group, and 7% of the concurrent speech/language disorder group. It is likely that the low prevalence figure for the concurrent group may have been partially due to the lower ages of the children.

Speech/language disorders. By definition, the three diagnostic groups differed from one another in the presence or absence of speech/language disorders. Thus, disorders involving language expression, comprehension, processing, or use were present in the pure language disorder group and the concurrent speech/language disorder group but not in the pure speech disorder group. Similarly, disorders involving voice, speech articulation, and speech fluency were present in the pure speech disorder group and the concurrent speech/language disorder group but not in the pure language disorder group.

Interestingly, however, the distributions of further subtypes of speech or language disorder were essentially the same between the concurrent disorder group and each of the corresponding pure disorder

Table 6-1. Medical and psychosocial correlates of speech/language diagnoses in the present research sample

	Signifi-cance[a]	Pure SD group (%)	Concurrent SD and LgD group (%)	Pure LgD group (%)
Medical disorders	*	49	64	49
CNS abnormalities		4	14	11
Speech mechanism problem		5	6	0
Febrile seizures		3	1	7
Perinatal problems	*	7	15	2
Congenital abnormalities		8	12	4
Ear disorders		24	25	9
Respiratory disorders		34	29	42
Psychosocial stressors (any)	*	56	68	67
Illness	*	16	27	31
Family discord		26	36	33
Changes		12	17	9
Deprivation		1	3	2
Significant events		9	13	9
Personal problems	*	6	7	22
Finances		2	5	2
Employment		7	4	7
Parental problems		2	0	7

Note. LgD = language disorder; SD = speech disorder.
[a]Significant difference (by chi-square test): *P < .0001.

groups. Thus, the distributions of voice, fluency, and articulation disorders were essentially the same among the pure speech disorder group and the concurrent speech/language disorder group. Similarly, the distributions of different types of language disorders (i.e., receptive disorder, expressive disorder, processing disorder) were the same between the pure language disorder group and the concurrent speech/language disorder group.

Medical and psychosocial factors. The data on the presence and types of medical disorders and psychosocial stressors in the three groups are presented in Table 6-1. Medical disorders in general were significantly more common among the concurrent speech/language–disordered children. However, specific types of medical disorders, with the exception of perinatal problems, were not significantly different across the three groups. Perinatal problems were significantly more common in the concurrent speech/language disorder group, possibly reflecting a biological etiology for at least some of the more global linguistic problems.

Psychosocial stress was significantly less common in the pure speech disorder group. There were no significant differences among the three groups with regard to the occurrence of most of the specific types of stressors. However, the distribution of two types of stressors was significantly different: personal problems of the children were significantly more common in the pure language disorder group, and illnesses of children and family members were significantly less common among the pure speech disorder group. It is again possible that the age differences of the three diagnostic groups may have played a role in the different distributions of these stressors.

Psychiatric diagnoses. The prevalence of Axis I psychiatric disorders was significantly different (chi-square test; $P < .0001$) across the three groups. The pure language disorder group had the highest prevalence of psychiatric disorder, with 73% of the children being psychiatrically ill. This prevalence rate was more than double the rate of psychiatric illness (31%) that was found in the pure speech disorder group. The concurrent speech/language disorder group had an intermediate rate of psychiatric illness (58%).

The data on levels of impairment and adaptive functioning in the three groups of children are presented in Table 6-2. The overall levels of impairment followed a pattern similar to that of psychiatric illness. Thus, significantly ($P < .0001$) more overall impairment was found in the pure language disorder group, and significantly less impairment was found in the pure speech disorder group. The data on levels of adaptive functioning in the three linguistic groups showed a similar pattern of involvement; however, these differences did not reach statistical significance.

The specific DSM-III diagnoses found in each group are also presented in Table 6-2. The numbers of children in the three groups who were diagnosed with the various specific disorders were generally too small to permit statistical analysis across groups. However, one disorder, attention-deficit disorder (ADD), did show significant differences in distribution across the three groups. This disorder was twice as common in the concurrent speech/language disorder group, and three times as common in the pure language disorder group, as it was in the pure speech disorder group. This finding reflects current reports in the literature of an association between attention-deficit hyperactivity disorder (ADHD) and language disorders (Beitchman et al. 1987; Love and Thompson 1988).

In addition to differences in the distribution of ADHD, the raw data suggest a trend toward differences in the distribution of certain other psychiatric diagnoses. For example, the children with pure lan-

Table 6-2. Psychiatric functioning in linguistic groups in the present research sample

	Signifi-cance[a]	Pure SD group (%)	Concurrent SD and LgD group (%)	Pure LgD group (%)
Overall level of impairment	**			
None		39	10	11
Mild		45	39	34
Moderate to severe		16	51	53
Overall level of adaptive functioning				
Superior or very good		29	4	7
Good		40	30	25
Fair		27	44	30
Poor or very poor		4	22	38
Psychiatric disorder	**	31	58	73
Psychiatric diagnosis[b]				
Attention-deficit disorder	**	10	23	33
Oppositional disorder		3	6	4
Conduct disorder		1	1	9
Pervasive developmental disorder		0	2	2
Anxiety disorders		7	12	9
Adjustment disorders		5	5	4
Affective disorders		3	3	18
Unspecified mental illness		2	4	2
Parent-child problem		2	5	4

Note. LgD = language disorder; SD = speech disorder.
[a]Significant difference (by chi-square test) between groups: **$P < .0001$.
[b]Diagnoses occurring in fewer than 1% of the children in each of the three groups were omitted from this table.

guage disorder had various behavioral and emotional disorders, with ADD and affective disorders being the two most common diagnoses. The children with concurrent speech and language disorders also had various behavioral and emotional disorders. However, the two most common diagnoses in this group were anxiety disorders and ADD. In the pure speech disorder group, however, all types of psychiatric diagnoses were less common. In this group, ADD was the only diagnosis that occurred in more than 10% of the children.

Psychiatric symptomatology. The data on psychiatric symptom clusters (derived from factor analyses of the parent and teacher questionnaires) in the three speech/language groups are presented in

Table 6-3. Symptoms in linguistic groups (questionnaire average factors) in the research sample

	Pure SD group		Concurrent SD and LgD group		Pure LgD group	
	Mean	SD	Mean	SD	Mean	SD
Conners parent questionnaire						
Conduct factor	0.38	0.41^a	0.39	0.49^a	0.71	0.76^b
Anxiety factor	0.54	0.48	0.50	0.51	0.65	0.61
Hyperactivity factor	0.41	0.46^A	0.81	0.67^B	0.85	0.80^B
Learning factor	0.16	$0.29^{a/A}$	0.24	0.38^b	0.70	0.78^B
Psychosomatic factor	0.41	0.41	0.36	0.40	0.43	0.59
Perfectionism factor	0.37	0.58	0.47	0.66	0.65	0.78
Antisocial factor	0.02	0.09	0.02	0.10	0.01	0.05
Tension factor	0.19	0.28^a	0.27	0.34^b	0.36	0.40^b
Conners teacher questionnaire						
Conduct factor	0.17	0.36^a	0.28	0.47	0.50	0.63^b
Passivity factor	0.51	0.55^A	1.05	0.72^B	1.17	0.79^B
Tension factor	0.42	0.47^A	0.63	0.60^B	0.66	0.59^B
Hyperactivity factor	0.43	0.62^A	0.77	0.71^B	1.06	0.93^B
Rutter parent questionnaire						
Neurotic factor	0.44	0.36	0.41	0.35	0.54	0.55
Antisocial factor	0.36	0.30	0.41	0.34	0.55	0.49
Total Score	0.41	$0.20^{A/a}$	0.49	0.25^B	0.59	0.34^b
Rutter teacher questionnaire						
Neurotic factor	0.22	$0.36^{A/a}$	0.41	0.50^B	0.54	0.51^b
Antisocial factor	0.21	0.35^a	0.34	0.40^b	0.49	0.54^b
Total score	0.28	0.26^A	0.49	0.29^B	0.57	0.38^B

Note. Groups with different letters are significantly different from each other (on *t* test); groups with the same letter are not significantly different. Upper-case letters denote probability levels of $P < .0001$; lower-case letters denote levels of $P < .01$. LgD = language disorder; SD = speech disorder.

Table 6-3. Approximately one-half of the factors were significantly different in at least one of the speech/language groups. All of the teacher factors (from both the Conners and the Rutter questionnaires) revealed some significant differences between groups. Of the parent questionnaire factors, those that were not significantly different across groups were the Conners anxiety, psychosomatic, perfectionism, and antisocial factors, and the Rutter neurotic and antisocial factors.

The majority of the factor differences were between the pure speech disorder group and the other two groups. For all factors, the pure speech disorder group had significantly lower mean scores than the other two groups. In most instances, the concurrent speech/language disorder group and the pure language disorder group did not differ significantly from each other in their factor scores. This was the situation with the Conners parent rating scale factors of hyperactivity, learning, and tension; the Conners teacher rating scale factors of tension, passivity, and hyperactivity; the Rutter total parent rating score; and the Rutter teacher neurotic, antisocial, and total scores.

However, the two Conners questionnaire conduct factors showed a different pattern of significant differences across groups. On the Conners parent rating scale, the conduct factor was significantly higher in the pure language disorder group than in the other two groups. On the Conners teacher rating scale, the conduct factor was significantly higher in the pure language disorder group than in the pure speech disorder group.

Symptoms associated with psychiatric illness. Tables 6-4 and 6-5 present the symptoms from the parent and teacher questionnaires that are significantly associated with psychiatric illness. On the parent questionnaire (Table 6-4), many symptoms significantly distinguished the psychiatrically well children from the psychiatrically ill children within the concurrent speech/language disorder group. In the other two linguistic groups, fewer parent-rated symptoms distinguished the psychiatrically well and psychiatrically ill children.

Fewer symptoms from the teacher questionnaire significantly distinguished the psychiatrically well and psychiatrically ill children than from the parent questionnaire. From the teacher questionnaire (Table 6-5), similar numbers of symptoms significantly distinguished the psychiatrically well versus ill children in the concurrent speech/language disorder group and the pure speech disorder group. As with the parent questionnaire data, fewer symptoms significantly distinguished the psychiatrically ill children in the pure language disorder group.

Controlled Comparisons
of Speech/Language Diagnoses

Comparison of Pure Speech Disorder
and Concurrent Speech/Language Disorders

Rationale and methods. The data presented above show that children with pure speech disorders differ from children with concurrent disorders of speech and language in a number of ways. Most important for the purposes of this study, the children with concurrent speech and language disorders had higher rates of psychiatric illness (in particular, higher rates of attention-deficit disorder with hyperac-

Table 6-4. Symptoms of psychiatric illness across speech/language groups (parent questionnaires) in the present research sample

	Pure SD group			Concurrent SD and LgD group			Pure LgD group		
	Well (%)	Ill (%)	P	Well (%)	Ill (%)	P	Well (%)	Ill (%)	P
Stomachaches	5	10		3	8	*	0	12	
Sleep problems	6	16	*	6	19	***	0	21	
Nightmares	5	3		6	15	*	0	15	
Eating: picky	12	19		13	23	*	18	24	
Daydreams	2	17	***	3	10	*	9	24	
Shy	12	26	*	11	26	***	10	15	
Fears not liked	6	14		3	11	**	0	33	*
Not liked	0	2		1	8	*	0	30	*
Quarrelsome	1	7		4	12	**	0	30	*
Sibling fights	12	28	*	8	22	***	18	37	
Sibling rivalry	4	17	**	1	12	***	9	33	
Dislikes school	2	5		1	7	**	0	30	*
Not learning	2	3		1	13	***	0	38	*
Mean, fights	0	2		0	7	**	0	12	
Keeps anger to self	6	10		1	7	*	0	21	
Unhappy	3	16	**	1	11	***	9	30	
Angry, irritable	7	28	***	8	29	***	9	48	*
Solitary	9	16		11	24	**	18	36	
Clings	2	4		7	20	**	0	9	
Tantrums	6	21	**	9	22	**	0	33	*
Overassertive	4	18	**	5	12	*	11	24	
Is bullied	5	5		6	17	**	9	15	
Often worried	4	13	*	2	7		0	21	
Immature	9	13		17	33	**	9	39	
Restless	7	28	***	16	47	***	0	48	**
Short attention span	7	28	***	19	51	***	18	61	*
Excitable	7	27	***	17	44	***	0	42	**
Drastic mood changes	4	14	*	5	25	***	0	33	*
Easily frustrated	13	40	***	24	50	***	0	48	**
Fears new situations	9	25	**	9	24	***	9	21	
Driven by motor	2	7		2	20	***	0	29	
Feelings easily hurt	25	42	*	26	41	**	18	52	
Disobeys often	4	19	**	9	35	***	9	36	
Lies	3	13	*	4	11	*	9	27	
Blames others	5	14	*	3	11	**	18	27	
Perfectionist	8	21	*	8	15		0	21	
Squirmy	2	16	**	9	32	***	0	30	*
Always climbing	7	14		15	26	*	0	12	
Intonation problem	2	15	**	8	13		18	3	
Abnormal speech	5	13		13	25	*	9	10	

Note. Significant difference (by chi-square test) between psychiatrically well and psychiatrically ill groups: *$P < .01$; **$P < .001$; ***$P < .0001$. LgD = language disorder; SD = speech disorder.

Table 6-5. Symptoms of psychiatric illness across speech/language groups (based on teacher questionnaire data) in the research sample

	Pure SD group			Concurrent SD and LgD group			Pure LgD group		
	Well (%)	Ill (%)	P	Well (%)	Ill (%)	P	Well (%)	Ill (%)	P
Restless, overactive	7	31	**	13	38	**	0	50	*
Disturbs others	5	33	**	4	30	**	0	56	*
Destroys property	1	9		0	8	*	0	12	
Daydreams	4	15		7	25	**	20	36	
Tics	2	13	*	11	4	*	10	12	
Disobedient	2	20	**	3	20	**	20	72	*
Short attention span	11	42	**	31	64	**	0	68	**
Constantly fidgets	7	29	**	8	39	**	0	32	
Hums	3	6		3	15	*	0	12	
Easily frustrated	7	25	*	1	0		0	28	
Poor coordination	5	19	*	25	33		0	32	*
Mood changes	1	9		3	15	*	0	32	*
Impulsive	7	21		7	36	**	0	48	*
Fights	3	17	*	6	17		0	40	
Not liked	3	14		1	13	*	10	36	
Solitary	9	15		13	36	**	30	48	
Bullies, teases	3	12		3	12		0	36	
Is bullied	6	14		7	24	*	0	32	
Lacks leadership	12	31	*	20	45	**	10	24	
Problems with same sex	3	19	*	3	8		20	32	
Sullen	3	17	*	6	8		10	26	
Worries	7	13		6	24	*	20	32	
Fearful	0	8	*	7	15		10	24	
Unresponsive	1	15	*	7	21	*	11	28	
Aches, pains	0	4		1	6		0	42	*
Resentful	1	23	**	13	16		0	10	*
Submissive	11	20		17	32		0	40	*
Defiant	1	21	**	7	20	*	10	52	
Demands attention	8	22	*	7	26	**	0	44	*
Stutters	15	19		11	27	*	10	32	
Speech hard to understand	3	21	**	18	28		10	48	
Limited language	4	13		5	24	*	0	25	
Sent to principal	5	20	*	45	56		40	38	

Note. Significant difference between psychiatrically well and psychiatrically ill groups by Fishers Exact test: *P < .01; **P < .0001. LgD = language disorder; SD = speech disorder.

tivity [ADDH]) and higher rates of developmental disorders than did the children with pure speech disorder. In addition, the children with concurrent speech and language disorders were somewhat younger when they presented for initial evaluation, had slightly younger parents, and came from families with slightly less education and slightly lower occupational levels. The children with concurrent speech and language disorders also had slightly more medical disorders, lower (but still normal) intelligence levels, and slightly more psychosocial stress than did the children with pure speech disorder.

These data thus support the hypothesis that children with different types of speech and language disorders are at differential risk for psychiatric and developmental disorders. In particular, children with pure speech disorder have lower risks of psychiatric and developmental disorders than do children with concurrent speech and language disorders. The differences that were found between the two groups of children in areas other than speech and language lend support to the validity of the clinical distinction between pure speech disorder and concurrent speech/language disorders.

Although the data suggest that it is language disorder that underlies the development of psychiatric and developmental disorders, they do not conclusively demonstrate a causal connection. This is because the elevated rates of psychiatric disorder in the children with language impairment were not the only factors associated with the presence of language disorder. Instead there were other correlates (including lower average age, SES, and performance intelligence levels) present in the group with language disorder that were not present in the group with pure speech disorder. As we noted in Chapter 4, such factors as these have also been suggested to be correlates of psychiatric disorder.

In the present study, mental retardation and psychosocial deprivation were both rare. Furthermore, the differences in age, performance intelligence, and background status that were found between the groups were rather small. Nonetheless, one must consider the possibility that these cognitive and/or background differences underlie the higher rate of psychiatric disorders in the language-disordered children.

In order to examine this possibility, two matched subgroups of pure speech-disordered children and of concurrent speech/language–disordered children were selected such that age, sex, and intelligence levels were controlled. The two matched subgroups each consisted of 134 children (92 boys and 42 girls) ranging in age from 2.3 to 12.0 years (mean = 5.57 years) and with performance intelligence levels ranging from 84 to 156.

Results.   Once the age and intelligence levels of the children were controlled for in the above way, the comparison between the pure speech disorder group and the concurrent speech/language disorder group revealed a somewhat different pattern of correlates. First, none of the background or demographic factors that had previously distinguished the groups (i.e., parental age, occupation, educational levels) continued to distinguish the two subgroups. Similarly, there were no longer significant differences between the subgroups in overall amount of psychosocial stressors, or in the frequency of occurrence of specific types of stressors.

However, significant differences still remained between the subgroups with regard to the prevalence of Axis II developmental disorders. Almost one-quarter of the children with concurrent speech/language disorders had some type of developmental disorder, compared with fewer than one-tenth of their matched counterparts with pure speech disorder. The different subtypes of developmental disorders did not occur in sufficient numbers for statistical comparisons to reach significance. Thus, it was not clear whether learning disorders in particular were significantly more prevalent in the concurrently disordered subgroup. However, achievement testing data (from the Wide Range Achievement Test) were available for 48 of the children, and statistical comparisons of these data indicated that significantly more children were behind in reading and in spelling (but not in arithmetic) in the concurrently disordered subgroup than in the other group.

In addition to these differences in developmental disorders, the two matched subgroups were significantly different in their prevalence rates of both medical and psychiatric disorders. The children with concurrent speech/language disorders had significantly more medical disorders than the children with pure speech disorder. However, the two subgroups had similar figures for the various subtypes of medical disorders, with only the overall totals showing a difference.

Finally, the clinical pictures of the two subgroups of children were quite distinct. There was significantly more psychiatric disorder among the children with concurrent speech and language disorders. More than one-half of the children in this subgroup had a diagnosable psychiatric disorder, compared with approximately one-third of the children in the pure speech disorder subgroup. Overall levels of impairment were also significantly different between the two groups, with the pure speech disorder subgroup tending to have no (37%) or mild (48%) impairments and the concurrently disordered subgroup tending to have mild (43%) or moderate-to-severe (40%) levels of impairment. The most common psychiatric diagnosis, ADDH, was also significantly more prevalent (approximately twice as common) in the concurrently disordered subgroup.

The key findings showing the significant differences between the matched pure speech disorder subgroup and the concurrent speech/language disorder subgroup are presented in Table 6-6. In addition, for convenience, this table summarizes the key associations that were previously found (reported in Tables 6-1 and 6-2 and in the above text) for the entire sample of children with pure speech disorder and children with concurrent speech/language disorders. It is of particular interest that the rates of psychiatric disorder, ADDH, developmental disorders, and medical disorders were essentially unchanged by the control of age and intelligence levels.

Even with the age levels and performance intelligence levels controlled, there were still strong associations between communication disorders involving language, and developmental and psychiatric disorders. This finding argues that it is language in particular (rather than some type of subtle cognitive deficit) that underlies the psychiatric and learning difficulties in these children.

Other Associations Between Types of Speech/Language Disorders and Psychiatric Disorder

Types of language disorders that are associated with psychiatric disorder. The above matched subgroup data show that, after controlling for age, sex, and performance intelligence, there is an association between concurrent speech/language disorders and psychiatric disorder. One question that remains is whether this association is with the language disorder per se, or whether it is unique to a language disorder that occurs concurrently with a speech disorder.

The previous data from the entire sample indicated that children with pure language disorder had significantly more psychiatric and developmental disorders than did children with either pure speech disorder or concurrent speech/language disorders. However, in the entire sample, the children with pure language disorder were significantly older than the children in the other two groups. Furthermore, average performance intelligence levels were higher in the pure language disorder group than in the concurrent speech/language disorder group.

Comparisons were made to examine the issue of whether pure language disorder is different from concurrent speech/language disorders with regard to psychiatric disorder. The comparisons are of two matched subgroups of children with pure language disorder and children with concurrent speech/language disorders, with age, sex, and intelligence levels controlled. The two matched subgroups each consisted of 32 children (21 boys and 11 girls) ranging in age from 2.7 to

Table 6-6. Summary of key associations with pure speech disorder and concurrent speech and language disorders in the present research sample

	Entire sample			Controlled groups		
	Pure SD group	Concurrent SD and LgD group	P	Pure SD group	Concurrent SD and LgD group	P
Number of children	203	352		134	134	
Psychiatric disorders (%)	31	58	*	34	56	*
Attention-deficit disorder (%)	10	23	*	11	24	*
Developmental disorder (%)	9	27	*	8	26	*
Medical disorders (%)	49	64	*	48	63	*

Note. All comparisons reported between the pure speech disorder groups and the concurrent speech/language disorder groups are significantly different (by chi-square test): $P < .0001$ for comparisons from the entire sample; $P < .001$ for comparisons between the matched subgroups. LgD = language disorder; SD = speech disorder.

14.0 years (mean = 7.0 years) and with performance intelligence levels again ranging from 84 to 156.

Once the age and intelligence levels of the children were controlled in the above way, it became clear that there were no particular factors uniquely associated with either pure language disorder or concurrent speech/language disorders. The key variables are presented in Table 6-7. The equally high rates of psychiatric illness in the two subgroups of children with language disorders suggest that language disorder (either alone or in combination with speech disorder) is what is associated with psychiatric disorder. Thus, having a "pure" language disorder therefore does not itself make a child more at risk for psychiatric disorder than having a language disorder in combination with a speech disorder.

Subtypes of language disorders associated with psychiatric disorder. The data presented in Chapter 4 showed a significant association between each of various types of language disorders (i.e., disorders of expression, comprehension, and processing) and psychiatric illness in the entire sample of 600 children. The association of these various subtypes of language disorders with psychiatric illness is examined further in Table 6-8. The pure language disorder and concurrent speech/language disorder groups from the sample of 600 children are further broken down to reveal the types of language disorders present. The prevalence rates for psychiatric illness have been determined for each of the language disorder subgroups.

The data in Table 6-8 show two consistent patterns in the rates of psychopathology between different types of language-disordered children in the concurrent speech/language disorder group and the pure language disorder group. First, children with expressive language disorder (and normal receptive functioning) have lower rates of psychopathology than do children with receptive language disorder. Thus, in both the concurrent speech/language disorder group and the pure language disorder group, children with expressive language disorder (and normal receptive functioning) have lower rates of psychopathology than do children with receptive language disorder. The rate of psychopathology for receptively disordered children was 63% in the concurrent speech/language disorder group and 81% in the pure language disorder group. Both of these figures were significantly higher than the rate of psychopathology for children with normal receptive functioning, which was 49% in both the concurrent speech/language disorder and the pure language disorder groups.

A second pattern found in the data is that children with an auditory processing impairment have higher rates of psychopathology than do children with normal language processing. Thus, for the children with receptive language disorder (and concurrent speech disorder), the rates of psychopathology were 59% when there was normal auditory processing and 70% when there was an auditory processing disorder. For children with receptive language disorder (and no concurrent speech disorder), the rates of psychopathology were 80% when there was normal auditory processing and 82% when there was an auditory processing disorder. When comparing children with pure expressive language disorder with and without an auditory processing

Table 6-7. Differences between matched subgroups with pure language disorder and concurrent speech and language disorders in the present research sample

	Pure LgD group	Concurrent SD and LgD group
Number of children	32	32
Psychiatric disorders (%)	75	69
Developmental disorder (%)	16	34
Medical disorders (%)	50	69
Psychosocial stressors (%)	78	75

Note. The matched pure language disorder and concurrent speech/language disorder subgroups were not significantly different on any of the above variables.

disorder, identical patterns of psychopathology were found in the concurrent and pure language disorder groups. Thus, in both the concurrent and pure language disorder groups, children with pure expressive language disorder and normal auditory processing had a psychiatric illness rate of 42%. In both the concurrent disorder and pure language disorder groups, children with expressive language disorder accompanied by some type of auditory processing impairment had a psychiatric illness rate of 68%.

Data from other classification studies. As mentioned above, a few studies have classified children according to their different types of speech/language disorders (Aram and Nation 1975; Feagans and Appelbaum 1986; Wilson and Risucci 1986; Wolfus et al. 1980). Unfortunately, these studies typically do not consider characteristics of the children outside of linguistic functioning. Similarly, as summarized in Chapter 1, a number of studies have looked for a possible association between psychiatric disorder and speech/language disorders. However, these studies typically have ignored the issue of subcategories of speech/language disorders.

One study, however, that has classified speech/language–disor-

Table 6-8. Psychiatric illness and language disorders in the present research sample

Language diagnosis (hierarchical groups)	Psychiatric illness (%)
Concurrent speech/language disorders	58
Expressive language disorder (receptive normal)	49
Expressive language disorder only	42
Expressive language and language processing disorders	68
Receptive and expressive language disorders	63
Receptive and expressive language disorders only	59
Receptive and expressive language disorders, and language processing disorder	70
Pure language disorder	73
Expressive language disorder (receptive normal)	49
Expressive language disorder only	42
Expressive language and language processing disorders	68
Receptive and expressive language disorders	81
Receptive and expressive language disorder only	80
Receptive and expressive language disorders, and language processing disorders	82

dered children and has examined the nonlinguistic features of the children in these classes has recently been reported (Beitchman et al. 1989a, 1989b). In this study, three groups of speech/language–disordered children were established using a cluster-analysis technique applied to language screening test data. It is of particular interest that the three clusters derived using this method closely paralleled the groups established in the present study using clinical intuition.

In the Beitchman et al. study, the cluster-analysis procedure categorized speech/language–disordered children into a "low overall" group; a "poor auditory comprehension" group; and a "poor articulation" group. The poor articulation group in Beitchman et al.'s study would have been classified as having pure speech disorder under the classification scheme used in the present study. These children obtained average scores on various tests of language function and low scores on speech articulation. The low overall group in Beitchman et al.'s study would have been classified as having concurrent speech/language disorder in the present study. These children had low measures on all tests of language function and low scores in speech articulation as well. In Beitchman et al.'s study, the group with poor comprehension was described as having "selectively impaired auditory comprehension." These children would have been classified as having pure language disorder in the present study. However, this final group in the Beitchman et al. study and the pure language disorder group in the present study do not correspond as closely as the other groups do, because children with "selectively impaired auditory comprehension" constituted only a portion of the children with pure language disorder in the present study. In the present study, the pure language disorder group frequently included children with word-finding difficulties and other expressive language impairments in addition to, or instead of, auditory comprehension problems.

Except for the fact that the children were all of kindergarten age, the Beitchman et al. study parallels the present study. Not only did these researchers use a similar tripartite classification of speech/language disorders, but they also used similar psychiatric methodology, and they obtained similar types of background and cognitive information regarding the children.

Of interest, Beitchman et al.'s findings regarding the nonlinguistic characteristics of their three speech/language groups parallel many of the results reported above from the present study. The low overall group in Beitchman et al.'s study (like the corresponding concurrent speech/language disorder group in the present study) had higher rates of DSM-III psychiatric illness, higher rates of ADHD, more behavioral-type disturbance, more medical disorders, slightly more social disadvantage, lower intelligence levels, and lower achievement functioning than did the other two groups. The group with poor articulation in Beitchman's study (like the corresponding group with pure speech disorder in the present study) had lower rates of psychiatric disorder and tended to do better on the other nonlinguistic measures than did the other two groups.

Summary

The data presented in Chapter 3 demonstrate that children with speech/language disorders have elevated rates of both learning disorders and psychiatric disorders. Furthermore, the data presented in Chapter 4 indicate that those speech/language–disordered children who are most likely to be psychiatrically ill are the ones whose speech/language disorder involves some type of impairment in language functioning.

The data from the present chapter confirm that children with impaired language functioning are different from children with pure speech disorder. In the present study, the children with impaired language functioning had elevated rates of psychiatric disorder and ADD. These differences were found both in the entire speech-clinic sample and in selected subsamples that were controlled for age and intelligence levels. Of interest, the similar study of younger children by Beitchman and colleagues found these same results.

The results of the present study also suggest that receptive language disorder and language processing disorder are further risk factors for psychiatric disorder, and that language disorder is a risk factor for developmental disorder. These findings were not replicated in Beitchman et al.'s study. However, it must be noted that the children in Beitchman et al.'s study were all of preschool age, an age at which it is more difficult to test for and to separate out functioning in areas such as receptive language, language processing, and learning. In the present study, more children were of school age, so these factors were more easily examined.

As was reported in Chapter 5, increased age was characterized by increasing rates of learning disorder. However, increased age was not associated with increased rates of psychiatric disorder. This is puzzling because learning disorders have been reported to be associated with increased rates of psychiatric disorder. This puzzle will be examined in more detail below.

Learning Factors in the Development of Psychopathology

The Relationship of Learning Disorder and Psychiatric Disorder

It has long been postulated that learning disorders and psychiatric disorders may be interrelated (Rutter 1974). However, there still is no definitive answer as to whether learning disorders and psychiatric disorders (or specific subtypes of either) are associated to a greater degree than would be predicted by chance. Furthermore, the nature of such associations, if they exist, is not understood.

One reason for this lack of understanding has to do with inconsistencies in the definitions of both psychiatric disorder(s) and learning disorder(s). For example, the present study defined psychiatric disorder as a disorder of behavior, emotions, relationships, cognitions, or interpersonal relationships severe enough and of long enough duration to cause distress, disability, or disadvantage to the individual. This definition is essentially equivalent to the inclusion criteria in DSM-III and DSM-III-R. In contrast, many of the studies in the literature have used general terms such as "emotionally disturbed" or "emotionally maladjusted." The lack of further definitions for such terms makes it difficult to compare results across studies.

The definition of learning disorder is even more problematic. As we have discussed elsewhere (Cantwell and Baker, in press), multiple terms have been used (e.g., learning disorder, learning disability, reading retardation, dyslexia, academic backwardness, educational backwardness, academic retardation, academic underachievement, academic performance problem). These terms are often used interchangeably, although they could better be used specifically to delineate different types of problems. For example, terms such as "academic performance problem" or "educational backwardness" are inclusive terms that do not take into account factors other than the child's manifest academic achievement. These terms do not distinguish between children who perform significantly below their grade level due to mental retardation, specific learning disability, or inadequate education, or because of being a younger age than their classmates.

Rutter (1974) has suggested that a better approach would be to take underlying characteristics such as the child's age and IQ into account. He proposes using terms such as "educational retardation," "academic retardation," or "academic underachievement" to refer to academic performance at a level significantly below that expected from the child's age and IQ. This approach requires first determining a child's expected level of performance in subjects such as reading, spelling, and math, and then determining what constitutes a significant deviance from that level. In the general population study of the Isle of Wight (Rutter et al. 1970b), for example, a regression-equation approach involving age and IQ was used to determine expected achievement levels. Then a cutoff for educational underachievement was set at an infrequently occurring level (i.e., 28 months below the expected level).

A useful distinction has been made between "learning disability" and "learning disorder." Learning disability refers to an underlying deficit in some particular ability, while learning disorder refers to the associated observable and quantifiable behavior (i.e., academic achievement). Thus, the DSM-III definitions are of learning disorders; they do not mention underlying inferred capacities or disabilities.

DSM-III and other definitions. One problem with the DSM-III definitions of learning disorders is that they do not specify the degree of performance deficit or the operational procedures required for determining the presence of the deficit. These are left to the individual clinician.

Another commonly used definition is that found in U.S. Public Law 94-142 (1975), The Education of the Handicapped Act, which defines "specific learning disability" as "a disorder in one or more of the basic psychological processes involved in understanding or in using language, spoken or written, which may manifest itself in an imperfect ability to listen, think, speak, read, write, spell, or to do mathematical calculations" (U.S. Office of Education 1977, p. 64). This definition is meant to include such conditions as perceptual handicaps, brain injury, minimal brain dysfunction, dyslexia, and developmental aphasia. Conversely, learning problems arising primarily from visual, hearing, or motor handicaps, mental retardation, emotional disturbance, or environmental, cultural, or economic disadvantage are specifically excluded.

As with the DSM-III definition, the federal definition does not specify how far behind a child must be, how to measure the basic psychological processes involved, or how to make the inclusions and exclusions. The latter is quite a serious problem, because many conditions overlap with learning disorders and with each other and are intertwined in such a way that it is impossible to disentangle the direction of effect. For example, in a child with both ADD and learning disorder, the learning disorder may be a result of the attention deficit, or both disorders may be co-occurring because of having similar underlying disabilities.

In 1981, the National Joint Committee for Learning Disabilities proposed a revised definition (see Interagency Committee on Learning Disabilities 1987) recognizing learning disabilities as a generic term for disorders intrinsic in an individual and presumably due to central nervous system dysfunction. This definition further recognized that even though a learning disability may occur concomitantly with other handicapping conditions (e.g., sensory impairment, mental retardation, social and emotional disturbance) or environmental influences (e.g., cultural differences, insufficient or inappropriate instruction), it is not the direct result of such conditions. This definition, considered by some to be an improvement over the U.S. Public Law 94-142 definition, has problems that are very similar to those of the previous definitions. Consequently, an amended version of the definition was published in 1987 (Interagency Committee on Learning Disabilities 1987). In this version, the manifestations were expanded to include difficulties in the acquisition and use of social skills, and the possible concomitant handicaps were expanded to include ADD. Work is currently at hand on further revisions.

Literature on the association of learning disorder and psychiatric disorder. Despite the methodological differences among the studies of the association between learning disorder and psychiatric disorder, it is possible to draw some tentative conclusions from the literature. First, studies looking at the behavioral and emotional characteristics of groups of learning-disordered children have reported high rates of problems with attention, concentration, and hyperactivity (Holborow and Berry 1986; Jorm et al. 1986); delinquency and conduct disorders (Cullinan et al. 1984; Epstein et al. 1985, 1986); problems with self-concept or self-esteem (Bingham 1980; Boersma and Chapman 1981; Hiebert et al. 1982); and emotional problems such as depression and anxiety (Bruck 1986; Dudek et al. 1987; Margalit and Shulman 1986).

Second, there are epidemiologic data pointing to a specific association between certain types of learning problems and psychiatric disorder. Thus, the Isle of Wight study (Rutter et al. 1970a, 1970b) found that specific reading retardation was strongly associated with disruptive behavioral disorder. Approximately one-quarter of the children with specific reading retardation in the Isle of Wight study also had antisocial behaviors. There was also some tendency for these children to have higher rates of internalizing or emotional disorders, but this association was less strong. Other epidemiologic studies (Berger et al. 1975; Clark 1970; Davie et al. 1972; Douglas et al. 1968; Sampson

1966; Sturge 1972) have reported similar results.

A third common finding is that children with learning disorders often suffer from impairments in interpersonal relations and "social skills" (Bryan and Bryan 1983; McConaughy and Ritter 1986; Pearl and Cosden 1982; Perlmutter et al. 1983; Pihl and McLarnon 1984). Thus, Rourke's recent (1988) review identified several ways in which learning-disabled children are different from their normally achieving classmates. These include the following:

1. Being perceived by parents, teachers, and peers as being less pleasant and less desirable

2. Receiving more negative communication from parents, teachers, and peers

3. Being ignored and rejected more often by teachers

4. Receiving more punitive and derogatory treatment from parents

5. Being more likely to live in disadvantaged family situations

Rourke concluded that studies of the relationship between psychiatric and learning disorders do not support an unequivocal relationship. Instead they suggest that learning-disabled children are heterogeneous in their skills and abilities, and do not manifest any one particular pattern of personality characteristics or psychiatric disorders. For example, Porter and Rourke's (1985) study of learning-disabled children, using the Personality Inventory for Children, found four major personality clusters independent of age. The most commonly occurring cluster, which involved approximately 50% of the sample, had no inventory elevations reflective of psychiatric disorder. The second cluster (approximately 25% of the subjects) had high scores in depression, withdrawal, and anxiety. The third cluster (approximately 15% of the sample) had elevated levels of hyperactivity and aggression, and the final and smallest cluster was characterized by a variety of somatic symptoms.

A similar study (Speece et al. 1986) used the Classroom Behavior Inventory with 63 learning-disabled children. One-third of these children were found to have normal profiles. The remaining children fell into four separate groups characterized by borderline or mild impairment, conduct disorder, withdrawal, and marked behavioral problems. A 3-year follow-up of this cohort (McKinney and Speece 1986) reported general stability of the subtypes over time, although with some changes in subtype membership among the pathological groups.

A general conclusion from these studies is that learning disability leads to psychiatric disturbance in some children but not necessarily in the majority of children. Thus, one research goal is to determine what factors are associated with the presence of psychiatric disorder in learning-disordered children. Along these lines, several authors (Glosser and Koppell 1987; McKinney 1985; Rourke 1988) have proposed that specific subtypes of learning disabilities (defined by neuropsychological tests) may be associated with specific patterns of personality structure and/or psychiatric disorder. In Rourke's model (1988), a specific causal connection is proposed between patterns of central processing deficits, particular subtypes of learning disabilities, and psychiatric disorder. In this model, children who have what is described as a nonverbal learning disability are considered to be most at risk for psychiatric illness. Glosser and Koppell (1987) suggested that children with left-hemisphere damage are most at risk for depressive and anxiety disorders; children with right-hemisphere damage are at risk for somatic symptomatology; and children with non-lateralized damage are at risk for behavioral and pervasive disorders. It has also been suggested (Rourke 1988) that learning-disabled children who have problems with social competence are most at risk for psychiatric disorder. However, it must be noted that social-skills problems may result from many mechanisms, including innate difficulties in cognitive or perceptual skills, attitude and motivation problems, and/or demands of the environment.

Similarly, the direction of cause and effect between psychiatric disorders and learning disorders is not a clear one. As we have pointed out elsewhere (Cantwell and Baker, in press), psychiatric and learning disorders may be related to each other in a variety of ways: 1) the psychiatric disorder might cause the learning disorder, 2) the learning disorder might cause the psychiatric disorder, or 3) there might be common underlying features predisposing a child to both learning disorder and psychiatric disorder. Aspects that must be considered include temperamental features, excess anxiety, psychosocial stress, lack of motivation, and avoidance of learning (Rutter 1974). In addition, various neuropsychological and neurocognitive features of the child (e.g., the rate of thinking, short-term memory, immediate memory, the ability to discriminate important from trivial stimuli) may be critical (Hunt and Cohen 1984).

In the next section, the characteristics of the learning-disordered children in the present research sample are examined with the hope of providing insight into the association of psychiatric illness and learning disorder.

Correlates of Learning Disorder

Correlates of learning disorder in the speech/language-disordered children. As reported in Chapter 3, a total of 42 of the speech/language–disordered children in the present study (7% of the sample) met the diagnostic criteria for a DSM-III specific developmental learning disorder. Of these 42 children, 13 had specific difficulties in reading, 1 had specific difficulties with arithmetic, 2 had "atypical" learning problems, and 26 had mixed learning difficulties. The 42 learning-disordered children were primarily young males (67% males; mean age = 9.9 years, SD = 3.4). The remaining (nonlearning-disordered) children in the sample consisted of 558 children, chiefly younger males (69% males; mean age = 5.5 years, SD = 2.6). Thus, in the present sample, the learning-disordered children were significantly (t test; P < .0001) older than the nonlearning-disordered children.

Those comparisons of the 42 learning-disordered children with the 558 nonlearning-disordered children that showed significant differences are presented in Table 6-9. There were no significant differences between the two groups in any socioeconomic measures, race, religion, birth order, or family size. However, there was a significant difference between the two groups with regard to certain family-structure configurations. In particular, the learning-disordered children lived more commonly with only their mother and less commonly with both biological parents. These data are consistent with the Isle of Wight finding that poor readers more often come from broken homes (Rutter et al. 1970b).

There were no significant differences between the two groups in the prevalence of overall medical disorders or psychosocial stressors, or in the prevalence of any specific subtypes of medical disorders or psychosocial stressors. There were also no significant differences between the learning-disordered children and the nonlearning-disordered children in any nonlanguage developmental variables, including performance intelligence levels, other DSM-III Axis II developmental diagnoses, and ages of attaining motor milestones.

In contrast, two of the linguistic measures significantly distinguished the learning-disordered and nonlearning-disordered children. The learning-disordered children had significantly more problems with language processing and significantly fewer problems in speech production. The learning-disordered children also showed significantly more overall impairment and significantly poorer overall levels of adaptive functioning. In addition, the learning-disordered children were characterized by significantly more psychiatric disorder and, specifically, more ADHD. Other types of psychiatric disorder were not

Table 6-9. Significant correlates of learning disorders in the present research sample

	Significance[a]	LD group (%)	Non-LD group (%)
Family structure			
Biological mother and father	*	54	72
Biological father absent	*	37	20
Mother alone	*	24	10
Linguistic abnormalities			
Speech	***	74	94
Language processing	***	76	30
Overall level of impairment	**		
None		7	20
Mild		26	42
Moderate to severe		67	38
Levels of adaptive functioning	*		
Good		24	47
Fair		43	37
Poor		33	16
Psychiatric illness	**	74	49
Attention-deficit disorders	**	40	18
Anxiety disorders		2	10
Adjustment disorders		2	5
Affective disorders		19	2

Note. LD = learning disorder.
[a]Significant difference (by chi-square test) between LD and non-LD groups: *$P < .01$;
**$P < .001$; ***$P < .0001$.

significantly different between the two groups; the data, however, showed a trend toward more affective disorders in the learning-disordered group and more anxiety disorders in the nonlearning-disordered group.

The data on the psychiatric symptomatology found in the learning-disordered and nonlearning-disordered children are reported in Tables 6-10 through 6-12. As would be expected from the DSM-III diagnoses described above, there were more symptoms (especially behavioral disorder symptoms) among the learning-disordered children.

The data on symptomatology in learning-disordered children according to the parent and teacher questionnaires are presented in Tables 6-10 and 6-11, respectively. According to both the parent and the teacher ratings of the children, a number of symptoms of psychiatric disorder were more common among the learning-disordered children than among the nonlearning-disordered children.

On the teacher questionnaire, those symptoms distinguishing the learning-disordered children tended to fall into two major groups: behavioral disorder symptoms (e.g., restlessness and overactivity, daydreaming, school truancy and absences, short attention span, bullying and teasing, fidgeting) and anxiety symptoms (e.g., worrying, aches and pains). Poor coordination was also reported by teachers as occurring more often in learning-disordered children, but this was the only developmental disorder so identified. The teacher questionnaire also revealed elevated rates of both behavioral and anxiety symptoms among the learning-disordered children. However, a larger variety of these symptoms, particularly of the behavioral-type symptoms, were significant on the parent questionnaire. Thus, the parents reported that the learning-disordered children had more problems with meanness, fighting, disobedience, tantrums, short attention span, excitability, squirming, and climbing. Dislike of school and difficulties with learning significantly distinguished the two groups according to the parents but not according to the teachers.

The factor scores from the parent and teacher questionnaires are reported in Table 6-12. None of the factors from the Rutter questionnaires significantly distinguished the learning-disordered children. However, the learning-disordered children had significantly higher scores in the hyperactivity, learning, tension, and passivity factors from the Conners questionnaires.

The data presented above show that in the speech-clinic sample, learning-disordered children were distinguished from nonlearning-disordered children by 1) being older, 2) coming more often from nonintact families, 3) having more language processing disorders, 4) having more psychiatric disorders and symptoms, and 5) having more behavioral symptoms and ADDs. These findings were not unexpected. However, the increased age of the children in the learning-disordered group was of some concern; the increased age of these children could explain their higher rates of nonintact families, their higher rates of language processing disorders, and their higher rates of psychopathology. In order to examine this possibility, the learning-disordered children are reexamined below in comparison to age-matched nonlearning-disordered children.

Correlates of learning disorder in matched subgroups.   In this section we compare the learning-disordered group with a group of nonlearning-disordered children who were pair-matched for age, sex, and (performance) intelligence level. These data have been published elsewhere (Cantwell and Baker 1985) and will only be briefly summarized here.

Table 6-10. Symptoms associated with learning disorders (based on parent questionnaires) in the present research sample

Symptom	Significance[a]	LD group (%)	Non-LD group (%)
Tics	**	20	6
Fears not being liked	***	57	27
Not liked	***	45	19
Dislikes school	***	45	15
Truant	**	12	1
Not learning	***	53	16
Mean, fights	*	31	16
Disobedient	***	38	14
Keeps anger to self	***	48	17
Tantrums	*	34	53
Health worries	*	31	14
Often worried	**	44	20
Short attention span	***	90	62
Excitable	*	77	55
Drastic mood change	*	46	30
Acts as if driven by motor	*	38	20
Feelings easily hurt	*	88	73
Squirmy	*	59	42
Always climbing	*	21	42

Note. LD = learning disorder.
[a]Significant difference (by chi-square test) between LD and non-LD groups: $*P < .01$; $**P < .001$; $***P < .0001$.

Once age, sex, and intelligence level were controlled in this way, a new set of correlates of learning disorder became apparent. No demographic-background, developmental, medical, or psychosocial factors distinguished the two matched groups of children. In particular, the family-structure differences (which distinguished the learning-disordered children from the rest of the large sample) were no longer present once age and intelligence level were controlled. In fact, the learning-disordered children differed from their matched counterparts in linguistic and psychiatric features.

The learning-disordered group had significantly $(P < .001)$ more concurrent speech/language disorders (68%) and less pure speech disorder (14%) than did the matched nonlearning-disordered group (in whom these prevalence rates were 29% and 61%, respectively). Furthermore, the learning-disordered children had significantly more auditory processing disorder (71%), more expressive language disorder (71%), and more receptive language disorder (46%) than did the control

Table 6-11. Symptoms associated with learning disorders (based on teacher questionnaires) in the present research sample

Symptom	Significance[a]	LD group (%)	Non-LD group (%)
Restless, overactive	*	70	49
Truant	*	13	3
Absent for trivial reasons	**	21	3
Daydreams	**	69	42
Short attention span	*	83	65
Constantly fidgets	*	73	49
Hums	*	40	21
Poor coordination	***	77	43
Bullies, teases	*	52	31
Worries	*	57	36
Aches, pains	*	27	12

Note. LD = learning disorder.
[a]Significant difference (by chi-square test) between LD and non-LD groups: $*P < .01$; $**P < .001$; $***P < .0001$.

children. (The rates of linguistic disorders in the control group were 20% for auditory processing disorder, 39% for expressive language disorder, and 25% for receptive language disorder.) Thus, the matched comparisons revealed more linguistic differences between learning-disordered children and nonlearning-disordered children.

As with the comparisons of the groups from the entire speech-clinic sample, the comparisons of the two matched groups revealed more psychiatric illness among the learning-disordered children. The learning-disordered group was characterized by significantly elevated rates of psychiatric symptomatology, psychiatric disorder, ADD, and overall impaired functioning. The prevalence rates for psychiatric illness were 68% for the learning-disordered group and 46% for the control group. The prevalence rates for ADD were 43% for the learning-disordered group and 18% for the control group. The factor symptom scores from the Conners and Rutter parent and teacher questionnaires showed significantly higher anxiety factor, hyperactivity factor, learning factor, and total factor scores in the learning-disordered group.

These data analyses, like those in the preceding chapters, demonstrate an association between language disorder, learning disorder, and psychiatric disorder. The learning-disordered children had more language disorder than their counterparts, as well as more psychiatric disorder.

Table 6-12. Symptomatology associated with learning disorders (questionnaire average factors) in the present research sample

Factor	Signifi-cance[a]	LD group Mean	SD	Non-LD group Mean	SD
Conners parent questionnaire					
Conduct factor		0.63	0.67	0.40	0.48
Anxiety factor		0.72	0.60	0.50	0.50
Hyperactivity factor	*	0.97	0.73	0.62	0.60
Learning factor	***	0.75	0.67	0.21	0.37
Psychosomatic factor		0.38	0.50	0.40	0.40
Perfectionism factor		0.50	0.80	0.45	0.60
Antisocial factor		0.02	0.07	0.02	0.07
Tension factor	*	0.41	0.45	0.22	0.30
Conners teacher questionnaire					
Conduct factor		0.29	0.52	0.26	0.45
Passivity factor	*	1.24	0.76	0.82	0.70
Tension factor		0.64	0.58	0.54	0.56
Hyperactivity factor		0.96	0.80	0.61	0.69
Rutter parent questionnaire					
Neurotic factor		0.58	0.48	0.42	0.36
Antisocial factor		0.50	0.42	0.40	0.34
Total score		0.57	0.29	0.45	0.24
Rutter teacher questionnaire					
Neurotic factor		0.55	0.55	0.32	0.45
Antisocial factor		0.41	0.41	0.27	0.38
Total score		0.57	0.31	0.39	0.31

Note. LD = learning disorder. SD = standard deviation.
[a]Significant difference (by *t* test) between LD and non-LD groups: $*P < .01$; $***P < .0001$.

The mechanism by which the psychiatric and learning disorders developed in these children is not clear. Of the three possible associations outlined in the previous section, the third possibility (i.e., the existence of common underlying features that predispose the child to both learning disorder and psychiatric disorder) seems best able to explain the present data.

Thus, it seems that a language disorder predisposes a child to both psychiatric disorder and learning disorder. The fact that the associations between these three problems remained present even after age and IQ were controlled suggests that the associations are not necessarily mediated by age or IQ. Furthermore, neither social-familial factors, nor other cognitive nonlinguistic factors, nor medical-biological factors appeared to play a significant role. The strongest factors underlying both psychiatric disorders and learning disorders in these children were, in fact, linguistic factors.

As noted above, Rourke (1988) proposed that children with "nonverbal learning disability" may be most at risk for psychiatric illness. In the present sample, however, the subgroup of children with language problems were the ones who were most likely to suffer from psychiatric (and learning problems). Thus, it seems a plausible hypothesis that deficits in either the processing or the production of communicative information have among their consequences both psychiatric and academic dysfunctions.

A promising area for further research would be to examine more closely the subtypes of language and learning disorders that tend to be associated, and, in turn, their associations with psychiatric disorder. The current speculations about the role of social-skills deficits in learning and psychiatric disorders also suggest a fruitful area for future work, because in many ways social skills parallel language skills. For example, language skills and social skills both require 1) a repertoire (or "lexicon") of specific and discrete verbal behaviors, 2) performance or use of the repertoire in social interactions, 3) processing or reading of verbal information from the social environment, and 4) adaptation of output according to demands of a specific social-verbal situation (Gresham and Reschly 1986; Michelson et al. 1983; Wilchesky and Reynolds 1986). Thus, it is a likely hypothesis that children with deficits in social skills will often have parallel deficits in language development. The degree to which such social skills deficits are associated with psychiatric disorder may be yet another indicator of the interrelationship between language disorder and psychiatric disorder.

Summary of Results, Discussion, and Conclusions

7

WE BEGAN OUR STUDY of psychiatric and developmental disorders in speech/language–disordered children with hypotheses based upon both clinical observations and reviews of the then-available literature. Clinical observations suggested that children with various types of communication disorders have elevated rates of both clinical psychopathology and learning difficulties. Literature reviews tended to confirm these clinical observations. For example, as noted in Chapter 1, the literature suggested that language plays a central role in many other areas of development in childhood. Thus, it would seem that a handicap in the development of speech and/or language would be associated with handicaps in other areas of development as well. This would be analogous to the high rates of psychiatric and learning disorders found in children with other types of handicap that are not as central to many areas of development as is the development of speech and language.

An underlying assumption of the present study, then, was that the presence of a communication disorder would be a "risk factor" for the development of both psychiatric disorders and learning disorders. The presence of a risk factor means that a group possessing that particular factor has a higher probability for the development of a particular type of a disorder than a group lacking that particular factor (Masten and Garmezy 1985).

As reviewed in Chapter 4, many factors (both biological and behavioral)—including genetic factors, biochemical factors, social factors, and cognitive-intellectual factors—have been identified as potential risk factors for the development of psychopathology. Environmental factors, especially stressful life events, the availability of social support, and family structure, have often been mentioned as potential risk factors for the development of psychopathology. However, as Regier and Allen (1981) have observed, no risk factors have been identified that are both highly sensitive and highly specific for the development of the major mental disorders, whether in adults, adolescents, or children.

The concept of "vulnerability" is related to the concept of risk, but it differs somewhat in that vulnerability refers to the predisposition of an individual to have a particular negative outcome. Masten and Garmezy (1985) point out that the basic distinction between risk and vulnerability has to do with the focus of emphasis on the individual rather than on the group. Thus, risk and risk factors are associated with group data, whereas vulnerability refers to individual susceptibility. When the term vulnerability is used in relation to the development of psychopathology, it can mean a general susceptibility to various types of stress factors, or it can mean a predisposition to the development of a specific disorder or type of disorder.

If, as hypothesized in the present study, children with speech/language disorders as a group are at risk for the development of clinical psychiatric syndromes and/or developmental learning disorders, this would make speech/language disorders a risk factor for the development of psychopathology. In order to examine the hypothesis, the study aimed to answer the following specific questions:

1. Do children with speech/language disorders, as a group, have higher rates of clinically significant psychiatric disorders than children in the general population?

2. Do children with speech/language disorders, as a group, have higher rates of any specific types of psychiatric disorders? That is, is there any type (or types) of psychiatric disorder that is uniquely more prevalent in children with speech/language disorders than in children in the general population?

3. Do children with speech/language disorders, as a group, have higher rates of specific developmental disorders, particularly developmental learning disorders?

4. If children with speech/language disorders, as a group, have higher rates of psychopathology than children in the general population, then what, if any, are the characteristics of those children who are psychiatrically ill that distinguishes them from those who are psychiatrically well?

5. Since children with speech/language disorders are not a homogeneous group linguistically, do various subtypes of speech/language disorders differ in their association with psychiatric and/or developmental disorders?

6. Since psychiatric disorder falls into several subtypes that may

each have its own specific correlates, do subtypes of psychiatric disorders have any unique characteristics associated with them in children with speech/language disorders?

7. What is the role of related factors—especially the age of the child and the sex of the child, and also the presence of various medical and neurological factors, family factors, and other demographic factors—in the development and maintenance of psychiatric and/or learning disorders?

The latter three questions begin to touch on the area of vulnerability, particularly vulnerability in the transactional perspective described by Sameroff and Chandler (1975). Thus, a child with a speech/language disorder may be vulnerable to the development of psychopathology in general and to the development of certain specific types of psychopathology. This vulnerability interacting with certain factors such as age, gender, presence of hearing impairment, low IQ, certain types of family factors, or environmental factors may produce certain distinct types of psychopathology in some children. Likewise, certain factors may be protective in nature—that is, their presence may protect an individual against the development of psychopathology even in the presence of other factors that produce vulnerability. Protective factors, which can then be conceptualized as the positive counterpart of risk factors, may be either individual or environmental.

Results of the Present Study

Prevalence of Psychiatric Disorder in Children With Speech/Language Disorders

The results of the present study (presented in Chapter 3) indicate that children with speech/language disorders, as a group, do have higher rates of Axis I clinical psychiatric syndromes than children in the general population. Approximately one-half of the children had some type of definable Axis I clinical psychiatric disorder. Reviews of previous epidemiologic studies suggest that this rate of psychiatric disorder is far above what one would find in this age-range in the general population. However, direct comparisons with children from the general population are difficult because different studies have used different definitions of psychiatric disorder and different methodology in determining whether the child had a disorder. It would have been desirable to have had a comparison group of children without speech/language disorders matched on relevant variables such as age, gender, and performance IQ, who could have been evaluated in a similar fashion for the presence and type of psychiatric disorders. Funding issues prevented this possibility. Nevertheless, it seems clear that, as a group, children with speech/language disorders are at risk for the development of psychiatric disorder.

The previous studies addressing the prevalence of psychiatric difficulties in children with speech/language disorders were summarized in Chapter 1 (see Appendix 2). Some of these studies did use comparison groups, but few used methodology that would be considered "state of the art" today in determining either prevalence or type of psychiatric disorder. Nonetheless, it is important to note that the results of a number of these studies correspond rather closely to the results of the present study.

For example, Griffiths (1969), using child and parent interviews, studied 49 language-delayed children. The ratings that were obtained were global ratings of emotional and social adjustment. Forty-five percent of the sample were rated as having poor emotional adjustment, and 25% were rated as having poor social adjustment. If "poor social and emotional adjustment" can be equated with an Axis I psychiatric disorder diagnosis, and if "poor emotional adjustment" can be equated with the emotional subtype of psychiatric disorder, then Griffiths's figures are very similar to those obtained in the present study.

Sheridan and Peckham's (1973) study examined 215 children with unintelligible speech but normal hearing at the age of 7. The only instrument used was the Bristol Social Adjustment Scales, on which 48% of the sample scored in the maladjusted range. Again, the 48% figure is uncannily similar to our figure for definable psychiatric disorder (50%), even though the age-range in Sheridan and Peckham's study was narrower. Unfortunately, the spectrum of speech/language disorder in Sheridan and Peckham's study is difficult to determine.

Stevenson and Richman (1978; Richman and Stevenson 1977) identified 24 children with a delay in expressive language, comparing them to the nonlanguage-delayed 3-year-olds from their epidemiologic sample. These researchers used a valid and reliable parent behavior rating instrument and an interview of the mother to determine the prevalence and type of behavioral problems in the children. They found that 59% of the language-delayed children (compared with only 14% of the nonlanguage-delayed children) had significant behavior problems. Again, their 59% figure is quite similar to our 50% figure. Although the children examined in this study were small in number, they were representative of the general population because of the epidemiologic selection procedures. The similarity between the rates of psychopathology found in these children and those found in the children in the present study suggests that the latter group (who were referred for clinical evaluation of their speech and language functioning) were most likely not referred because they had increased rates of psychopathology.

Another relevant epidemiologic study was conducted in Britain by Fundudis and colleagues (1979). They investigated 102 children selected from the general population who had an inability to use three-word sentences at 36 months (a somewhat vague definition of speech/language impairment). However, valid and reliable methodology (including teacher questionnaires, the Jr. Eysenck Personality Inventory, and parent and child interviews) was used to determine the presence of psychopathology. Eighteen of the children had severe problems such as retardation, elective mutism, and autism. The remainder of the group had abnormal average scores on all of the measures used. These findings again suggest that children selected from the general population with significant speech/language delay are likely to be disturbed in other areas.

Two other epidemiologic studies support this view. Beitchman and his colleagues (1983, 1986a, 1986b) investigated 142 kindergarten children with speech/language disorders and 142 age- and sex-matched control subjects. Reliable and valid parent and teacher questionnaires and a child interview were used to determine psychopathology. The rate of psychiatric disorder was 53% in the speech/language disorder group versus 12% in the control group. Again, the figure obtained for psychopathology in this epidemiologic sample was strikingly similar to that obtained in the present study.

Finally, Silva and colleagues (1984), as part of the ongoing Dunedin epidemiologic study, compared 57 3-year-olds with delayed speech development to the rest of an epidemiologic sample. The same Rutter parent and teacher questionnaires that were used in the present study were employed by Silva et al. Again, the speech-delayed children were found to have significantly more behavioral problems, as rated by both parents and teachers, than the general population group.

In summary, the data from the present study suggest very strongly that speech/language–disordered children are at risk for the development of psychopathology. The fact that the present sample was a clinical sample does raise the question of whether one would find similar rates of psychopathology in children with speech/language disorders who were selected from the general population. The answer is that the available data from various epidemiologic studies show strikingly similar rates of psychopathology.

Types of Psychiatric Disorder
in Children With Speech/Language Disorders

The second aim of the study was to determine whether or not there was a specific type (or types) of psychiatric disorder associated with childhood speech/language disorders. Previous work with physically handicapped children (such as brain-damaged children and epileptic children) found no unique type of psychiatric disorder associated with the handicaps. However, certain types of defined psychiatric disorders were more common among these children. In the case of brain-damaged children, the Isle of Wight study (Rutter et al. 1970a, 1970b) found high rates of psychiatric disorder but no unique "brain damage" behavior syndrome. Rather, the types of psychiatric disorders in these children closely approximated those found in children without brain damage. The same can be said of studies of children with other types of handicaps such as epilepsy and mental retardation. Thus, no evidence exists for the concept of an "epileptic personality" or a "retarded personality." Although there are certain types of psychiatric disorders that are more common in retarded children than in nonretarded children, these disorders are not uniquely associated with intellectual retardation.

It was hypothesized that the types of psychiatric disorders found in speech/language–disordered children would be the same types found in children in the general population. Generally, this hypothesis was confirmed. The data presented in Chapter 3 show that the two most common types of psychiatric disorders were disruptive behavioral disorders and emotional disorders. These types correspond to "externalizing disorders" and "internalizing disorders," respectively, two large categories of disturbance that have been identified in numerous factor-analysis and cluster-analysis studies of children in the general population (Achenbach 1980; Achenbach and Edelbrock 1978, 1981, 1989).

Nonetheless, as might be expected, certain psychiatric diagnoses were disproportionately more common in the speech/language–disordered children than they were in the general population. An example is the pervasive developmental disorders (PDDs): eight children (of the 600 studied) received this diagnosis, six having classical infantile autism and two having childhood onset PDD. The prevalence rate for PDDs obtained in the present study (1.3%) is far above the rates (usually less than 0.1%) reported in the general population (Graham and Rutter 1973; Lotter 1966; Wing et al. 1976). Since the children in the present study were presenting with one of the core disturbances of PDDs (i.e., speech/language development), it is not surprising to find that they had an increased prevalence rate of PDDs. For the most part, however, the present data support the view that the types of disorders found in children with speech/language disorders are representative of those found in children in the general population. The data on previous studies reviewed in Appendix 2 also support this conclusion.

Prevalence of Developmental Disorders in Children With Speech/Language Disorders

A third issue is whether or not children with speech/language disorders are at risk for other types of developmental disorders and, in particular, for developmental learning disorders. There are several reasons for hypothesizing this risk for developmental disorders. First, as reviewed above, it is clear that the development of speech and language is related to other areas of development. Beitchman (1985) and others subsequently (Bishop and Edmundson 1987a; Tallal et al. 1989) have proposed the concept of a global "neurodevelopmental immaturity" to explain the association of developmental disorders of speech and language and other disorders. Additionally, several follow-up studies of children with early disorders of communication have reported that one of the outcomes over time is difficulties in academic achievement (Aram et al. 1984; Cantwell and Baker 1987c; Hall and Tomblin 1978; Paul and Cohen 1984). Finally, as summarized in Appendix 3, studies of learning-disordered children that employ a variety of speech/language assessment instruments indicate that learning-disabled children do have difficulties in a variety of areas of linguistic functioning.

The data presented in Chapter 3 also indicate that speech/language–disordered children as a group have elevated rates of developmental disorders in general and of developmental disorders of learning in particular. However, because the children in our sample were predominantly preschool-age, the majority had not yet entered into a true academic environment and thus were not able to receive a diagnosis of a developmental learning disorder. Nonetheless, it is clear that in the older subsample of children with speech/language disorders described in Chapter 5, the rate of learning disorders is considerably higher.

Risk Factors for Psychopathology in Children With Speech/Language Disorders

Although children with speech/language disorders constitute a group at risk for psychopathology, not all speech/language–disordered children are equally vulnerable. Similarly, even among "high-risk" children such as offspring of schizophrenic parents, not all children are vulnerable to psychopathology or indeed develop it. Thus, the issue arises of identifying within the high-risk group of speech/language–disordered children those particular children most likely to develop psychopathology. By identifying those factors significantly associated with clinical psychiatric disorder, it may be possible to efficiently target preventive maneuvers. In addition, identification of specific risk factors could provide clues as to the mechanisms by which speech/language disorders and psychiatric disorders are associated.

Theoretically, psychiatric disorder and speech/language disorder could be associated through several different mechanisms: 1) the speech/language disorder could lead directly or indirectly to the psychiatric disorder; 2) the psychiatric disorder could lead to the speech/language disorder; or 3) the speech/language disorder and the psychiatric disorder could arise independently because of common etiological factors (Cantwell and Baker 1977).

Other possible mechanisms of association may involve longitudinal phenomena. For example, the speech/language disorder may lead to an intermediate problem (e.g., learning disorders) that in turn is associated with the development of psychiatric disorder. This is a plausible hypothesis, because children with speech/language disorders are at risk for the development of learning disorders and children with learning disorders are at risk for the development of clinical psychopathology. Or, following the transactional model of Sameroff and Chandler (1975), it may be that the development of psychopathology in a speech/language–disordered child depends upon his or her degree of individual vulnerability and upon a transactional effect between the child and his or her environment over time.

The comparisons of psychiatrically well children to psychiatrically ill children in terms of background factors, developmental factors, linguistic factors, biological factors, and psychosocial factors were presented in Chapter 4. The key findings and their significance will be discussed below.

Background and demographic factors.   The data revealed surprisingly few background factors that significantly distinguished the psychiatrically ill from the psychiatrically well children. The background variable that most strongly distinguished between the two groups was family structure, with the psychiatrically ill children being significantly more likely to come from "broken homes." However, nearly 70% of ill children came from intact families. Thus, although risk studies of the general population indicate that children from broken homes have higher rates of psychopathology, it is not clear how much of a contributing factor this is in the present sample.

The psychiatrically ill children were also significantly older than the psychiatrically well children, but the actual age difference was small (approximately 6 months average difference). We had hypothesized that the psychiatrically ill group would be substantially older than the well group. This would have allowed more opportunity for a transactional process in which the speech/language–disordered child would have had to cope with his or her communication disorder at home, in school, with peers, and so on. It is not clear, however, that this occurred. In fact, the specific age data (presented in Chapter 6) showed that the preschool-age children had rates of psychiatric illness similar to those of the older children. Furthermore, the younger children had higher rates of behavioral disorders than did the older children. It is also relevant that the selection criteria for the sample required first presentation for speech/language evaluation. Thus, it is not clear that the older children in this study had a longer duration of communication disorder.

Somewhat surprisingly, male sex was not positively associated with psychopathology. In the general population in this age-range, psychopathology is more prevalent in males than in females. However, in the present study, a psychiatric diagnosis was just as likely to be present in females as in males. Apparently whatever protective factors there are that generally lower the rate of clinical psychopathology in young girls are ineffective in the presence of a speech/language disorder. Similar phenomena have been reported for other risk factors, including brain damage and environmental deprivation (Rutter et al. 1970a, 1970b; Wolkind and Rutter 1973).

Developmental factors. There are certain developmental factors that have been thought to underlie psychiatric disorder in children with speech/language disorder (Cantwell and Baker 1977). Intellectual retardation is one such variable because it is a common cause of speech/language disorders and because the mentally retarded are themselves at risk for high rates of psychiatric disorder (Rutter et al. 1970a, 1970b). Thus, one might expect that in the present study, the psychiatrically ill children would be the ones who would have mental retardation. In fact, the psychiatrically ill and well subgroups did not differ in their prevalence rates for the clinical diagnosis of mental retardation. Also, while verbal and performance intelligence levels were both significantly lower in the psychiatrically ill children, the mean intelligence levels of both groups were well within the normal range. Furthermore, in the present sample of speech/language–disordered children, mental retardation was not a common cause of the communication disorders. Thus, the data do not indicate that either intellectual retardation or a clinical diagnosis of mental retardation plays a major role in the development of psychopathology.

As stated above, another plausible hypothesis is that a communication disorder could lead to a learning disorder and that the learning disorder would then be associated with high rates of psychiatric disorder. In fact, those children in the sample with an Axis I psychiatric diagnosis were approximately twice as likely to have any Axis II developmental disorder diagnosis, a significant difference from the psychiatrically well group.

Speech/language factors. A number of linguistic factors distinguished the psychiatrically well and psychiatrically ill children. Those children with some degree of language involvement were far more likely to have clinical psychiatric diagnoses than were the children with pure speech disorder. Nevertheless, children with pure speech disorder had higher rates of psychiatric disorder than did children in the general population.

Abnormalities in language expression, in language comprehension, and in language processing were all strongly associated with the presence of psychiatric illness. This finding suggests that within the general high-risk group, those who were most vulnerable to psychopathology were the ones with some degree of language involvement. Those who have involvement in multiple areas of language (e.g., expression, comprehension, processing) may be most vulnerable to psychopathology.

Delays in expressive and receptive language were more strongly associated with the development of psychopathology than was a delay in articulation. Nevertheless, delays in articulation tended to be more severe among the psychiatrically ill children (averaging 1.8 years compared to 1.4 years among the psychiatrically well children).

Thus, the presence of certain specific aspects of language impairment and severity of impairment within those domains seem to be risk factors for the development of psychopathology. These data suggest that speech/language disorders per se (and especially language disorders) play a strong direct etiological role in the development of clinical psychopathology in children. A closer look at children with different types of speech/language diagnoses (presented in Chapter 6) supports this hypothesis.

Biological-medical factors. There are a number of biological factors that theoretically might be related to the presence of psychiatric disorder in children with speech/language disorder. For example, brain damage or brain dysfunction may lead to both the speech/language disorder and the psychiatric disorder, producing an association of the two. Likewise, deafness is a common cause of speech/language disorder, and deaf children are at elevated risk for development of psychiatric problems.

Ear and hearing problems, which occurred at some time in approximately one-quarter of the sample, were equally common among the psychiatrically ill and the psychiatrically well children. Similarly, definite diagnoses of brain damage or brain dysfunction were equally prevalent among the psychiatrically ill and the psychiatrically well children. On the other hand, the psychiatrically well children performed better overall on the developmental neurological examination. However, these developmental neurological findings (or "soft signs") cannot be taken clearly as evidence of either brain damage or brain dysfunction (Landman et al. 1986; Neeper and Greenwood 1987). The association between soft signs and psychopathology is somewhat controversial (Hadders-Algra et al. 1985; Kindlon et al. 1988; Shafer et al. 1983).

A greater proportion of psychiatrically ill children had histories of chronic respiratory problems. The link between respiratory problems, speech/language disorders, and psychiatric disorders is unclear. It is possible that these chronic respiratory difficulties were associated with intermittent problems that were in turn associated with serous otitis media. Intermittent serous otitis media has been thought to be associated with delayed speech/language development, intermittent hearing problems, auditory processing problems, and attentional and behavioral difficulties (Bennett et al. 1980; Eimas and Kavanagh 1986; Hagerman and Falkenstein 1987). However, there are methodological problems with many of the studies on this topic (Ayukawa and Rudmin 1983; Bench 1979; Bishop and Edmundson 1986; Hall and Hill 1986). At any rate, in the present study, the prevalence of reported histories of ear infections per se was not significantly different between the psychiatrically well and psychiatrically ill groups.

Psychosocial factors. There are a variety of psychosocial factors that are known risk factors for psychopathology in children. In the present study, psychiatrically ill children were significantly more likely to have psychosocial stressors than were psychiatrically well children. However, some of these psychosocial stressors could also have been a by-product of the child's psychiatric disorder (e.g., less warm relations with parents and siblings, less sibling play). Thus, it is difficult to disentangle direction of causality.

What is possibly most noteworthy is that the severity of psychosocial stressors was greater in the psychiatrically ill children as well as the number of psychosocial stressors present. Illness in the family and family discord were two specific types of stressors strongly associated with the presence of psychiatric disorder. These stressors are associated with psychopathology in children in the general population as well.

Somewhat surprisingly, parental mental illness in general did not significantly distinguish the psychiatrically well from the psychiatrically ill children. In fact, many more children in the well group had two parents who were psychiatrically well than did children in the ill group, but this difference did not reach statistical significance. However, certain specific types of psychiatric disorder in fathers, including antisocial spectrum disorders and substance abuse disorders, were significantly more common among the psychiatrically ill children. In the general population, such disorders are common in the families of children with disruptive behavioral disorders, and this was likewise true of children in the present sample. However, once other factors were controlled (such as nature and severity of the children's speech/language disorders), the relationship between type of paternal psychiatric diagnosis and presence of childhood psychopathology became nonsignificant (Cantwell and Baker 1984).

Comparison of Behavioral and Emotional Psychiatric Disorders

Until now, this discussion has treated the psychiatrically ill children as if they were a homogeneous group. However, it is clear from the data presented in Chapters 3 and 4 that they were not. The two large groups of psychiatrically disordered children found were those with overt or disruptive behavioral disorders and those with disorders characterized by emotional symptomatology. These two types of childhood psychiatric disorders have been identified in numerous other epidemiologic and clinical studies (Achenbach and Edelbrock 1978, 1981, 1983, 1989; Hewitt and Jenkins 1946; Peterson 1961; Quay 1964, 1979). Furthermore, there is some evidence that in the general population, the two types of disorders have different background, developmental, and other correlates (Rutter 1975).

The comparison of these two groups (presented in Chapter 4) revealed few differences with regard to background and demographic factors. The one major difference was that the behavioral disorder group was significantly more likely to be male. Because behavioral disorders are more common in males in the general population, this finding was not surprising.

With regard to developmental factors, both the behavioral and emotional groups were delayed in ages of saying first words and first sentences and lower in both verbal and performance IQ levels in comparison with psychiatrically well children. The behavioral and emotional disorder groups were not significantly different from each other in these (or most other) developmental variables. However, the behavioral disorder group was significantly more likely than either the psychiatrically well group or the emotional disorder group to have an Axis II developmental disorder. There is some evidence that in the general population developmental learning disorders are more strongly associated with behavioral disorders than with emotional disorders (Baker and Cantwell 1990; Cantwell and Baker, in press; Rutter 1975). The reasons for this are not quite clear.

In the present study, both groups of psychiatrically ill children were more likely than the psychiatrically well children to have language impairment (as opposed to pure speech impairment). But the general type of speech/language diagnosis (i.e., pure speech disorder, concurrent speech/language disorders, or pure language disorder) did not distinguish the two ill groups. Similarly, the presence of specific speech/language deficits distinguished both groups of psychiatrically ill children from the psychiatrically well children but not from each other. Thus, both groups of psychiatrically ill children were significantly more likely to have disorders of language expression, language comprehension, and language processing, and significantly less likely to have disorders of speech production, than were the psychiatrically well children.

Overall, few developmental or linguistic factors particularly predisposed these at-risk children to the specific development of either a behavioral disorder or an emotional disorder. The general presence of a developmental disorder stands out in this regard in its association with behavioral disorders and its lack of association with emotional disorders.

Medical and neurological abnormalities also did not distinguish significantly between the behaviorally and emotionally disordered children. Similarly, there were significantly more psychosocial stressors in both psychiatrically ill groups than in the psychiatrically well group, but they did not distinguish the two ill groups.

Types of Speech/Language Disorders

As described in Chapter 1, there are a variety of different ways of classifying childhood speech/language disorders. The present study opted for a clinically simple distinction based on the phenomenology of predominant linguistic involvement. Thus, the sample of 600 children was divided into three subgroups: a pure speech disorder subgroup; a pure language disorder subgroup; and a subgroup of children with concurrent speech/language disorders. It should be noted that these groups could have been subdivided even further (e.g., disorders of receptive language, expressive language, and language processing; various types of speech disorders). However, a first step was to compare the three larger groups to determine what factors significantly distinguished them.

Comparisons across these three subgroups revealed that children in the concurrent speech/language disorder group were somewhat younger at the time they presented for initial evaluation. Children in the pure language disorder group tended to be older, and those in the pure speech disorder group were intermediate in age. It appears that there were more subtle ("higher level") disorders in the pure language disorder group, and because these children did not manifest overt speech difficulties (i.e., did not "sound funny"), they were not taken for evaluation until a later age. Children in the concurrent speech/language disorder group, on the other hand, were globally impaired in both speech and language functioning, and therefore received the earliest referral.

The three groups did not differ in gender ratio. However, several other background variables were weakly significantly different among the three groups. The parents of the concurrent speech/language-disordered children tended to be younger than the parents in the other two groups (as did their children). The parents of the concurrently disordered children also tended to have less education and to have lower–socioeconomic-status (SES) occupations than did the parents of the pure speech-disordered children.

There were several developmental differences across the three linguistic groups, including intelligence levels and prevalence of developmental disorders. Verbal intelligence was lowest in the concurrent speech/language disorder group; highest in the pure speech disorder group; and intermediate in the pure language disorder group. Performance intelligence followed a similar pattern but was not significantly different between the pure speech disorder group and the pure language disorder group.

Psychosocial stress was significantly more common in the concurrent speech/language disorder group than in the other two groups. Furthermore, two specific types of psychosocial stressors were different across groups. Parental illness was significantly more common in both groups of children with language involvement than it was in the pure speech disorder group. Personal problems were significantly more common in the pure language disorder group than in the two other groups. In summary, the concurrent speech/language disorder group came from lower SES families, were younger at the time of initial evaluation, and had slightly lower mean and verbal performance intelligence levels. The pure speech disorder group had lower prevalence rates of developmental disorders. Thus, in some key areas of background factors, developmental factors, and psychosocial and medical factors, the three major linguistic subgroups differed significantly.

Most important, the three groups differed in prevalence rate of psychiatric diagnosis. Higher rates of psychiatric disorder were found in the children with language involvement. In particular, these children had elevated rates of disruptive behavior symptoms and disorders, especially attention-deficit hyperactivity disorder (ADHD).

These findings, like the comparisons of psychiatrically well and psychiatrically ill children, suggest an association between impairments in language acquisition and psychiatric and learning disorders. Comparisons of subgroups of children controlled for age and intelligence levels revealed the same associations between language functioning and psychiatric functioning. Thus, when age and intelligence are controlled, there is still a strong association between psychiatric disorder and language disorders of all types. This means that differing intelligence levels cannot completely explain the differences in prevalence of psychiatric disorder between the speech/language disorder groups.

The data presented in Chapter 6 (especially in Table 6-8) show that disorders of language and concurrent disorders of speech and language are more strongly associated with psychopathology than are disorders of pure speech. Furthermore, concurrent disorders of expressive and receptive language are more strongly associated with the development of psychopathology than are disorders involving only expressive abilities (with receptive abilities within normal limits).

There is further support for some of these findings in the work of Beitchman and colleagues (1989a, 1989b). These researchers reported that psychiatric disorder, and in particular attention-deficit disorder, were more likely to be found in children with "low overall" linguistic disorder (i.e., concurrent speech/language disorders) than in children with "poor articulation" (i.e., pure speech disorder).

Sex and Age Differences

Finally, associations with age and sex were examined (see Chapter 5). There were many more males in the sample than females, reflecting the greater prevalence of males for developmental speech/language disorders. The boys and the girls in the sample did not differ with regard to demographic and background factors, psychosocial stressors, medical disorders, or linguistic factors.

One significant difference was that the overall prevalence of developmental disorders was greater in the girls than in the boys. However, the specific types of developmental disorders (including learning disorders and mental retardation) were not individually significantly different in prevalence between the boys and girls. What is noteworthy is that childhood developmental disorders are generally much more common in boys, suggesting that the presence of a speech/language disorder may make a girl more vulnerable to developmental disorders.

On the parent and teacher behavior ratings, the boys were rated as having significantly more hyperactivity factor symptoms than the girls. Boys were rated on the Rutter teacher questionnaire as having more antisocial factor symptoms. The antisocial factor of the Rutter teacher questionnaire and the hyperactivity factor of the Conners teacher questionnaire overlap to a large degree. Because disruptive behavior is more common in boys in the general population for this age-range, these findings are not surprising.

Levels of impairment and overall adaptive functioning did not significantly distinguish the boys from the girls, nor did the prevalence of psychiatric disorder in general. However, there were differences between the sexes in the types of psychiatric illnesses found. Thus, the boys were significantly more likely to have disruptive behavior disorders, whereas the girls were more likely to have emotional disorders. Again, these sex differences in behavioral and emotional disorders have been reported in the literature for the general population.

These data suggest that the presence of a speech/language disorder makes girls as vulnerable as boys to the development of psychiatric and developmental disorders. In this way, speech/language–disordered children are different from children in the general population. However, the types of disorders that the speech/language–disordered children develop tend to be the same as those occurring in the general population.

The analysis of age factors also revealed some interesting material. The preschool-age, elementary school–age, and older children all had similar rates of psychiatric illness, similar rates of psychosocial stress, and similar demographic and background characteristics. Because of disparities in the numbers of children in the three different age groups, particularly the small number of children over age 12, statistical analyses across the three groups were not always valid.

However, the raw data (presented in Tables 5-5 and 5-6 in Chapter 5) suggest age differences in types of psychiatric disorders, presence and types of developmental disorders, and types of speech/language disorders.

The findings on prevalence of psychiatric disorder were counter to the hypothesis that the older the child (and thus the greater the length of time the child's speech/language disorder would have been interacting with the environment), the greater the likelihood of psychiatric disorder. However, it must be remembered that this sample consisted of children who were first-referrals for speech/language evaluation. Thus, the older children did not necessarily manifest speech/language disorder for a longer time than the younger children.

There were significant differences associated with age for certain specific psychiatric symptoms. Primarily these differences were consistent with known developmental trends (e.g., drops in prevalence for wetting, clinging, and throwing tantrums).

While there were no differences with age in the overall prevalence of an Axis I diagnosis, certain specific diagnoses were more common in certain age groups. Attention-deficit disorder with hyperactivity (ADDH) was more common in younger and grade school–age children, whereas affective disturbances, as might be expected, were disproportionately more common in older children.

Clinical Implications and Research Questions

Overall, the findings of the present study strongly suggest that children with speech/language disorders are a group at risk for both psychiatric disorder and learning disorder. Insofar as the epidemiologic data (summarized in Chapter 1) suggest that childhood speech/language disorders may be relatively common, childhood speech/language disorders may have considerable impact upon society. A considerable number of children are affected by speech/language disorders, and, in terms of the duration and severity of their problems, they may suffer long-term linguistic, psychiatric, and learning problems.

The findings of the present study have implications for professionals in many areas, including primary-care practitioners, pediatricians, family practitioners, speech/language pathologists, educators, and mental health practitioners (such as child psychiatrists, child psychologists, and social workers). Because normal speech and language development progresses rapidly during the preschool period, it is most likely that the primary-care practitioners (either pediatricians or family practitioners) will be the first ones presented with the young speech/language–impaired child.

We have outlined elsewhere (Cantwell and Baker 1985, 1987a) specific guidelines for when children should be referred for detailed speech/language evaluation. Such guidelines would permit the primary-care practitioner to recognize and identify as early as possible a child with problems in speech/language development.

Unfortunately, appropriate training for serving emotionally and behaviorally disordered children is typically limited in communication-disorders training programs (Prizant et al., in press). Speech/language pathologists need to become aware that the children that they see for evaluation and intervention are likely to have psychiatric and/or learning problems. Such problems will have multiple implications for the speech/language pathologist in terms of assessment, diagnosis, treatment, and referral. For example, treatment plans for these children may need to be modified to take into account the possibility of attention, concentration, or other emotional or behavioral problems that would affect treatment progress. Furthermore, a major focus of speech/language therapy may need to be in areas having to do with interpersonal interactions (e.g., "social skills" and/or pragmatic development).

Children with speech/language disorders are most often seen at specialty speech-and-hearing clinics where the practitioners may have little expertise in the recognition or assessment of learning or psychiatric disorders. The introduction of screening measures into these clinics would be useful in helping to identify those children most at risk for learning disorders and/or psychiatric disorders. Guidelines for appropriate educational or psychiatric referral for these children are also needed. Finally, it is incumbent upon speech/language professionals to develop a network for appropriate referrals (Prizant et al., in press).

Educators similarly need to recognize that children with speech/language problems who are in preschool, kindergarten, or grade school are likely to be at risk for psychiatric and learning problems. These children will most likely need some type of special educational intervention geared toward their multiple problems in the speech/language, learning, and psychiatric areas. Special educational programs in the public schools are often categorically based, so that speech/language–disordered children may be placed into an "aphasia class" or other classroom setting in which they may receive help only for speech/language difficulties. Another problem is that placement in a class for children with speech/language disorders may be determined by rather arbitrary cutoff scores. Sometimes the scores may be too high, resulting in children being returned to a regular classroom even though they are not able to function well there. The child mental health practitioner should be especially alert to the fact that a significant proportion of patients referred for psychiatric problems will have underlying communication difficulties that could be quite subtle. Such patients will require help in the speech/language area in addition to psychiatric intervention. Moreover, children with speech/language disorders will have difficulties in the verbal skills often essential for play therapy, individual therapy, family therapy, and even behavior modification programs. Because such therapeutic approaches depend upon the ability to understand commands and interpret meanings, some modification of therapeutic techniques may be necessary for children with underlying communication problems.

The present study was cross-sectional, looking at children at one point in time (i.e., at first referral for evaluation of a speech/language disorder). Most of these children subsequently went on to receive speech/language intervention. However, little is known about the continuity and natural history of childhood speech/language disorders or about the effectiveness of their treatments. There are many questions about the long-term effects of speech/language disorders on educational and academic functioning as well as on psychiatric functioning. The natural history of psychiatric disorders in children with speech/language disorders and the natural history of learning disorders in children with speech/language disorders are particularly unclear. For example, it is not known whether the natural history of ADDH in a child with speech/language disorder is different from the natural history of ADDH in an otherwise nondisordered child. The same is true for all other childhood psychiatric disorders. Similarly, it is not known whether the child with a significant reading disability and an underlying language disorder will have a worse outcome, a better outcome, or the same outcome as a reading-disabled child without any underlying and linguistic problem. We also need to know the correlation, if any, between improvements in speech/language and improvements in any psychiatric or learning status.

Little is currently known about the efficacy of various interventions for speech/language disorders. We need to know, for example, the effect that speech/language therapy of various types has upon various aspects of speech/language functioning and upon behavioral, emotional, and/or learning problems. Similarly, we need to know the possible effects of psychiatric intervention for a psychiatric disorder, or educational programs for a learning disorder, on linguistic functioning. We need to know more about the impact of nonlanguage variables (e.g., medical status, educational status, psychosocial stressors, neurological status, family factors) upon educational, psychiatric, and linguistic outcomes of speech/language–disordered children. The majority of the literature dealing with the natural history of childhood communication disorders consists of case reports or naturalistic follow-up or follow-back reports on small groups of children from specialized inpatient schools. Only a few outcome studies have used any type of control group or comparison group. Furthermore, almost all of these studies dealt only with the nature of speech/language functioning at follow-up; few mentioned educational adjustment, and fewer mention psychiatric outcome.

We have previously reviewed the outcome literature (Baker and Cantwell 1984; Cantwell and Baker 1987a) and found that (at the time of the review) only 12 follow-up studies of speech/language–disordered children had examined educational outcome. Furthermore, the age-range of the samples studied, the initial size of the samples, the sources from which the samples were obtained, the percentage of children followed up, the ages at follow-up, and the methodology for both speech/language assessment and educational assessment, had all varied greatly from study to study. Thus, firm conclusions were difficult to draw. The same can be said of the nine follow-up studies of speech/language–disordered children that assessed aspects of psychiatric outcome. Nevertheless, the literature tends to indicate that over time, children with speech/language disorders are at risk for both educational disorders and psychiatric disorders.

The chief outcome finding in the literature with regard to linguistic functioning is that there generally tends to be improvement over time. Speech disorders seem more likely to improve than language disorders. However, whether speech/language intervention is effective or not, and, if it is effective, whether it has any effect upon psychiatric and learning problems, still need to be assessed.

It is tempting to think that the present data point to areas of preventive intervention. Since the psychiatrically ill children differed the most from the psychiatrically well children in the nature and severity of their speech/language problems, one could argue that the speech/language problem is primary and therefore should be treated first.

The appropriately controlled study of prevention would include random assignment of speech/language–disordered children to different therapeutic interventions (e.g., speech/language intervention alone, psychiatric intervention alone, the combination of psychiatric intervention plus speech/language intervention, speech/language intervention plus educational intervention, educational intervention alone, etc.). All of the therapeutic groups would need to be matched not only for type and severity of speech/language diagnosis, psychiatric diagnosis, and educational diagnosis, but also for the relevant background factors that could alter outcome. Standardized intervention procedures would need to be employed, and these would need to be monitored over time, with standardized evaluation of outcomes being done by professionals who are blind to both the initial diagnosis and the types of intervention, and using evaluation instruments of known reliability and validity. Comparison groups receiving either no intervention or placebo intervention (e.g., the same amount of time in contact with outside individuals who do not use a special intervention technique) would also be desirable.

Reviews of the learning disorder area by Schonhaut and Satz (1983) and by Gittelman (1985) suggest that the prognosis for children with learning disabilities over time is rather poor. Further, there is little research to suggest that different types of treatment of reading disorders are any better or worse than each other or indeed any better or worse than no intervention at all. With the exception of some behavior modification literature and psychopharmacological literature, essentially the same thing can be said for the study of intervention of psychiatric disorders in childhood. Review of the speech/language intervention literature leads to essentially the same conclusions.

As we have suggested before, a review of the available literature does not provide definite answers to the question of whether or not intervention in speech/language can prevent the development of psychiatric and/or learning disorders. However, the present data do suggest some intervention guidelines. The data indicate that of the large group of children with speech/language disorders, it is those with language difficulty (and in particular difficulties involving the areas of comprehension, production, and processing of language) who are most at risk for the development of psychiatric and learning disorders. Children who have problems solely involving the speech mechanism are less at risk. It is imperative, then, that when resources are limited, therapeutic effort should be concentrated on those children whose disorders involve language. However, it is not clear that intervening solely in the speech/language area will affect psychiatric disorder outcome or learning disorder outcome. The present data showing an association between speech/language disorders, learning problems, and psychiatric disorder (particularly disruptive behavioral disorder) are consistent with the literature on the relationship between learning disorders (particularly reading disorder) and disruptive behavior disorders. This suggests that educational intervention to decrease the learning problem, coupled with appropriate speech/language therapy, may be an effective mode to prevent the development of a disruptive behavior disorder or at least to ameliorate it to some degree once it has developed. Speech/language intervention in children is thus appropriate before grade school. It is our hope that intense work with these children before they develop severe remedial academic problems may alter the need for later educational and/or psychiatric intervention.

Appendix 1

Prevalence of Childhood Speech/Language Disorders: A Review of the Literature

Reference	Disorder studied; definition used	Sample: size, age range, source	Prevalence
Beitchman et al. 1986a	Delay in speech and language development; defined by standardized tests	1-in-3 sample of 5,000 5-year-olds from kindergartens in Ottawa area	Estimated prevalence of 16.2% to 21.8%
Bendel et al. 1989	Speech and language disorders diagnosis in medical charts; methods of diagnosis not stated	Israeli birth cohort followed by chart review at age 3 years (N = 9,854)	16.5 per 1,000
Blanton 1916	Speech defects (mutism, stuttering, motor aphasia, thick/indistinct speech, lisp, nasality) rated by speech therapists during sentence-repetition task	4,862 parochial and public school students (kindergarten through 12th grade) in Madison, WI	5.6% for any defect
Brady and Hall 1976	Stuttering, defined by questionnaire responses of school speech therapists regarding excessive involuntary speech disruptions or blockings	Random sample of school speech therapists in IL and PA, serving a population of normal (n = 187,420) and mentally retarded (n = 3,511) students	0.35% in normal students; 1.60% in educable mentally retarded students; 3.08% in trainable mentally retarded students
Butler et al. 1973	Speech defects; per screening by a physician, teachers, or nurses	7-year-olds; national cohort in Great Britain	10%–13% had speech impairment
Calnan and Richardson 1976	Speech problem; defined by teachers' or doctors' ratings and by sentence-imitation task scored for mispronunciations	10,921 11-year-olds born during 1 week in March 1958 in Great Britain	Physician estimate = 4.6%; teacher estimate = 10.5%
Carhart 1939	Speech defects, rated by high school teachers	Adolescents from 405 high schools in IL	20.8% in all students; seniors = 17.8%, freshmen = 23.3%
Chazan et al. 1980	Speech or language problems, per screening by health visitors	Children 3.75 to 4.25 years of age in Great Britain (N = 7,320)	Definite = 3.2%; maybe = 12.4%

Reference	Disorder studied; definition used	Sample: size, age range, source	Prevalence
Dickson 1971	Stuttering, defined as repetitions of sounds or words, or as getting stuck on or between words, as reported by parents	Questionnaires sent to parents of 3,276 elementary and 647 junior high school students in a suburb	9% overall: 10% elementary school; 8% junior high school
Drillien and Drummond 1983	Specific expressive, receptive, or articulation delay	Cohort of 3-year-olds in Dundee, UK ($N = 4,191$)	Overall prevalence of 57 per 1,000
Fundudis et al. 1979	Speech retardation, defined by failure to use sentences of 3 or more words by age 36 months	3-year-old children born in Newcastle (Great Britain) in 1962 ($N = 3,300$)	4%
Gillespie and Cooper 1973	Speech problems, identified by a self-rating questionnaire and by subsequent ratings of speech and oral reading by speech pathologists	All junior and senior high school students from a city in AL ($N = 5,054$)	5.5% overall: 7.9% in 7th grade; 3.0% in 12th grade
Herbert and Wedell 1970	Severe, specific language delay (defined as not forming sentences by age 3 years)	733 children 3 to 3.5 years of age in Great Britain	0.8%
Hull et al. 1971	Articulation impairment, determined by speech pathologists' ratings of taped speech sample	38,802 schoolchildren (grades 1 to 12) from 100 school districts across the United States	34% overall: 63% in 1st grade; 20% in 12th grade
Ingram 1963	Severe language retardation, defined as normal intelligence, only single-word speech at 3 years, indicated by referrals from various professionals	Speech pathologists, psychiatrists, psychologists, and audiologists in Edinburgh and Aberdeen, UK	0.75% for Aberdeen; 0.71% for Edinburgh
Irwin 1948	Speech defects (stuttering, articulation problems, and aphasia) diagnosed by speech therapists with individual testing	6,000 children from grades 1 to 6 in Cleveland, OH, schools	10%
Louttit and Halls 1936	Speech defects, including stuttering, cleft palate, or other; defined by positive responses on questionnaires by school principals	1,223 school principals in IN, polling a total of 694,428 schoolchildren	3.7% for any speech defect
Miller et al. 1974	Significant articulation defects or stuttering (per health visitor)	Cohort in Great Britain followed from birth to age 5 years	Articulation problem = 5%; stuttering = 4%
Mills and Streit 1942	Speech disorders, including dyslalia, stuttering, dysphonia, cleft palate, slobbering, and mutism	Every child in grades 1 to 3 in Holyoke, MA, 1940–1941 ($n = 1,196$); 3,469 children in grades 3 to 6	12.6% in grades 1–3; 10.1% in grades 1–6

Reference	Disorder studied; definition used	Sample: size, age range, source	Prevalence
Morley 1965	Retarded language development (defined as limited use of language at 3.75 years and incomplete sentences at 6 years of age)	Cohort of 114 children from Newcastle; 3.75 and 6.0 years of age	6%
National Center for Health Statistics 1981	Speech impairments (not associated with deafness) as reported to census interviewers by heads of households	Random sample of families across the United States	1.1%
Pronovost 1951	Speech problems (articulation, stuttering, and cleft palate) per teacher or physician questionnaires	Staff of 3,870 schools and hospitals in New England states	Overall prevalence of 7.8%
Randall et al. 1974	Articulation, comprehension, and expression difficulties as determined by test scores at least two SDs below mean	160 3-year-olds from a London area, born during March 1968	6% were below norms in any of the tests
Rescorla 1984	Language delay; defined by fewer than 30 words and/or no word combinations at 2 years of age	2-year-olds from private pediatrician or pediatric-clinic patient caseloads ($N = 351$)	14% overall; range = 1%–17% in various clinics
Richman and Stevenson 1977; Stevenson and Richman 1976	Expressive language delay (i.e., cannot name 7 pictures, use word combination, use 20-word vocabulary, use sentences longer than 4 syllables, use adjectives and adverbs)	1-in-4 random sample of 3-year-olds living in a London borough ($N = 705$ from indigenous families)	2.3% to 3.1% depending on criteria
Rutter et al. 1970a	Specific developmental language disorder; defined by referral to a speech therapist	All children in school in September 1965 in the Isle of Wight, UK	0.08%
Silva et al. 1984	Delayed speech; defined as scores below the 7th percentile on a standardized articulation test	7-year-olds followed from a representative sample of 3-year-olds in the city of Dunedin, New Zealand ($N = 872$)	6%
Silva and Williams 1983	Language delay (i.e., at or below 5th percentile in tested language comprehension or expression) ($N = 1,027$)	3-year-olds from Dunedin, New Zealand	Any delay = 7.6%; pure comprehension = 26%; expression = 2.3%
Stewart 1981	Speech, language, or hearing handicaps, as noted in school records	School records of 77,328 children in public schools in TN	2.88% with any speech or language problems

Reference	Disorder studied; definition used	Sample: size, age range, source	Prevalence
Stewart et al. 1979	Speech or language per standardized articulation or language tests	Patient population from a large health care facility in Nashville, TN (N = 1,638)	Any speech/language problem = 32%; articulation problem = 17.5%; language problem = 9.8%
Tuomi and Ivanoff 1977	Articulation or language problems, based on cursory screening	Kindergartners and 1st-graders in Canada (N = 900)	Articulation problems = 7%–24%; language problems = 7%
White House Conference on Child Health and Protection 1931	Speech defects, including articulation defects, stuttering, and voice disorders, diagnosed by speech pathologists' tests	10,033 schoolchildren from Madison, WI	Speech defect = 6.9%
Williams et al. 1980	Speech/language impairment (criteria not defined)	Preschool children in Ontario (N = 411)	Speech/language problem = 15%

Appendix 2

Psychiatric Disorders in Children With Speech/Language Disorders: A Review of the Literature

Reference	Sample studied; comparison group	Psychiatric method	Findings
Affolter et al. 1974	30 3- to 10-year-olds with specific language problems; 30 control subjects with no language problems	Battery of perceptual and processing tests	No significant differences among groups except that group with language problems had lower attention spans.
Aimard et al. 1973	100 children under 5 years of age: 50 from a speech clinic and 50 from a psychiatric clinic	Examination of case records	Concluded that language and psychiatric disturbances are part of a complex of symptoms indicating deficiencies in personality maturation.
Alessi and Loomis 1988	25 hospitalized depressed children	Psychiatric hospitalization	40% had language disorders; 24% had both receptive and expressive problems.
Alessi et al. 1990	97 child psychiatric patients	Psychiatric hospitalization	42% had language disorders; 32% had expressive problems and 24% had receptive problems.
Anders 1945	53 functionally articulation-disordered 6- to 12-year olds	California Test of Personality	Articulation-disordered children had above-average adjustment.
Aram et al. 1984	20 language-disordered teenagers 13 years, 3 months, to 16 years, 10 months of age	Parental questionnaire	The language-disordered teenagers were significantly more schizoid, immature, obsessive-compulsive, hostile, and withdrawn than the norm.
Baltaxe and Simmons 1988	125 psychiatric-clinic patients 15–72 months old	Chart review (psychiatric records)	Expressive and receptive problems were present in 65% of patients.
Barrett and Hoops 1974	30 misarticulating 1st-graders; 15 recovered and 15 did not on follow-up at 3rd grade	Index of Adjustment and Values Test	The recovered subgroup had significantly lower self-concepts and higher standards and goals.

213

Reference	Sample studied; comparison group	Psychiatric method	Findings
Bartak et al. 1975	23 dysphasic children, 4 years, 6 months, to 9 years, 11 months, of age	Vineland Social Maturity Scale; parent interviews	Average social quotient = 91. Common problems were quasi-obsessional activities, attachments to odd objects, ritualistic activities, and resistance to change.
Baumgartner 1980	426 speech-impaired children from special schools in Bavaria	Parent questionnaires	Common problems were difficulties with: concentration or attention (49%); shyness or clinging (50%); fears (32%); self-concept (45%); and social relations (36%).
Beckey 1942	50 nursery school–age children with retarded language; 50 control subjects	Semistructured interviews with parents	More crying and solitary behaviors in the children who were language retarded.
Beitchman et al. 1983, 1986a	142 speech/language–disordered kindergartners; 142 age- and sex-matched control subjects	Parent and teacher questionnaires; child interviews	Rate of psychiatric disorder was 53% in the speech/language–disordered group—significantly more than in the control group.
Bennett and Runyan 1982	282 educators	Questionnaire for educators	39% said communication disorder had adverse effect on academic and social skills; 9.6% said it had adverse effects on social development only.
Blood and Seiden 1981	Elementary school speech pathologists with 1,060 stuttering patients	Questionnaire surveying opinions	Therapists' impressions were that emotional problems were rare in these patients.
Brickman et al. 1984	64 institutionalized adolescent delinquents	Luria-Nebraska Neuropsychological Battery	Expressive language scores were abnormal (but no statistics were reported).
Broad and Bar 1973	Stutterers; articulation-impaired and hearing-impaired patients	Bender Visual Motor Gestalt Test; Children's Apperception Test	Concluded that there were underlying psychological conflicts in all three groups.
Bubenickova 1977	86 stutterers; 170 classmates	School records	Stutterers did not have more negative relationships with school, but had more fears of speaking in class.
Butler 1965	15 articulation-disordered children 5 to 8 years of age	Bender Visual Motor Gestalt Test	63% of sample had a significant degree of emotional disturbance.

Reference	Sample studied; comparison group	Psychiatric method	Findings
Caceres 1971	25 children, 3 to 13 years of age, with expressive language disorders	Examination of case records	84% had psychiatric problems, usually either hyperactive, destructive, and aggressive, or timid and inhibited.
Cantwell and Baker 1980	250 children with language delay from a psychiatric clinic; 250 age- and sex-matched patients	Examination of charts (psychiatric records)	7 psychiatric symptoms were significantly more common in the language-delayed patients than in the other psychiatric-clinic patients.
Chess 1944	7 psychiatric patients, 5 to 8 years of age, with language disorder	Case reports	All had distortions in personality; aggression and neurosis were common.
Chess and Rosenberg 1974	563 patients from a child psychiatry practice	Chart review	139 children (24%) had some type of speech/language problem.
Clifford 1969	39 children with cleft palate; 68 asthmatic control subjects	Self-ratings; sentence-completion task	No significant differences between groups in symptom impact or in overall self-concept.
Cohen et al. 1988, 1989, 1990	Samples of $n = 37$, 50, and 110 psychiatric outpatients, 4 to 12 years of age	Teacher and parent questionnaires; DSM symptom screenings	Approximately 1/3 of outpatients had known language problems at referral; approximately 1/3 more had previously undetected moderate to severe language impairments.
Cozard and Rousey 1968	10- to 18-year-olds from schools for delinquent youths	Presence in school for delinquents	58.3% of all students had a speech (voice, articulation, stuttering) disorder.
de Ajuriaguerra et al. 1976	17 dysphasic adolescents (followed since 4.5 years of age)	Not stated	Most serious problems at follow-up were in nonlinguistic areas (e.g., IQ and social behavior).
Demb 1980	2 language-disordered preschoolers	Case reports	Both children manifested serious emotional problems.
Despert 1946	50 stutterers, 6 to 15 years of age; school sample	Comprehensive psychiatric evaluation	Majority had anxiety: 50% had compulsions; 50% had sleep problems; 75% had fears.
Duncan 1947	22 hoarse speakers; 22 nonhoarse speakers (ages not specified)	Bell Adjustment Inventory	Home maladjustment was significantly more common in voice-disordered speakers than in normal speakers.

Reference	Sample studied; comparison group	Psychiatric method	Findings
English 1961	30 children with cleft palate; control subjects matched for normal age, sex, IQ, etc. (8–12 years of age)	Projective tests; parent and teacher ratings; sentence completion	No significant differences between groups on parent and teacher ratings; "more extrapunitive needs" for cleft-palate group on projective tests.
Ferry et al. 1975	60 dyspraxic children, most between 4 and 10 years of age	Not specified	Over 50% of sample had tantrums. Other common problems included depression and autistic features.
Fitzsimons 1958	70 articulation-impaired 1st-graders; 70 control subjects matched for age, sex, IQ, and school	CAT; Vineland Social Maturity Scale	Significantly more destructiveness, fears, tantrums, refusals to obey, shyness, and school failure in the articulation-impaired group.
Fundudis et al. 1979	102 children with inability to use three-word sentences at 36 months (follow-up study)	Rutter Teacher Questionnaire; Jr. Eysenck Personality Inventory; child and parent interviews	18 were extremely abnormal (autistic, mute, mentally retarded); the remaining group had abnormal mean scores on all measures.
Funk and Ruppert 1984	Boy, 3 years, 8 months of age, with receptive and expressive language disorder	Single case report	Extreme overactivity and tantrums associated with language disorder.
Garbee 1973	58 13- to 18-year-old boys: 29 having an articulation defect; 29 normal control subjects	Dignan Ego Identity Scale	Boys with articulation defects were not significantly different from control subjects in "ego identity."
Gemelli 1982	30 stuttering children from a psychiatric practice	Maternal interviews	Psychodynamic difficulties and "developmental conflicts" were common in children who stutter.
Glasner 1949	70 stutterers under 5 years of age, referred to a psychiatrist	Parent and child interviews	All had some emotional problems; 37% were anxious or overly sensitive.
Gluck et al. 1965	50 children with cleft palate; compared with Wylie et al.'s (1965) guidance-clinic patients	Chart review	Children with cleft palate had more shyness and enuresis than child guidance-clinic patients.
Griffiths 1969	49 children with language delay	Child, parent, and teacher interviews	45% had poor emotional adjustment; 25% had poor social adjustment.
Grinnell et al. 1983	Preadolescent and adolescent psychiatric hospital patients ($N = 115$)	Psychiatric hospital admission	34% had language problems and hearing loss; of nonhearing-impaired individuals, 80% had speech/language pathology.

Reference	Sample studied; comparison group	Psychiatric method	Findings
Gualtieri et al. 1983	26 psychiatric-clinic inpatients, 4 years, 11 months, to 13 years, 2 months of age	Psychiatric hospital admission	50% of the admissions had moderate to severe language dysfunctions.
Harper and Richman 1978	14- to 19-year-olds: 52 with cleft palate and 46 control subjects with orthopedic disabilities	MMPI	Significantly more self-doubt and self-concern in the children with cleft palate.
Holroyd 1968	26 children with a verbal IQ of 25+ points below performance IQ	Review of medical charts	Children with significantly lower verbal IQs did not have more psychiatric illness.
Ierodiakonou 1970	65 children who stutter, 3 to 15 years of age, from a child guidance clinic	Psychiatric files; CAT, Rorschach, school report	Prestuttering personality typically timid, shy, and withdrawn, but at home obstinate and overly active.
Ingram 1959	80 speech-clinic children with specific developmental language disorders	Speech-clinic case records	11 children were withdrawn, and 7 were immature or overly dependent; smaller numbers had tantrums or were excessively excitable.
Jenkins et al. 1980	Epidemiologic sample, children, 2 to 4.9 years of age ($N = 168$)	Maternal interview; physician ratings	18% of normally behaving children had speech/language problems vs. 35% of children with behavior problems.
Kapp 1979	34 11- to 14-year-old children with cleft palate; matched control subjects	Self-concept self-rating	No significant difference in self-concept, but group with cleft palate was significantly less happy and less satisfied with appearance.
King et al. 1982	50 preschoolers with speech/language delays, followed up at ages 13 to 20 years	Telephone interviews with parents	At follow-up, only 8% of the patients with speech/language delays had "interpersonal problems."
Klackenberg 1980	52 speech-retarded 3-year-olds followed up in 3rd and 6th grades; control subjects	Teacher ratings	Children with speech retardation were chosen as playmates significantly less often and were significantly more destructive than control children.
Kotsopoulos and Boodoosingh 1987	46 psychiatric-clinic patients, 6 to 12 years of age	DSM-III diagnoses from patient charts	71.7% of the children had speech/language impairment severe enough to require therapy.
Lerea and Ward 1966	20 1st- and 2nd-graders with articulation disorders; 20 matched control subjects	Figure-placement task	Group with articulation disorders put more space between figures, suggesting social reluctance.

Reference	Sample studied; comparison group	Psychiatric method	Findings
Lerner et al. 1985	88 normal preschoolers followed up 11.5 years later	DICA parent and child interviews	Speech/language problem at ages 3 to 5 years was a strong predictor of psychiatric illness at follow-up.
Lindholm and Touliatos 1979	106 speech-therapy patients (grades K–8); 2,991 classmates	Teacher questionnaire	Speech-therapy patients had significantly more personality problems, psychotic signs, and immaturity.
Livingood and Cohen-Sandler 1980	2 communication-disordered 6-year-olds in psychiatric treatment	Psychiatric case records	School phobias and impaired peer relationships were present.
Lolley 1975	5- to 11-year-olds: 50 with voice disorders and 50 with normal speech	Devereux teacher ratings	Groups were significantly different in only one factor of classroom behavior—comprehension.
Loomis and Alessi 1988	75 psychiatric inpatient children	Psychiatric hospitalization	49% had articulation and/or language disorders; 62% of these not previously identified.
Love and Thompson 1988	116 preschool-age psychiatric outpatients (no mental retardation or PDD)	Psychiatric diagnoses per DSM-III	64.7% had some type of speech/language disorder.
McHale 1967	Boys from school psychological service: 24 with stammering; also enuretic, phobic, and normal groups	Vineland Social Maturity Scale	Each group had characteristic pattern (not specified) of adjustment.
McWilliams and Matthews 1979	226 children with cleft palate	Vineland Social Maturity Scale	Children with cleft palate were within normal limits on the scale.
McWilliams and Musgrave 1972	170 cleft-palate children with and without articulation impairments	Maternal questionnaires	Normally speaking children with cleft palate had no marked behavior problems; cleft-palate children with articulation disorders had significantly more behavior problems, bad temper, and bed-wetting.
Mehrhof and Rousey 1971	12 patients with "pathognomonic speech difficulties"; 12 psychiatric-patient control subjects (4–35 years of age)	Chart review; psychiatric records	Patients with speech disorders had histories of suicidal acts and/or histories of self-assault.
Moller 1960	20 stutterers; 20 normal children; 20 "predelinquents"— all 10 to 12 years of age	Rorschach	More indications of maladjustment in stutterers than in predelinquents.

Reference	Sample studied; comparison group	Psychiatric method	Findings
Morley 1973	5 receptive/expressive developmental aphasic individuals	Case summaries	Reasonably normal emotional relationships; some children had frustration and tantrums.
Muma et al. 1968	40 high school–age adolescents with harsh, nasal, hoarse, or breathy voices; 38 control subjects	MMPI; peer ratings	No relationships between voice qualities and any of the personality ratings.
Neeper 1985	75 children with learning disorders; 11 inattentive children	Teacher ratings	Inattentive group was 2 SDs below mean in linguistic-processing rating.
Nelson 1953	3rd-, 5th-, and 7th-graders: 35 with articulation disorders; 35 sex- and IQ-matched control subjects	California Test of Personality; teacher ratings	Group with articulation problems were not significantly different from controls on the CTP; however, they had less desirable behavior according to teachers.
Ollendick 1979	121 incarcerated male delinquents, 13.5 to 16.2 years of age	WISC performance and verbal IQ scores	Average verbal IQ scores were significantly lower than performance IQ scores among the delinquents.
Paul and Cohen 1984; Paul et al. 1983	28 children with developmental language disorder, followed up approximately 7 years after diagnosis	Observations, tests, questionnaires	More than 50% had attention, activity, and motor problems that persisted; 50% had autistic features at follow-up.
Petrie 1975	11 children with severe receptive language disorder	Bristol Social Adjustment Scales	7 children were "maladjusted"; all had shyness, social withdrawal, and depression.
Prins 1972	66 stutterers (8–21 years of age); 23 control subjects with speech/language disorder	California Test of Personality	Neither group showed marked maladjustment; more problems were present in control subjects.
Richman 1976, 1978; Richman and Harper 1978, 1979; Harper and Richman 1978	Compared cleft-palate children with normal children and/or orthopedically handicapped children	Teacher and parent ratings; MMPI; self-ratings of interests	Cleft-palate group had more personality disorders and more inhibition than did the normal children, and more inhibition and self-concern than did orthopedic control subjects.
Rousey 1974	Articulation-impaired children from psychiatric practice	Observations from psychotherapy sessions	Author concluded types of articulation errors predict presence and types of psychiatric disorders.

Reference	Sample studied; comparison group	Psychiatric method	Findings
Ruess 1965	49 children with cleft palate, 7 to 12 years of age; normal siblings	Teacher and parent ratings	No significant differences between cleft-palate children and siblings on any measures.
Rutter et al. 1970a	5- to 15-year-old schoolchildren with brain disorders in Isle of Wight	Teacher and parent ratings; child and parent interviews	69% of psychiatrically ill children had articulation problems and 75% had language problems; vs. only 50% and 30% of the psychiatrically well.
Santostefano 1960	26 stutterers; 26 age-, sex-, and IQ-matched control subjects	Rorschach (anxiety/hostility scores)	Significantly more anxiety and hostility in stutterers.
Schweckendiek and Danzer 1970	200 7- to 14-year-old children with cleft palate	Parent and teacher ratings; examination of report cards	Most common problems were tantrums (according to parents), and concentration and learning difficulties (according to teachers).
Sermas and Cox 1982	19 stutterers, 16 to 48 years of age	Psychiatric interviews and tests	Most had psychopathology, but no particular personality type was present.
Sheridan and Peckham 1973	215 7-year-olds with unintelligible speech and normal hearing	Bristol Social Adjustment Guide	48% of children scored in "maladjusted" range.
Sherrill 1967	53 elementary school–age children with severe functional articulation disorder; 53 sex- and age-matched control subjects	Teacher and peer ratings; self-ratings	Children with articulation disorder were not perceived as being significantly different from peers in anxiety, academic functioning, or social acceptance.
Shriberg et al. 1986	114 children with "phonologic disorders of unknown origin"	Chart reviews (speech-therapy records)	33% were manipulative; 29% were noncompliant; 35% had delayed psychosocial development; 35% were distractible; 41% were overly sensitive; and 46% were immature.
Silva et al. 1984	57 speech-delayed 3-year-olds; compared with rest of epidemiologic sample	Rutter Parent and Teacher Questionnaires	Speech-delayed children had significantly more behavior problems according to teacher and parent reports than did control subjects.
Simonds and Heimburger 1978	40 children, 6 to 18 years of age, with cleft palate; 40 age-, sex-, and SES-matched control subjects	Maternal ratings and child interviews	Cleft-palate group was significantly more likely to have psychiatric problems; those with serious articulation problems had the highest prevalence of psychiatric problems.

Reference	Sample studied; comparison group	Psychiatric method	Findings
Solomon 1961	49 1st-graders with impaired articulation; 49 age-, sex-, and IQ-matched control subjects	Interviews with mothers rated by two judges	Significantly more problems in the group with impaired articulation.
Spriesterbach 1973	175 children with cleft palate; matched control subjects	Interviews with families	Children with cleft palate characterized by shyness and dissatisfaction.
Stevenson and Richman 1978; Richman and Stevenson 1977; Richman et al. 1982	24 children with delay in expressive language from an epidemiologic sample of 750 3-year-olds; compared with rest of sample	Parent behavior ratings; interviews with mothers	59% of children with language delay had significant behavior problems vs. only 14% of children with no language delay.
Tallal et al. 1989a	81 4-year-olds with language delay; 49 control subjects	Parent behavior ratings	Children with language delay had significantly higher mean total symptoms and internalizing disorder scores.
Teja et al. 1972	539 child guidance-clinic patients in India	Chart review	6.6% of patients had speech problems.
Thorley 1984	73 hyperkinetic boys; psychiatric patient controls	Chart review	Hyperactive group had significantly more speech/language disorders.
Trapp and Evan 1960	54 articulation-impaired and normal 8- to 10-year-olds	Score on WISC Digit Symbol Subtest	Severely articulation-impaired children were more anxious (i.e., scored worse) than normal children.
Varbiro and Engelmayer 1972	14 3rd- to 8th-grade stutterers; 14 control subjects	California Achievement Test	Significantly more situational fears in stutterers.
Voorhees 1981	15 delinquent; 13 control teenagers	Luria-Nebraska Neuropsychological Battery	Delinquent teenagers scored significantly lower on language tasks.
Watson 1964	Cleft-palate (n = 34), physically handicapped, and normal children	Personal Adjustment Inventory	No differences between groups on any inventory scales.
Weber 1965	104 4- to 12-year-old psychiatric patients	Patient records; speech/language tests	More than 75% of the patients had speech/language problems.
Wilson and Lamb 1974	12 children with hoarse voice; 12 age-, sex-, IQ-, and SES-matched control subjects	Rorschach	More difficulty in adjustment in the children with voice disorder; no consistent personality types.

Reference	Sample studied; comparison group	Psychiatric method	Findings
Wing 1969	4- to 16-year-old children with expressive (n = 10) or receptive language (n = 11) disorder; normal children (n = 25)	Parent ratings	Groups with language disorders were characterized by social problems, lack of play, and inappropriate behaviors.
Wirls and Plotkin 1971	66 children with cleft palate and their siblings	CAT; Draw-a-Person Test; Rorschach	On CAT, cleft-palate group referred to themselves significantly more frequently and had more negative stories.
Wolff et al. 1982	56 delinquent 14- and 15-year-old boys; 96 control subjects	Delinquency	Delinquent adolescents had significantly more impairments in all language measures.
Woods 1970	48 3rd- and 6th-grade stutterers; 562 nonstuttering classmates	Social position ratings by classmates	No significant differences between stutterers and classmates.
Wyatt 1958	20 stutterers; 20 normal speakers	Story-telling battery	Stutterers manifested more anxiety and fears.
Wylie et al. 1965	45 speech/language–disordered patients from a child guidance clinic; rest of clinic patients	Examination of chart notes (child guidance-clinic charts)	Speech/language–disordered patients were significantly different from other patients in 17 symptoms; different symptoms were associated with different speech/language disorders.
Yanagawa 1973–1974	42 Japanese junior high school–age stutterers; 41 nonstuttering control subjects	Manifest Anxiety Scale; other projective tests	Significantly more emotional symptoms in the stutterers, especially depression, neurosis, lability, and feelings of inferiority.
Zinkus and Gottlieb 1983	30 13- to 18-year-old institutionalized male delinquents	Delinquency history	Articulation, auditory processing, and comprehension problems present in over 60%.

Note. CAT = Children's Apperception Test; DICA = Diagnostic Interview for Children and Adolescents; MMPI = Minnesota Multiphasic Personality Inventory; PDD = pervasive developmental disorder; SES = socioeconomic status; SD = standard deviation; WISC = Wechsler Intelligence Scale for Children.

Appendix 3

Association Between Learning Disorders and Speech/Language Disorders: A Review of the Literature

Reference	Subjects studied	Methods	Findings
Alessi et al. 1990	41 language-disordered psychiatric patients; 56 psychiatric patients with no language disorders	Woodcock-Johnson Psychoeducational Test	Language-disordered group was significantly worse in reading, writing, math, and knowledge.
Anderson 1982	5 4th-graders with learning disorders; 5 nonlearning-disordered 4th-graders	Peabody Language Development Kit	Group with learning disorders was significantly more deficient in syntax.
Andolina 1980	80 7- to 12-year-old students with learning disorders; normal classmates	Children's oral stories analyzed for syntax and vocabulary	Syntactic development showed different pattern in students with learning disorders.
Aram and Nation 1980	63 language-disordered preschoolers followed 4 to 5 years later	Parent and teacher questionnaires; school records	At follow-up, 40% were behind in reading, and 28% were behind in spelling.
Aram et al. 1984	20 teenagers with language disorders (10-year follow-up)	Classroom placements; WISC IQ scores	At follow-up, 20% appeared mentally retarded; of rest, 69% had learning problems.
Blalock 1982	80 adults with learning disorders who requested evaluation	Formal and informal speech and language assessment	Over 78% had an auditory language problem.
Bryan 1977	23 3rd- to 5th-graders with learning disorders; 11 normal 3rd- to 5th-graders	Children's Profile of Nonverbal Sensitivity	Group with learning disorders had less accurate understanding of nonverbal communication.
Bubenickova 1977	86 stutterers; 170 classmates	School records	No significant difference between groups in school achievement.
Butler et al. 1973	215 7-year-olds with defective speech	Teacher reports	86% were poor in reading, and 80% were poor in arithmetic.
Byrne 1981	24 poor and 20 good readers from a 2nd-grade class	Sentence-comprehension task	Poor readers had certain comprehension deficits.

Reference	Subjects studied	Methods	Findings
Calnan and Richardson 1976	Epidemiologic study of 512 11-year-olds	School records; speech/language screening	Subgroup with speech disorders scored lower in reading, math, and general ability.
Cambourne and Rousch 1982	120 2nd-, 4th-, 6th-, and 8th-graders: proficient, average, or disabled in reading	Miscue research paradigm	Group with reading disorders had marked problems retaining grammatical structure and meaning of text.
Ceci 1982	10-year-olds with learning disorders; 4-, 7-, and 10-year-olds without learning disorders	Semantic-decision task	Semantic processing of children with learning disorders was like that of younger nonlanguage-disordered children.
de Ajuriaguerra et al. 1976	17 dysphasic adolescents (follow-up study)	Not stated	Over 82% had scholastic delays.
Dean and Kundert 1981	16 children with learning disorders; matched normal children (all 6–11 years of age)	Paired-associate learning task	Children with learning disorders showed specific difficulties with abstract nouns.
Denckla et al. 1981	10 dyslexic boys; 10 nondyslexic learning-disordered boys	Tests of naming, paired-associate learning, perception, and matching	Dyslexic boys were slow in naming and had other dysphasic errors.
Dickstein and Warren 1980	38 learning-disordered children, 5 to 8 years of age; age-matched control subjects	Interpretation of characters' thoughts and feelings	Learning-disordered children had problems with role taking.
Donahue 1981, 1983; Donahue and Bryan 1983; Donahue et al. 1980, 1982	1st- through 8th-grade learning-disordered children (separated by grade levels); normal classmates	Various language tasks: requesting, responding to limited information, syntax production, initiating conversations	Children with learning disorders were less proficient on all language measures.
Everhart 1953	Children with articulation disorder; control subjects	Iowa Test of Basic Skills	No significant differences between groups.
Fayne 1981	75 learning-disordered and nonlearning-disordered 10th- and 11th-graders	Pronoun reference-comprehension task	Group with learning disorders had specific problems.
Fundudis et al. 1980	102 3-year-olds with speech/language disorders (follow-up at age 7 years)	Achievement and intelligence tests	"Average reading quotient" = 80.
Gambrell and Heathington 1981	28 adult good readers; 28 adult poor readers	Interviews about reading	Poor readers were unaware of reading comprehension strategies.

Reference	Subjects studied	Methods	Findings
Garvey and Gordon 1973	58 children with language delay (follow-up)	School placement	Approximately 50% were in special schools.
German 1979	30 learning-disordered and 30 normal 8- to 11-year-olds with comparable IQs	Word-finding tasks	Group with learning disorders had significantly more word-finding errors than did the normal children.
Gillam and Johnston 1985	10 language-disordered and 10 normal 3- to 6-year-olds	Print-matching tasks	Children with language disorders were poorer on print-matching tasks.
Godfrey et al. 1981	17 dyslexic and 17 normal 10-year-olds	Speech-perception tasks	Dyslexic children were poorer in speech perception.
Griffiths 1969	49 children with speech/language delay (follow-up study)	Achievement tests; teacher interviews	Most children had learning problems; 61% were in special schools.
Hall and Tomblin 1978	Adult follow-up of 18 articulation-impaired and 18 language-impaired children	Parent reports; school records	Language-impaired children had significantly lower achievement in all areas.
Hook and Johnson 1978	14 learning-disordered and 12 nonlearning-disordered boys in grades 3 and 4	Various tasks involving oral language skills	Learning-disordered group had problems abstracting features and forming oral language rules.
Hresko 1975, 1979	40 learning-disordered and 40 normal 5- to 6-year-olds	Elicited-imitation task	Group with learning disorders had significantly more errors and ungrammatical repetitions.
Israel 1984	Learning-disordered and nonlearning-disordered children, 7.5 to 12.3 years of age	Word-association task	Group with learning disorders had significantly more nonparadigmatic and clang responses.
Jerger et al. 1987	Case study: 11-year-old with learning disorder	Various language processing measures	Evidence of auditory phonological disorder.
Kavale 1982	25 learning-disordered and 25 normal 1st-graders	Boehm Test of Basic Concepts	Group with learning disorders had significantly lower comprehension of basic concepts.
Kean 1984	6 adult dyslexic individuals; various control subjects	Reaction time for word recognition	Dyslexic individuals showed specific problems with determiners.
King et al. 1982	15-year follow-up of 50 speech/language–impaired 3- to 6-year-olds	Questionnaire or telephone interview with mothers	52% of children had problems in one or more academic subjects.
Klackenberg 1980	52 3-year-olds with retarded speech followed up in 3rd and 6th grades; compared with normal 3-year-olds	Teacher ratings	Group with retarded speech had significantly poorer school performance than did control subjects.

Reference	Subjects studied	Methods	Findings
Klein-Konigsberg 1984	60 learning-disordered and 60 normal 7- to 11-year-olds	Questions about information contained in sentences read aloud	Group with learning disorders attended to smaller units and had problems recalling critical information.
Knight-Arest 1984	Boys, 10 years to 12 years, 11 months of age: 25 with learning disorders and 25 without learning disorders	Instructional task (teach examiner to play checkers)	Group with learning disorders was less informative and adaptable to the listener.
Lapointe 1976	32 learning-disordered and 20 normal adolescents	Token Test	Group with learning disorders scored lower, suggesting receptive language problem.
Levi et al. 1982	32 6- to 7.8-year-olds who had language disorder at 3 to 4 years of age	Sentence reading and writing task	Reading/writing problem at 6 to 7 years of age was related to semantic problem at ages 3 to 4.
Levi et al. 1984	8- to 10-year-olds: 36 reading disabled; 18 with normal reading	Story-telling task	Children with reading disability had less lexical diversity.
Lewis and Kass 1982	44 learning-disordered and 40 average students, 4 to 9 years of age	Labeling, recalling, and relabeling objects	Pupils with learning disorders used significantly more inappropriate labels.
Lorsbach 1982	20 learning-disordered and 20 matched nonlearning-disordered 9.5- to 11.5-year-olds	Word-categorization task; free-recall tasks	Students with learning disorders had difficulties with semantic recall.
Lyle 1970	54 retarded readers and 54 matched control subjects, 6 to 12 years of age	Retrospective study of developmental variables	Early speech problems were best predictor of later learning disorder.
Mann 1984	68 kindergartners followed up 1 year later	Word-repetition task	Initial word repetition problems correlated with follow-up reading ability.
Markoski 1983	15 learning-disordered children and 15 nonlearning-disordered peers, 7 to 9 years of age	Persuasion task	Group with language disorders used significantly more requests.
Matthews et al. 1982	25 learning-disordered 15- to 18-year-olds; 25 control subjects	Various role-playing tasks	Group with learning disorders was significantly less capable at many interactional skills.
Moore and Simpson 1983	4th- to 6th-graders; 15 learning disordered, 15 behavior disordered, and 15 normal	Interactions with peers, teachers, and aides	Group with learning disorders interacted differently from normal children, and the same as group with behavior disorders.

Reference	Subjects studied	Methods	Findings
Moran and Byrne 1977	60 learning-disordered and 60 nonlearning-disordered children (mean age = 7.9 years)	Test of verb-tense markers	Group with learning disorders used different response pattern than did nonlearning-disordered group.
Morris and Crump 1982	72 learning-disordered and 72 nonlearning-disordered boys, 9 to 15 years of age	Syntactic analyses of written stories	Group with learning disorders had significantly lower syntax scores and significantly less variety in word usage.
Nelson 1953	3rd-, 5th-, and 7th-graders with articulation disorders; control subjects	Teacher ratings	Group with articulation disorders was significantly worse in educational achievement.
Noel 1980	40 learning-disordered and 40 nonlearning-disordered boys, 9 to 11 years of age	Explanation task	Group with learning disorders was deficient in referential skills, especially labeling.
Olsen et al. 1983	30 learning-disordered and 15 nonlearning-disordered 5th-graders	Spontaneous speech during board game	Group with learning disorders used significantly fewer of certain syntactic structures.
Pajurkova et al. 1976	20 learning-disordered and 40 nonlearning-disordered boys, 9 to 10 years of age	Word-finding test	Group with learning disorders had significantly poorer performance on test.
Reid and Hresko 1980	60 learning-disordered and 60 nonlearning-disordered children, 5 to 7 years of age	Test of Early Language Development	Children learning normally had significantly higher test scores.
Richman et al. 1982	22 language-delayed 3-year-olds and 22 nonlanguage-delayed control subjects; followed up at 4 and 8 years of age	Reading accuracy; reading comprehension; spelling tests	Language-delayed 3-year-olds had significantly lower reading and spelling scores at follow-up.
Rudel 1980	128 learning-disordered children (74 having dyslexia, 74 having other learning disorders); 120 normal control subjects	Naming task	Group with learning disorders performed significantly more poorly on naming task than did control subjects.
Rudel et al. 1981	41 learning-disordered (dyslexic and other) children, 10 to 14 years of age; 20 control subjects, 10 to 13 years of age	Supplying names for pictures, for definitions, for objects, and for incomplete sentences	Groups with learning disorders were significantly worse than control subjects at all types of naming.
Ruess 1965	49 children with cleft palate, 7 to 12 years of age; normal siblings	Teacher and parent ratings; achievement scores	No significant differences between groups on any measures.

Reference	Subjects studied	Methods	Findings
Semel and Wiig 1975	34 learning-disordered children, 7 to 11 years of age; 17 control subjects	Northwestern Syntax Screening Test	Group with learning disorders was significantly lower on receptive portion of test.
Sheridan and Peckham 1975, 1978	215 speech-defective 7-year-olds, followed up at 11 and 16 years of age	Educational placement records	35% and 30% of the group were in special schools by ages 11 and 16, respectively.
Silva 1986; Silva and Williams 1983; Silva et al. 1984	Epidemiologic study (see Appendixes 1 and 2, this volume): 851 children seen at 3, 5, 7, 9, and 11 years of age	Parent and teacher questionnaires; IQ, language, and achievement tests	Language tests at 3 and 5 years correlated with educational achievement tests at ages 7, 9, and 11.
Snowling 1981	33 dyslexic children, 8 to 17 years of age; 22 nondyslexic subjects (matched reading age)	Repetition task with nonsense words	Dyslexic group had repetition problems suggestive of a phonemic deficit.
Soensken et al. 1981	2 learning-disordered and 2 nondisabled 3rd-graders	Pragmatic analysis of spontaneous language	Learning-disordered children did not switch codes, unlike nondisabled children.
Spekman 1981	12 learning-disordered and 36 nonlearning-disordered 4th- and 5th-graders	Verbal-communication task (relay a block arrangement)	Group with learning disorders was significantly less effective and efficient at communication task.
Vogel 1983	20 learning-disordered and 20 nonlearning-disordered children, 7 and 8 years of age	Grammar comprehension test	Group with learning disorders was delayed in acquisition of morphology.
Whitehouse 1983	42 dyslexic and 42 nondyslexic 4th- to 12th-graders	Token Test (of language comprehension)	Some but not all dyslexic individuals had impaired syntactic processing.
Wiig 1976; Wiig and Semel 1973, 1975, 1980; Wiig et al. 1973, 1982, 1983	Learning-disordered adolescents; age-, grade-, IQ-, and sex-matched control subjects	Various language tests: repetition, production, comprehension, opposites, association, naming, words, morphemes, and sentences	Groups with learning disorders scored significantly worse than nonlearning-disordered groups on all of the language measures.
Williams et al. 1969	100 6th-grade male stutterers; 300 control subjects	Iowa Test of Basic Skills	Stutterers were behind control subjects in all subtests.
Wolpaw et al. 1979	5-year follow-up of 30 language-disordered patients (follow-up average age = 9 years)	School placement	23.3% were in classes for educable mentally retarded at follow-up; another 43.3% had learning problems.

References

Abbie MH, Douglas MH, Ross KE: The clumsy child: observations in cases referred to the gymnasium of the Adelaide Children's Hospital over a three year period. Med J Aust 1:65–68, 1978

Achenbach TM: DSM-III in light of empirical research on the classification of child psychopathology. Journal of the American Academy of Child Psychiatry 19:395–412, 1980

Achenbach TM: Assessment and Taxonomy of Child and Adolescent Psychopathology. New York, Sage Publications, 1986

Achenbach TM, Edelbrock CS: The classification of child psychopathology: a review and analysis of empirical efforts. Psychol Bull 85:1275–1301, 1978

Achenbach TM, Edelbrock CS: Behavioral Problems and Competencies Reported by Parents of Normal and Disturbed Children Aged 4 Through 16. Monographs of the Society for Research in Child Development, Vol 46 (ser no 188), 1981

Achenbach TM, Edelbrock CS: Manual for the Child Behavior Checklist and Revised Child Behavior Profile. Burlington, VT, Department of Psychiatry, University of Vermont, 1983

Achenbach TM, Edelbrock CS: Diagnostic, taxonomic, and assessment issues, in Handbook of Child Psychopathology, 2nd Edition. Edited by Ollendick TH, Hersen M. New York, Plenum, 1989, pp 53–73

Achenbach TM, McConaughy SH: Empirically Based Assessment of Child and Adolescent Psychopathology: Practical Applications. Beverly Hills, CA, Sage Publications, 1987

Achenbach TM, Verhulst FC, Baron GD, et al: Epidemiological comparisons of American and Dutch children, I: behavioral/emotional problems and competencies reported by parents for ages 4 to 16. J Am Acad Child Adolesc Psychiatry 26:317–325, 1987a

Achenbach TM, Verhulst FC, Edelbrock CS, et al: Epidemiological comparisons of American and Dutch children, II: behavioral/emotional problems reported by teachers for ages 6 to 11. J Am Acad Child Adolesc Psychiatry 26:326–332, 1987b

Ackerman PT, Anhalt JM, Dykman RA, et al: Effortful processing deficits in children with reading and/or attention disorders. Brain Cogn 5:22–40, 1986

Ackerson L: Children's Behavior Problems. Chicago, IL, University of Chicago Press, 1931

Adler S: Developmental patterns as a function of ethnicity. J Commun Disord 6:184–192, 1973

Affolter F, Brubaker R, Bischofberger W: Comparative studies of normal and language disturbed children based on performance profiles. Äcta Otolaryngol (Stockh) 323 (suppl):1–32, 1974

Agras WS, Sylvester D, Oliveau D: The epidemiology of common fears and phobias. Compr Psychiatry 10:151–156, 1969

Agrawal R, Kaushal K: Attention and short-term memory in normal children, aggressive children, and non-aggressive children with attention-deficit disorder. J Gen Psychol 114:335–344, 1987

Aimard P, Bringuier N, Cotte MF, et al: Les troubles de l'expression verbale comme signal d'alarme chez l'enfant de moins de 5 ans. Revue de Neuropsychiatrie Infantile et d'Hygiene Mentale de l'Enfance 21:611–640, 1973

Alberman E: The early prediction of learning disorders. Dev Med Child Neurol 15:202–204, 1973

Alessi NE, Loomis S: The frequency and severity of language disturbances in depressed children. Paper presented at the 35th annual meeting of the American Academy of Child and Adolescent Psychiatry, Seattle, WA, October 1988

Alessi NE, Eisner SJ, Knight C: The association of language disturbances with cognitive and motoric impairments in psychiatrically hospitalized children. Poster session presented at the meeting of the Society for Research in Child and Adolescent Psychopathology, Costa Mesa, CA, January 1990

Algozzine B, Ysseldyke JE, Shinn M: Identifying children with learning disabilities: when is a discrepancy severe? Journal of School Psychology 20:299–305, 1982

Alin-Akerman B: The expectation and parentage of twins: a study on the language development of twin infants. Acta Genet Med Gemellol (Roma) 36:223–232, 1987

Allen DV, Robinson DO: Middle ear status and language development in preschool children. ASHA 26:33–37, 1984

Allen R, Wasserman GA: Origins of language delay in abused infants. Child Abuse Negl 9:335–340, 1985

Aman MG: Hyperactivity: nature of the syndrome and its natural history. J Autism Dev Disord 14:39–56, 1984

American Psychiatric Association: Diagnostic and Statistical Manual of Mental Disorders. Washington, DC, American Psychiatric Association, 1952

American Psychiatric Association: Diagnostic and Statistical Manual of Mental Disorders, 2nd Edition. Washington, DC, American Psychiatric Association, 1968

American Psychiatric Association: Diagnostic and Statistical Manual of Mental Disorders, 3rd Edition. Washington, DC, American Psychiatric Association, 1980

American Psychiatric Association: Diagnostic and Statistical Manual of Mental Disorders, 3rd Edition, Revised. Washington, DC, American Psychiatric Association, 1987

Amorosa H, vonBenda U, Dames M, et al: Deficits in fine motor coordination in children with unintelligible speech. Eur Arch Psychiatry Neurol Sci 236:26–30, 1986

Anders QA: Study of the personal and social adjustment of children with functional articulatory defects. Unpublished master's thesis, University of Wisconsin, Madison, 1945

Anderson JC, Williams S, McGee R, et al: DSM-III disorders in preadolescent children. Arch Gen Psychiatry 44:69–76, 1987

Anderson PL: A preliminary study of syntax in the written expression of learning disabled children. Journal of Learning Disabilities 15:359–362, 1982

Andolina C: Syntactic maturity and vocabulary richness of learning disabled children at four age levels. Journal of Learning Disabilities 13:372–377, 1980

Angold A, Weissman MM, John K, et al: Parent and child reports of depressive symptoms in children at low and high risk of depression. J Child Psychol Psychiatry 28:901–915, 1987

Aram DM, Nation JE: Patterns of language behavior in children with developmental language disorder. J Speech Hear Res 18:229–241, 1975

Aram DM, Nation JE: Preschool language disorders and subsequent language and academic difficulties. J Commun Disord 13:159–170, 1980

Aram DM, Nation JE: Child Language Disorders. St. Louis, MO, CV Mosby, 1982

Aram DM, Ekelman B, Nation JE: Preschoolers with language disorders: 10 years later. J Speech Hear Res 27:232–244, 1984

Arbib MA, Caplan D, Marshall JC (eds): Neural Models of Language Processing. New York, Academic, 1982

Arieti S, Bemporad J: Severe and Mild Depression. New York, Basic Books, 1978

August GJ: Production deficiencies in free recall: a comparison of hyperactive, learning-disabled, and normal children. J Abnorm Child Psychol 15:429–440, 1987

Ayres AJ: Types of sensory integrative dysfunction among disabled learners. Am J Occup Ther 26:13–18, 1972

Ayukawa H, Rudmin F: Does early middle ear pathology affect auditory perception skills and learning? Comment on Brandes and Ehinger (1981). J Speech Hear Disord 48:222–223, 1983

Baker HJ, Leland B: Detroit Tests of Learning Aptitude (DTLA). Indianapolis, IN, Bobbs-Merrill, 1967

Baker L: Speech/language assessment of mentally retarded preschoolers. Seminars in Speech and Language 9:73–80, 1988

Baker L, Cantwell DP: Language acquisition, cognitive development and emotional disorder in childhood, in Children's Language, Vol 3. Edited by Nelson KE. Hillsdale, NJ, Erlbaum, 1982, pp 286–321

Baker L, Cantwell DP: Primary prevention of the psychiatric consequences of childhood communication disorders. Journal of Preventive Psychiatry 2:75–97, 1984

Baker L, Cantwell DP: Developmental articulation disorder, in Comprehensive Textbook of Psychiatry IV. Edited by Kaplan HI, Sadock BJ. Baltimore, MD, Williams & Wilkins, 1985a, pp 1705–1708

Baker L, Cantwell DP: Developmental language disorder, in Comprehensive Textbook of Psychiatry IV. Edited by Kaplan HI, Sadock BJ. Baltimore, MD, Williams & Wilkins, 1985b, pp 1700–1704

Baker L, Cantwell DP: A prospective psychiatric follow-up of children with speech/language disorders. J Am Acad Child Adolesc Psychiatry 26:546–553, 1987

Baker L, Cantwell DP: Association between emotional/behavioral disorders and learning disorders in a sample of speech/language impaired children. Advances in Learning and Behavioral Disorders 6:27–46, 1990

Baltaxe CAM, Simmons JQ: Language in childhood psychosis: a review. J Speech Hear Disord 40:439–458, 1975

Baltaxe CAM, Simmons JQ: Communication deficits in preschool children with psychiatric disorders. Seminars in Speech and Language 9:81–90, 1988

Barkley RA: Hyperactive Children: A Handbook for Diagnosis and Treatment. New York, Guilford, 1981

Barkley RA: The social interactions of hyperactive children: developmental changes, drug effects, and situational variation, in Childhood Disorders: Behavioral-Developmental Approaches. Edited by MacMahon F, Peters R. New York, Brunner/Mazel, 1985, pp 218–243

Barkley RA, Cunningham CE: The parent-child interactions of hyperactive children and their modification by stimulant drugs, in Treatment of Hyperactive and Learning Disordered Children. Edited by Knights R, Bakker D. Baltimore, MD, University Park Press, 1980, pp 219–236

Barkley RA, Ullman D: A comparison of objective measures of activity level and distractibility in hyperactive and nonhyperactive children. J Abnorm Child Psychol 3:231–244, 1975

Barkley RA, Cunningham CE, Karlsson J: The speech of hyperactive children and their mothers: comparisons with normal children and stimulant drug effects. Journal of Learning Disabilities 16:105–110, 1983

Barnes SB, Gutfreund M, Satterly DJ, et al: Characteristics of adult speech which predict children's language development. Journal of Child Language 10:65–84, 1983

Barrett CM, Hoops HR: The relationship between self-concept and the remission of articulatory errors. Language, Speech, and Hearing Services in Schools 2:67–70, 1974–1975

Bartak L, Rutter M: Language and cognition in autistic and "dysphasic" children, in Language, Cognitive Deficit and Retardation. Edited by O'Connor N. London, Butterworths, 1975, pp 193–202

Bartak L, Rutter M, Cox A: Comparative study of infantile autism and specific developmental receptive language disorder, I: the children. Br J Psychiatry 7:127–145, 1975

Bartolucci G, Albers R: Deictic categories in the language of autistic children. Journal of Autism and Childhood Schizophrenia 14:131–141, 1974

Bates E, Benigni L, Bretherton I, et al: Cognition and Communication in Infancy. New York, Academic, 1979

Battle E, Lacey BA: Context for hyperactivity in children over time. Child Dev 43:757–772, 1972

Baumgartner S: The social behavior of speech disordered children as viewed by parents. Int J Rehabil Res 3:82–84, 1980

Beardslee WR, Bemporad J, Keller MB, et al: Children of parents with major affective disorder: a review. Am J Psychiatry 140:825–832, 1983

Beck AT, Emery G: Anxiety Disorders and Phobias: A Cognitive Perspective. New York, Basic Books, 1985

Beckey R: A study of certain factors related to retardation of speech. Journal of Speech Disorders 7:223–249, 1942

Bee HL, Barnard KE, Eyres SJ, et al: Prediction of IQ and language skill from perinatal status, child performance, family characteristics, and mother-infant interaction. Child Dev 53:1134–1156, 1982

Beitchman JH: Speech and language impairment and psychiatric risk: toward a model of neurodevelopmental immaturity. Psychiatr Clin North Am 8:721–735, 1985

Beitchman JH, Patel PG, Ferguson B, et al: A survey of speech and language disorders among five-year-old kindergarten children. Unpublished manuscript, University of Ottawa, Montreal, 1983

Beitchman JH, Nair R, Clegg M, et al: Prevalence of psychiatric disorders in children with speech and language disorders. Journal of the American Academy of Child Psychiatry 25:528–535, 1986a

Beitchman JH, Nair R, Clegg M, et al: Prevalence of speech and language disorders in 5-year-old kindergarten children in the Ottawa-Carleton region. J Speech Hear Disord 51:98–110, 1986b

Beitchman JH, Tuckett M, Batth S: Language delay and hyperactivity in preschoolers: evidence for a distinct subgroup of hyperactives. Can J Psychiatry 32:683–687, 1987

Beitchman JH, Peterson M, Clegg M: Speech and language impairment and psychiatric disorder: the relevance of family demographic variables. Child Psychiatry Hum Dev 18:191–207, 1988

Beitchman JH, Hood J, Rochon J, et al: Empirical classification of speech/language impairment in children, I: identification of speech/language categories. J Am Acad Child Adolesc Psychiatry 28:112–117, 1989a

Beitchman JH, Hood J, Rochon J, et al: Empirical classification of speech/language impairment in children, II: behavioral characteristics. J Am Acad Child Adolesc Psychiatry 28:118–123, 1989b

Belenchia TA, Crowe TA: Prevalence of speech and hearing disorders in a state penitentiary population. J Commun Disord 16:279–285, 1983

Bellman M: Studies on encopresis. Acta Paediatr Scand [Suppl] 170:1–150, 1966

Bemporad JR, Pfeifer CM, Gibbs L, et al: Characteristics of encopretic patients and their families. Journal of the American Academy of Child Psychiatry 10:272–292, 1971

Bench J: Auditory deprivation—an intrinsic or extrinsic problem? Some comments on Kyle (1978). Br J Audiol 13:51–52, 1979

Bendel J, Palti H, Winter S, et al: Prevalence of disabilities in a national sample of 3-year-old Israeli children. Isr J Med Sci 25:264–270, 1989

Bennett CW, Runyan CM: Educator's perceptions of the effects of communication disorders upon educational performance. Language, Speech, and Hearing Services in Schools 13:260–263, 1982

Bennett FC, Ruska SH, Sherman R: Middle ear function in learning disabled children. Pediatrics 66:254–260, 1980

Berger M, Yule W, Rutter M: Attainment and adjustment in two geographical areas, II: the prevalence of specific reading retardation. Br J Psychiatry 126:510–519, 1975

Bernthal JE, Bankson NW: Articulation and Phonological Disorders, 2nd Edition. Englewood Cliffs, NJ, Prentice-Hall, 1988

Berry CA, Shaywitz SE, Shaywitz BA: Girls with attention deficit disorder: a silent minority? A report on behavioral and cognitive characteristics. Pediatrics 76:801–809, 1985

Bettes BA, Walker E: Symptoms associated with suicidal behavior in childhood and adolescence. J Abnorm Child Psychol 14:591–604, 1986

Bingham G: Self-esteem among boys with and without specific learning disabilities. Child Study Journal 10:41–47, 1980

Bishop DVM: Using non-preferred hand skill to investigate pathological left-handedness in an unselected population. Dev Med Child Neurol 26:214–226, 1984

Bishop DVM: The causes of specific developmental language disorders. J Child Psychol Psychiatry 28:1–8, 1987

Bishop DVM, Edmundson A: Is otitis media a major cause of specific developmental language disorders? Br J Disord Commun 21:321–338, 1986

Bishop DVM, Edmundson A: Language impaired 4-year-olds: distinguishing transient from persistent impairment. J Speech Hear Disord 52:156–173, 1987a

Bishop DVM, Edmundson A: Specific language impairment as a maturational lag: evidence from longitudinal data on language and motor development. Dev Med Child Neurol 29:442–459, 1987b

Blager F, Martin HP: Speech and language of abused children, in The Abused Child. Edited by Martin HP, Kempe CH. Cambridge, MA, Ballinger, 1976, pp 83–92

Blalock J: Persistent auditory language deficits in adults with learning disabilities. Journal of Learning Disabilities 15:604–609, 1982

Blank M, Rose SA, Berlin LJ: Preschool Language Assessment Instrument: The Language of Learning in Practice. New York, Grune & Stratton, 1978

Blanton S: A survey of speech defects. Journal of Educational Psychology 7:581–592, 1916

Bleuler M: The Schizophrenic Disorders: Long-Term Patient and Family Studies. New Haven, CT, Yale University Press, 1978

Blood GW, Seiden R: The concomitant problems of young stutterers. J Speech Hear Disord 46:31–33, 1981

Bloom L, Lahey M: Language Development and Language Disorders. New York, John Wiley, 1978

Bloomfield L: Language. New York, Holt, Rinehart & Winston, 1933

Boersma F, Chapman J: Academic self-concept, achievement expectations, and locus of control in elementary learning disabled children. Canadian Journal of Behavioural Science 13:349–358, 1981

Borland BL, Heckman HK: Hyperactive boys and their brothers: a 25-year follow-up study. Arch Gen Psychiatry 33:669–675, 1976

Boucher J: Articulation in early childhood autism. Journal of Autism and Childhood Schizophrenia 6:297–302, 1976

Bradley L: Reading, spelling and writing problems: research on backward readers, in Helping Clumsy Children. Edited by Gordon N, McKinlay I. New York, Churchill Livingstone, 1980, pp 135–154

Bradley S, Sloman L: Elective mutism in immigrant families. Journal of the American Academy of Child Psychiatry 14:510–514, 1975

Brady WA, Hall DE: The prevalence of stuttering among school-age children. Language, Speech, and Hearing Services in Schools 7:75–81, 1976

Brandes P, Ehinger D: The effects of early middle ear pathology on auditory perception and academic achievement. J Speech Hear Disord 46:301–307, 1981

Brent DA: Correlates of the medical lethality of suicide attempts in children and adolescents. J Am Acad Child Adolesc Psychiatry 26:87–89, 1987

Bresnan J: The Mental Representation of Grammatical Relations. Cambridge, MA, MIT Press, 1983

Brickman AS, McManus M, Grapentine WL, et al: Neuropsychological assessment of seriously delinquent adolescents. Journal of the American Academy of Child Psychiatry 23:453–457, 1984

Broad RD, Bar A: Personality correlates of communication disorders as revealed by projective assessment and verbal expression. Folia Phoniatr (Basel) 25:405–415, 1973

Broman S, Brien E, Shaughnessy P: Low Achieving Children: The First Seven Years. Hillsdale, NJ, Erlbaum, 1985

Brookhouser PE, Hixson PK, Matkin ND: Early childhood language delay: the otolaryngologist's perspective. Laryngoscope 89:1898–1913, 1979

Brown GW, Harris TO, Peto J: Life events and psychiatric disorders, Part 2: nature of causal link. Psychol Med 3:159–176, 1973

Brown JB, Lloyd H: A controlled study of children not speaking in school. Journal of the Association of Workers for Maladjusted Children 18:49–54, 1975

Brown JB, Redmond A, Bass K, et al: Symbolic play in normal and language-impaired children. Paper presented at the convention of the American Speech and Hearing Association, Las Vegas, NV, November 1975

Brown R: A First Language: The Early Stages. Cambridge, MA, Harvard University Press, 1973

Brown RT, Borden KA, Schleser R, et al: The performance of attention-deficit disordered and normal children on conservation tasks. J Genet Psychol 146:535–540, 1985

Bruck M: Social and emotional adjustments of learning disabled children: a review of the issues, in Handbook of Cognitive, Social and Neuropsychological Aspects of Learning Disabilities, Vol 1. Edited by Ceci S. Hillsdale, NJ, Erlbaum, 1986, pp 361–380

Bruininks VL: Peer status and personality characteristics of learning disabled and non-disabled students. Journal of Learning Disabilities 11:484–494, 1978

Brumback RA, Staton RD: Learning disability and childhood depression. Am J Orthopsychiatry 53:269–281, 1983

Bruner JS: Beyond the Information Given: Studies in the Psychology of Knowing. New York, WW Norton, 1973

Bruner JS, Roy C, Ratner N: The beginnings of request, in Children's Language, Vol 3. Edited by Nelson KE. Hillsdale, NJ, Erlbaum, 1982, pp 91–138

Bryan JH, Bryan TH: The social life of the LD youngster, in Current Topics in Learning Disabilities. Edited by McKinney JD, Feagans L. Norwood, NJ, Ablex, 1983, pp 57–86

Bryan TH: Learning disabled children's comprehension of non-verbal communication. Journal of Learning Disabilities 10:501–506, 1977

Bryan TH: Social relationships and verbal interactions of learning disabled children. Journal of Learning Disabilities 7:107–115, 1978

Bubenickova M: The stuttering child's relation to school. Psychologia a Patopsychologia Dietata 12:535–545, 1977

Butler KG: The Bender Gestalt Visual Motor Test as a diagnostic instrument with children exhibiting articulation disorders. ASHA 7:380–381, 1965

Butler NR, Peckman C, Sheridan MD: Speech defects in children aged 7 years: a national study. Br Med J 1:253–257, 1973

Butler RJ: Nocturnal Enuresis: Psychological Perspectives. Bristol, UK, John Wright, 1987

Byrne BM: Deficient syntactic control in poor readers: is a weak phonetic memory code responsible? Applied Psycholinguistics 2:201–212, 1981

Byrne BM, Willerman L, Ashmore LL: Severe and moderate language impairment: evidence for distinctive etiologies. Behav Genet 44:331–345, 1974

Bzoch KR, League RL: Receptive-Expressive-Emergent Language Scale for the Measurement of Language Skills in Infancy. Baltimore, MD, University Park Press, 1971

Caceres VA: Retardo del lenguaje verbal. Revista de Neuropsiquiatria 34:210–226, 1971

Callaghan S: Symbolic play abilities of normal and language disordered 4- to 6-year-olds. Paper presented at the eighth annual Boston University Conference on Language Development, Boston, MA, October 1983

Calnan M, Richardson K: Speech problems in a national survey: assessment and prevalences. Child Care Health Dev 2:181–202, 1976

Cambourne BL, Rousch PD: How do learning disabled children read? Topics in Learning and Learning Disabilities 1:59–68, 1982

Camp BW: Verbal mediation in young aggressive boys. J Abnorm Psychol 86:145–153, 1977

Campbell SB: Mother-child interaction in reflective, impulsive and hyperactive children. Developmental Psychology 8:341–349, 1973

Campbell SB: Developmental issues in childhood anxiety, in Anxiety Disorders of Childhood. Edited by Gittelman R. New York, Guilford, 1986, pp 24–57

Campbell SB, Douglas VI, Morgenstern G: Cognitive styles in hyperactive children and the effect of methylphenidate. J Child Psychol Psychiatry 12:55–67, 1971

Campbell SB, Breaux AM, Ewing LJ, et al: Correlates and predictors of hyperactivity and aggression: a longitudinal study of parent-referred problem preschoolers. J Abnorm Child Psychol 14:217–234, 1986

Cantwell DP: The Hyperactive Child: Diagnosis, Management, Current Research. New York, Spectrum Publications, 1975

Cantwell DP: Hyperactivity and social behavior. Journal of the American Academy of Child Psychiatry 1:252–262, 1978

Cantwell DP: Implications of research in child psychiatry, in Basic Handbook of Child Psychiatry, Vol 4. Edited by Noshpitz JD, Berlin IN, Stone LA. New York, Basic Books, 1979, pp 458–465

Cantwell DP: The diagnostic process and diagnostic classification in child psychiatry—DSM-III. Journal of the American Academy of Child Psychiatry 19:345–355, 1980

Cantwell DP: Family genetic factors, in Affective Disorders in Childhood and Adolescence. Edited by Cantwell DP, Carlson GA. New York, Spectrum Publications, 1983, pp 249–264

Cantwell DP: Childhood disorders, in An Annotated Bibliography of DSM-III. Edited by Skodol AE, Spitzer RL. Washington, DC, American Psychiatric Press, 1987a, pp 59–68

Cantwell DP: Clinical child psychopathology: diagnostic assessment, diagnostic process, and diagnostic classification—DSM-III studies, in Assessment and Diagnoses in Child Psychopathology. Edited by Rutter M, Tuma AH, Lann IS. New York, Guilford, 1987b, pp 3–36

Cantwell DP: Conduct disorder, in Comprehensive Textbook of Psychiatry V, Vol 2. Edited by Kaplan HI, Sadock BJ. Baltimore, MD, Williams & Wilkins, 1989, pp 1821–1828

Cantwell DP, Baker L: Psychiatric disorder in children with speech and language retardation: a critical review. Arch Gen Psychiatry 34:583–591, 1977

Cantwell DP, Baker L: Psychiatric and behavioral characteristics of children with communication disorders. J Pediatr Psychol 5:161–178, 1980

Cantwell DP, Baker L: Parental mental illness and psychiatric disorders in "at-risk" children. J Clin Psychiatry 45:503–507, 1984

Cantwell DP, Baker L: Interrelationship of communication, learning, and psychiatric disorders in children, in Communication Skills and Classroom Success. Edited by Simon C. San Diego, CA, College-Hill Press, 1985, pp 43–61

Cantwell DP, Baker L: Clinical significance of childhood communication disorders: perspectives from a longitudinal study. J Child Neurol 2:257–264, 1987a

Cantwell DP, Baker L: Developmental Speech and Language Disorders. New York, Guilford, 1987b

Cantwell DP, Baker L: Prevalence and type of psychiatric disorder and developmental disorders in three speech and language groups. J Commun Disord 20:151–160, 1987c

Cantwell DP, Baker L: Issues in the classification of child and adolescent psychopathology. J Am Acad Child Adolesc Psychiatry 27:521–533, 1988

Cantwell DP, Baker L: Association between attention-deficit hyperactivity disorder and learning disorders. Journal of Learning Disabilities (in press)

Cantwell DP, Satterfield JH: The prevalence of academic underachievement in hyperactive children. Pediatric Psychology, Special Issue 4, 1978, pp 168–171

Cantwell DP, Baker L, Rutter M: A comparative study of infantile autism and specific developmental receptive language disorder, IV: an analysis of syntax and language functioning. J Child Psychol Psychiatry 19:351–362, 1978

Carey G: Big genes, little genes, affective disorder, and anxiety. Arch Gen Psychiatry 44:486–491, 1987

Carhart R: A survey of speech defect in Illinois high schools. J Speech Hear Disord 4:61–70, 1939

Carlson CL: Attention deficit disorder without hyperactivity, in Advances in Clinical Child Psychology, Vol 9. Edited by Lahey BB, Kazdin AE. New York, Plenum, 1986, pp 153–175

Carlson CL, Lahey BB, Neeper R: Direct assessment of the cognitive correlates of attention deficit disorders with and without hyperactivity. Journal of Psychopathology and Behavioral Assessment 8:69–86, 1986

Carlson CL, Lahey BB, Frame CL, et al: Sociometric status of clinic-referred children with attention deficit disorders with and without hyperactivity. J Abnorm Child Psychol 15:537–547, 1987

Carlson GA, Cantwell DP: A survey of depressive symptoms, syndrome, and disorder in a child psychiatric population. J Child Psychol Psychiatry 21:19–25, 1980

Carlson GA, Garber J: Developmental issues and the classification of depression in children, in Depression in Young People. Edited by Rutter M, Izard C, Read P. New York, Guilford, 1986, pp 399–434

Carlson GA, Strober M: Affective disorders in adolescence. Psychiatr Clin North Am 2:511–526, 1979

Carrow E: Carrow Elicited Language Inventory. New York, Teaching Resources Corporation, 1974

Carrow E: Test of Auditory Comprehension of Language (1973). Austin, TX, Learning Concepts, 1978

Carrow-Woolfolk E, Lynch J: An Integrative Approach to Language Disorders in Children. New York, Grune & Stratton, 1982

Casby M, Ruder K: Symbolic play and early language development in normal and mentally retarded children. J Speech Hear Res 26:404–411, 1983

Ceci S: Extracting meaning from stimuli: automatic and purposive processing of the language-based learning disabled. Topics in Learning and Learning Disabilities 2:46–53, 1982

Cermak SA, Ward EA, Ward LM: The relationship between articulation disorders and motor coordination in children. Am J Occup Ther 40:546–550, 1986

Chamberlain R, Chamberlain G, Howlett B, et al: British Births, 1970, Vol 1: The First Week of Life. London, Heinemann, 1975

Charles L, Schain RJ: A 4-year follow-up study of the effects of methylphenidate on the behavior and academic achievement of hyperactive children. J Abnorm Child Psychol 9:495–505, 1981

Chase R: Neurological aspects of language disorders in children, in Principles of Childhood Language Disabilities. Edited by Irwin JV, Marge M. Englewood Cliffs, NJ, Prentice-Hall, 1972, pp 96–136

Chawla PL, Sahasi G, Sundaram KR, et al: A study of prevalence and pattern of hyperactive syndrome in primary school children. Indian Journal of Psychiatry 23:313–323, 1981

Chazan M, Laing AF, Bailey MS, et al: Some of Our Children: The Early Education of Children With Special Educational Needs. London, Open Books, 1980

Chess S: Developmental language disability as a factor in personality distortion in childhood. Am J Orthopsychiatry 14:483–490, 1944

Chess S, Rosenberg M: Clinical differentiation among children with initial language complaints. Journal of Autism and Childhood Schizophrenia 4:99–109, 1974

Chess S, Thomas A: Differences in outcome with early intervention in children with behavior disorders, in Life History Research in Psychopathology, Vol 2. Edited by Roff M, Robins LN, Pollack M. Minneapolis, University of Minnesota Press, 1972, pp 35–46

Chess S, Thomas A, Birch HG: Behavior problems revisited: findings of an anterospective study. Journal of the American Academy of Child Psychiatry 6:321–331, 1967

Chiat S, Hirson A: From conceptual intention to utterance: a study of impaired language output in a child with developmental dysphasia. Br J Disord Commun 22:37–64, 1987

Chomsky N: Recent contributions to the theory of innate ideas. Synthese 17:2–11, 1967

Chomsky N: Language and Mind. New York, Harcourt, Brace & World, 1968

Chomsky N: Rules and Representations. New York, Columbia University Press, 1980

Cicchetti D, Aber JL: Early precursors of later depression: an organizational perspective, in Advances in Infancy Research, Vol 4. Edited by Lipsitt LP, Rovee-Collier C. Norwood, NJ, Ablex, 1986, pp 87–131

Cicchetti D, Beeghly M: Symbolic development in maltreated youngsters: an organizational perspective, in Atypical Symbolic Development. Edited by Cicchetti D, Beeghly M. San Francisco, CA, Jossey-Bass, 1987, pp 47–68

Clark MM: Reading Difficulties in Schools. Harmondsworth, UK, Penguin, 1970

Clifford E: The impact of symptom: a preliminary comparison of cleft lip and palate and asthmatic children. Cleft Palate J 6:221–227, 1969

Cloninger CR, Christiansen KO, Reich T, et al: Implications of sex differences in the prevalences of antisocial personality, alcoholism, and criminality for familial transmission. Arch Gen Psychiatry 35:941–951, 1978

Cohen NJ, Weiss G, Minde K: Cognitive styles in adolescents previously diagnosed hyperactive. J Child Psychology Psychiatry 13:203–209, 1972

Cohen NJ, Davine M, Meloche-Kelly M: Psychiatrically disturbed children with unsuspected language disorders: background and language characteristics. Paper presented at the 35th annual meeting of the American Academy of Child and Adolescent Psychiatry, Seattle, WA, October 1988

Cohen NJ, Davine M, Meloche-Kelly M: Prevalence of unsuspected language disorders in a child psychiatric population. J Am Acad Child Adolesc Psychiatry 28:107–111, 1989

Cohen NJ, McDonald J, Horodezky N, et al: Patterns of psychopathology in disturbed children with unsuspected language disorders. Poster session presented at the meeting of the Society for Research in Child and Adolescent Psychopathology, Costa Mesa, CA, January 1990

Cohen P, Velez CN, Garcia M: The epidemiology of childhood depression. Paper presented at the annual meeting of the American Academy of Child Psychiatry, San Antonio, TX, October 1985

Coleman J, Wolkind S, Ashley L: Symptoms of behavioral disturbance and adjustment to school. J Child Psychol Psychiatry 18:201–209, 1977

Coltheart M: Functional architecture of the language-processing system, in The Cognitive Neuropsychology of Language. Edited by Coltheart M, Sartori G, Job R. Hillsdale, NJ, Erlbaum, 1987, pp 1–25

Coltheart M, Sartori G, Job R (eds): The Cognitive Neuropsychology of Language. Hillsdale, NJ, Erlbaum, 1987

Compas BE: Stress and life events during childhood and adolescence. Clinical Psychology Review 7:275–302, 1987

Connell P, Myles-Zitzer C: An analysis of elicited imitation as a language evaluation procedure. J Speech Hear Disord 47:390–396, 1982

Conners CK: A teacher rating scale for use in drug studies with children. Am J Psychiatry 126:884–888, 1969

Conners CK: Symptom patterns in hyperkinetic, neurotic, and normal children. Child Dev 41:667–682, 1970

Conti-Ramsden G: Mothers in dialogue with language-impaired children. Topics in Language Disorders 5:58–68, 1985

Copeland AP: Types of private speech produced by hyperactive and nonhyperactive boys. J Abnorm Child Psychol 7:169–177, 1979

Costello AJ, Edelbrock CS, Dulcan M, et al: Diagnostic Interview Schedule for Children (DISC). Pittsburgh, PA, Western Psychiatric Institute, 1984

Cotugno AJ: Cognitive control functioning in hyperactive and nonhyperactive learning disabled children. Journal of Learning Disabilities 20:563–567, 1987

Cox AD, Rutter M: Diagnostic appraisal and interviewing, in Child and Adolescent Psychiatry: Modern Approaches, 2nd Edition. Edited by Rutter M, Hersov L. Oxford, UK, Blackwell Scientific Publications, 1985, pp 233–248

Cox AD, Rutter M, Yule B, et al: Bias resulting from missing information: some epidemiological findings. British Journal of Preventive and Social Medicine 31:131–136, 1977

Cox AD, Puckering C, Pound A, et al: The impact of maternal depression in young children. J Child Psychol Psychiatry 28:917–928, 1987

Cozard R, Rousey CL: Hearing and speech among delinquent children. Journal of Corrective Psychiatry and Social Therapy 12:250–257, 1968

Crookes T, Greene M: Some characteristics of children with two types of speech disorder. Br J Educ Psychol 33:31–40, 1963

Crowther JH, Bond LA, Rolf JE: The incidence, prevalence, and severity of behavior disorders among preschool-aged children in day care. J Abnorm Child Psychol 9:23–42, 1981

Cullen KJ, Boundy CAP: The prevalence of behavior disorders in the children of 1,000 western Australian families. Med J Aust 2:805–808, 1966

Cullinan D, Schultz RM, Epstein MH, et al: Behavior problems of handicapped adolescent female students. Journal of Youth and Adolescence 13:57–65, 1984

Cytryn L, McKnew D, Bunney WE: Diagnosis of depression in children: a reassessment. Am J Psychiatry 137:22–25, 1980

Dadds MR: Families and the origins of child behavior problems. Family Process 26:341–357, 1987

Daniels D, Moos RH, Billings AG, et al: Psychosocial risk and resistance factors among children with chronic illness, healthy siblings, and healthy controls. J Abnorm Child Psychol 15:295–308, 1987

Davie CE, Hutt SJ, Vincent E, et al: The Young Child at Home. Windsor, Ontario, NFER-Nelson, 1984

Davie R, Butler N, Goldstein H: From Birth to Seven. London, Longman, 1972

de Ajuriaguerra J, Jaeggi A, Guignard F, et al: The development and prognosis of dysphasia in children, in Normal and Deficient Child Language. Edited by Morehead D, Morehead A. Baltimore, MD, University Park Press, 1976, pp 345–385

Dean RS, Kundert DK: The effects of abstractness in mediation with learning problem children. Journal of Clinical Child Psychology 10:173–176, 1981

DeFries JC, Plomin R: Adoption designs for the study of complex behavioral characters, in Genetic Aspects of Speech and Language Disorders. Edited by Ludlow CL, Cooper JA. New York, Academic, 1983, pp 121–138

de Hirsch K, Jansky JJ, Langford WS: The oral language performance of premature children and controls. J Speech Hear Disord 29:60–69, 1964

Deluty RH: Consistency of assertive, aggressive, and submissive behavior for children. J Pers Soc Psychol 49:1054–1065, 1985

Demb HB: A language disturbance as a possible indicator of serious mental illness in young school-age children. Int J Pediatr Otorhinolaryngol 2:329–335, 1980

Denckla MB: Revised Physical and Neurological Examination for Subtle Signs. Psychopharmacol Bull 21:773–779, 1985

Denckla MB, Rudel RG: Anomalies of motor development in hyperactive boys. Ann Neurol 3:231–233, 1978

Denckla MB, Rudel RG, Broman M: Tests that discriminate between dyslexic and other learning-disabled boys. Brain Lang 13:118–129, 1981

DeQuiros J: Diagnosis of developmental language disorders. Folia Phoniatr (Basel) 26:13–32, 1974

Deshler DD, Schumaker JB: Social skills of learning disabled adolescents: characteristics and interventions. Topics in Learning and Learning Disabilities 3:15–23, 1983

Despert JL: Psychosomatic study of 50 stuttering children. Am J Orthopsychiatry 16:100–113, 1946

Deutsch F: Observational and sociometric measures of peer popularity and their relationship to egocentric communication in female preschoolers. Developmental Psychology 10:745–747, 1974

de Zwart HS: Language acquisition and cognitive development, in Cognitive Development and the Acquisition of Language. Edited by Moore TE. New York, Academic, 1973, pp 9–25

Dickson S: Incipient stuttering and spontaneous remission of stuttering speech. J Commun Disord 4:99–110, 1971

Dickstein EB, Warren DR: Role-taking deficits in LD children. Journal of Learning Disabilities 13:378–382, 1980

DiSimoni F: The Token Test for Children. Boston, MA, Teaching Resources Corporation, 1978

DiSimoni FG, Mucha R: Language comprehension of pre-school children reared in one-parent families: a preliminary report. J Aud Res 23:9–12, 1983

Donahue M: Requesting strategies of learning disabled children. Applied Psycholinguistics 2:213–234, 1981

Donahue M: Learning-disabled children as conversational partners. Topics in Language Disorders 4(1):15–27, 1983

Donahue M, Bryan TH: Conversational skills and modeling in learning disabled boys. Applied Psycholinguistics 4:251–278, 1983

Donahue M, Bryan TH: Communicative skills and peer relations of learning disabled adolescents. Topics in Language Disorders 4(2):10–21, 1984

Donahue M, Pearl R, Bryan TH: Learning disabled children's conversational competence: responses to inadequate messages. Applied Psycholinguistics 1:387–403, 1980

Donahue M, Pearl R, Bryan TH: Learning disabled children's syntactic proficiency on a communicative task. J Speech Hear Disord 47:397–403, 1982

Douglas JWB, Ross JM, Simpson HR: All Our Future. London, Peter Davies, 1968

Douglas VI: Research on hyperactivity: stage two. J Abnorm Child Psychol 4:307–308, 1976

Drillien C, Drummond M: Developmental screening and the child with special needs. Clinics in Developmental Medicine 86:1–284, 1983

Drumwright AF: The Denver Articulation Screening Exam. Denver, CO, University of Colorado Medical Center, 1971

DuBose RF, Langley MB: Developmental Activities Screening Inventory. New York, Teaching Resources Corporation, 1977

Dudek SZ, Strobel M, Thomas AD: Chronic learning problems and maturation. Percept Mot Skills 64:407–429, 1987

Dukes P: Developing social prerequisites to oral communication. Topics in Learning and Learning Disabilities 1:47–58, 1981

Duncan MH: Personality adjustment techniques in voice therapy. Journal of Speech Disorders 12:161–167, 1947

Dunn LM: Peabody Picture Vocabulary Test. Circle Pines, MN, American Guidance Service, 1965

Durkin K: Language and social cognition during the school years, in Language Development in the School Years. Edited by Durkin K. London, Croom Helm, 1986, pp 203–233

Dwyer JT, Delong GR: A family history study of twenty probands with childhood manic-depressive illness. J Am Acad Child Adolesc Psychiatry 26:176-180, 1987

Earls F: Prevalence of behavior problems in 3-year-old children. Arch Gen Psychiatry 37:1153–1157, 1980

Earls F: Sex differences in psychiatric disorders: origins and developmental influences. Psychiatr Dev 5:1–23, 1987

Edelbrock CS, Costello AJ, Dulcan MK, et al: Parent-child agreement on child psychiatric symptoms assessed via structured interview. J Child Psychol Psychiatry 27:181–190, 1986

Eimas PD, Kavanagh JF: Otitis media, hearing loss, and child development: a NICHD conference summary. Public Health Rep 101:289–293, 1986

Eisenson J: Aphasia in Children. New York, Harper & Row, 1972

Elliott L: Epidemiology of hearing impairment and other communicative disorders. Adv Neurol 19:399–420, 1978

Eme RF: Sex differences in childhood psychopathology: a review. Psychol Bull 86:574–595, 1979

Endicott J, Spitzer RL: A diagnostic review. Arch Gen Psychiatry 35:837–844, 1978

English RH: Cleft palate children compared with non-cleft palate children: a personality study. Unpublished doctoral dissertation, University of Oregon, Eugene, 1961

Epps S, McGue M, Ysseldyke JE: Interjudge agreement in classifying students as learning disabled. Psychology in the Schools 19:209–220, 1982

Epstein MH, Bursuck W, Cullinan D: Patterns of behavior problems among the learning disabled: in boys aged 12–18, girls aged 8–11, and girls aged 12–18. Learning Disability Quarterly 8:123–131, 1985

Epstein MH, Cullinan D, Lloyd JW: Behavior-problem patterns among the learning disabled, III: replication across age and sex. Learning Disability Quarterly 9:43–54, 1986

Essen J, Peckham C: Nocturnal enuresis in childhood. Dev Med Child Neurol 18:577–589, 1976

Everhart RW: The relationship between articulation and other developmental factors in children. J Speech Hear Disord 18:332–338, 1953

Fay D, Mermelstein R: Language in infantile autism, in Handbook of Applied Psycholinguistics: Major Thrusts of Research and Theory. Edited by Rosenberg S. Hillsdale, NJ, Erlbaum, 1982, pp 393–428

Fay W, Schuler AL: Emerging Language in Autistic Children. Baltimore, MD, University Park Press, 1980

Fayne H: A comparison of learning disabled adolescents with normal learners on an anaphoric pronomial reference task. Journal of Learning Disabilities 14:597–599, 1981

Feagans L, Appelbaum MI: Validation of language subtypes in learning disabled children. Journal of Educational Psychology 78:358–364, 1986

Feighner J, Robins E, Guze SB, et al: Diagnostic criteria for use in psychiatric research. Arch Gen Psychiatry 26:57–63, 1972

Fein G: Imagination and language: some relationships in early development. Paper presented at the annual convention of the American Speech and Hearing Association, San Francisco, CA, November 1978

Felton FH, Wood FB, Brown IS, et al: Separate verbal memory and naming deficits in attention deficit disorder and reading disability. Brain Lang 31:171–184, 1987

Fergusson DM, Dimond ME, Horwood LJ: Childhood family placement history and behaviour problems in 6-year-old children. J Child Psychol Psychiatry 27:213–226, 1986

Ferrari M: Childhood autism: deficits of communication and symbolic development, I: distinctions from language disorders. J Commun Disord 15:191–208, 1982

Ferry PC, Hall SM, Hicks JL: Dilapidated speech: developmental verbal dyspraxia. Dev Med Child Neurol 17:749–756, 1975

Feshbach S: Aggression, in Carmichael's Manual of Child Psychology, Vol 2. Edited by Mussen PH. New York, John Wiley, 1970, pp 159–259

Fine G: Friends, impression management, and preadolescent behavior, in The Development of Children's Friendships. Edited by Asher S, Gottman J. Cambridge, UK, Cambridge University Press, 1981, pp 29–52

Fischer M, Rolf JE, Hasazi JE, et al: Follow-up of a preschool epidemiological sample: cross-age continuities and predictions of later adjustment with internalizing and externalizing dimensions of behavior. Child Dev 55:137–150, 1984

Fischler RS, Todd NW, Feldman CM: Otitis media and language performance in a cohort of Apache Indian children. Am J Dis Child 139:355–360, 1985

Fitzhardinge PM, Ramsay M: The improving outlook for the small prematurely born infant. Dev Med Child Neurol 15:447–459, 1973

Fitzsimons R: Developmental, psychosocial, and educational factors in children with nonorganic articulation problems. Child Dev 29:481–489, 1958

Fletcher P: The basis of language impairment in children: a comment on Chiat and Herson. Br J Disord Commun 22:65–72, 1987

Fodor JA: The Modularity of Mind. Cambridge, MA, MIT Press, 1983

Fodor JA, Bever T, Garrett MF: The Psychology of Language. New York, McGraw-Hill, 1974

Forness S, Sinclair E, Guthrie D: Learning disability discrepancy formulas: their use in actual practice. Learning Disability Quarterly 6:107–114, 1983

Fox L, Long SH, Langlois A: Patterns of language comprehension deficit in abused and neglected children. J Speech Hear Disord 53:239–244, 1988

Frank Y, Ben-Nun Y: Toward a clinical subgrouping of hyperactive and nonhyperactive attention deficit disorder: results of a comprehensive neurological and neuropsychological assessment. Am J Dis Child 142:153–155, 1988

Freeman FJ, Silver LB: Developmental articulation disorder, in Comprehensive Textbook of Psychiatry V, Vol 2. Edited by Kaplan HI, Sadock BJ. Baltimore, MD, Williams & Wilkins, 1989, pp 1804–1809

Freud A: Normality and Pathology in Childhood. New York, International Universities Press, 1965

Friedlander BZ, Wetstone HS, McPeek DL: Systematic assessment of selective language listening deficit in emotionally disturbed children. J Child Psychol Psychiatry 15:1–12, 1974

Friedrich D, Fuller GB, Davis D: Learning disability: fact and fiction. Journal of Learning Disabilities 17:205–209, 1984

Friman PC, Mathews JR, Finney JW, et al: Do encopretic children have clinically significant behavior problems? Pediatrics 82:407–409, 1988

Fundudis T, Kolvin I, Garside R: Speech Retarded and Deaf Children: Their Psychological Development. New York, Academic, 1979

Fundudis T, Kolvin I, Garside R: A follow-up of speech retarded children, in Language and Language Disorders in Childhood. Edited by Hersov L, Berger M, Nicol A. New York, Pergamon, 1980, pp 97–114

Funk JB, Ruppert ES: Language disorders and behavioral problems in preschool children. J Dev Behav Pediatr 5:357–360, 1984

Gabel S, Hegedus AM, Wald A, et al: Prevalence of behavior problems and mental health utilization among encopretic children: implications for behavioral pediatrics. J Dev Behav Pediatr 7:293–307, 1986

Gabel S, Chandra R, Shindledecker R: Behavioral ratings and outcome of medical treatment for encopresis. J Dev Behav Pediatr 9:129–133, 1988

Gambrell LB, Heathington BS: Adult disabled readers' metacognitive awareness about reading tasks and strategies. Journal of Reading Behavior 13:215–222, 1981

Garai J, Scheinfeld A: Sex differences in mental and behavioral traits. Genetic Psychology Monographs 77:169–299, 1968

Garbee FE: Ego identity in adolescent males with articulatory disorders. Unpublished doctoral dissertation, Claremont College, Claremont, CA, 1973. Cited in Dissertation Abstracts International 34:1719(4B), 1973

Garfield JL (ed): Modularity in Knowledge Representation and Natural-Language Understanding. Cambridge, MA, MIT Press, 1987

Garfinkel BD, Froese A, Hood J: Suicide attempts in children and adolescents. Am J Psychiatry 139:1257–1261, 1982

Garmezy N: Children vulnerable to major mental disorders: risk and protective factors, in Psychiatry Update: The American Psychiatric Association Annual Review, Vol 3. Edited by Grinspoon L. Washington, DC, American Psychiatric Press, 1984, pp 91–103

Garmezy N, Rutter M: Acute reactions to stress, in Child and Adolescent Psychiatry: Modern Approaches, 2nd Edition. Edited by Rutter M, Hersov L. Oxford, UK, Blackwell Scientific Publications, 1985, pp 152–176

Garvey M, Gordon N: A follow-up study of children with disorders of speech development. Br J Disord Commun 8:17–28, 1973

Gath D, Cooper B, Gattoni F, et al: Child Guidance and Delinquency in a London Borough. Institute of Psychiatry Maudsley Monograph No 24. London, Oxford University Press, 1977

Geffen G, Sexton MA: The development of auditory strategies of attention. Developmental Psychology 14:11–17, 1978

Gemelli RJ: Classification of child stuttering, I: transient developmental, neurogenic acquired, and persistent child stuttering. Child Psychiatry Hum Dev 12:220–253, 1982

Gemelli RJ: Understanding and helping children who do not talk in school. Pointer 27:18–23, 1983

German D: Word finding skills in children with learning disabilities. Journal of Learning Disabilities 12:43–48, 1979

Gershon ES, Targum SD, Kessler LR, et al: Genetic studies and biologic strategies in the affective disorders, in Progress in Medical Genetics, Vol 2. Edited by Bearn AG, Motulsky AG, Childs B. Philadelphia, PA, WB Saunders, 1977, pp 101–164

Gersten JC, Langner TS, Eisenberg JG, et al: Stability and change in types of behavioral disturbance of children and adolescents. J Abnorm Child Psychol 4:111–127, 1976

Gillam RB, Johnston JR: Development of print awareness in language-disordered preschoolers. J Speech Hear Res 28:521–526, 1985

Gillberg IC, Gillberg C: Generalized hyperkinesis: follow-up study from age 7 to 13 years. J Am Acad Child Adolesc Psychiatry 27:55–59, 1988

Gillespie SK, Cooper EB: Prevalence of speech problems in junior and senior high schools. J Speech Hear Res 16:739–743, 1973

Gittelman R: The role of psychological tests for differential diagnosis in child psychiatry. Journal of the American Academy of Child Psychiatry 19:413–438, 1980

Gittelman R: Ratings for anxiety disorders. Psychopharmacol Bull 21:933–950, 1985

Gittelman R, Mannuzza S, Skenker R, et al: Hyperactive boys almost grown up, I: psychiatric status. Arch Gen Psychiatry 42:937–947, 1985

Glasner PJ: Personality characteristics and emotional problems of stutterers under the age of five. J Speech Hear Disord 14:135–138, 1949

Glosser G, Koppell S: Emotional-behavioral patterns in children with learning disabilities: lateralized hemispheric differences. Journal of Learning Disabilities 20:365–368, 1987

Gluck M, McWilliams BJ, Wylie HL, et al: Comparison of clinical characteristics of children with cleft palates and children in a child guidance clinic. Percept Mot Skills 21:806, 1965

Godfrey JJ, Syrdal-Lasky AK, Millay KK, et al: Performance of dyslexic children on speech perception tests. J Exp Child Psychol 32:401–424, 1981

Goldman R, Fristoe M: Goldman-Fristoe Test of Articulation (GFTA) (1969), Revised Edition. Circle Pines, MN, American Guidance Service, 1972

Golinkoff RM, Gordon L: In the beginning was the word: a history of the study of language acquisition, in The Transition From Prelinguistic to Linguistic Communication. Edited by Golinkoff RM. Hillsdale, NJ, Erlbaum, 1983, pp 1–25

Goodenough FL: Anger in Young Children. Minneapolis, MN, University of Minnesota Press, 1931

Goodglass H: The Assessment of Aphasia and Related Disorders, 2nd Edition. Philadelphia, PA, Lea & Febiger, 1983

Goodglass H, Kaplan E: The Assessment of Aphasia and Related Disorders. Philadelphia, PA, Lea & Febiger, 1972

Goodman R: The developmental neurobiology of language, in Language Development and Disorders. Edited by Yule W, Rutter M. Philadelphia, PA, JB Lippincott, 1987, pp 129–145

Goodson BD, Greenfield PM: The search for structural principles in children's manipulation play: a parallel with linguistic development. Child Dev 46:734–746, 1975

Goodyer IM, Kolvin I, Gatzanis S: Do age and sex influence the association between recent life events and psychiatric disorders in children and adolescents?: a controlled enquiry. J Child Psychol Psychiatry 27:681–687, 1986

Gopnik A, Meltzoff AN: Relations between semantic and cognitive development in the one-word stage: the specificity hypothesis. Child Dev 57:1040–1053, 1986

Gottfried AW, Gottfried AE: Home environment and cognitive development in young children of middle socioeconomic status families, in Home Environment and Early Cognitive Development. Edited by Gottfried AW. Orlando, FL, Academic, 1984, pp 57–115

Gottlieb MI, Zinkus PW, Thompson A: Chronic middle ear disease and auditory perceptual deficits: is there a link? Clin Pediatr 18:725–732, 1979

Gottman J, Gonso J, Rasmussen B: Social interaction, social competence, and friendship in children. Child Dev 46:709–718, 1975

Gould MS, Wunsch-Hitzig R, Dohrenwend BP: Formulation of hypotheses about the prevalence, treatment, and prognostic significance of psychiatric disorders in children in the United States, in Mental Illness in the United States: Epidemiological Estimates. Edited by Dohrenwend BP, Dohrenwend MB, Gould MS, et al. New York, Praeger, 1980, pp 9–44

Gould MS, Wunsch-Hitzig R, Dohrenwend BP: Estimating the prevalence of childhood psychopathology. Journal of the American Academy of Child Psychiatry 20:462–476, 1981

Gove W, Herb T: Stress and mental illness among the young: a comparison of the sexes. Social Forces 53:256–265, 1974

Goyette CH, Conners CK, Ulrich R: Normative data on Revised Conners Parent and Teacher Rating Scales. J Abnorm Child Psychol 6:221–236, 1978

Graham P, Rutter M: Psychiatric disorder in the young adolescent. Proceedings of the Royal Society of Medicine 66:1226–1229, 1973

Gray WS: Gray Oral Reading Tests. Indianapolis, IN, Bobbs-Merrill, 1967

Green R: Sexual Identity Conflict in Children and Adults. Baltimore, MD, Penguin, 1974

Gresham FM, Reschly DJ: Social skill deficits and low peer acceptance of mainstreamed learning disabled children. Learning Disability Quarterly 9:23–32, 1986

Griffin GW: Childhood predictive characteristics of aggressive adolescents. Exceptional Children 54:246–252, 1987

Griffiths CPS: A follow-up study of children with disorders of speech. Br J Disord Commun 4:46–56, 1969

Grinnell SW, Scott-Hartnett D, Glasier JL: Language disorders (letter). Journal of the American Academy of Child Psychiatry 22:580–581, 1983

Grodzinsky Y: Language deficits and the theory of syntax. Brain Lang 27:135–159, 1986

Gross RT, Dornbusch SM: Enuresis, in Developmental-Behavioral Pediatrics. Edited by Levine MD, Carey WB, Crocker AC, et al. Philadelphia, PA, WB Saunders, 1983, pp 573–586

Grossman HJ, Begab MJ, Cantwell DP, et al (eds): Classification in Mental Retardation. Washington, DC, American Association on Mental Deficiency, 1983

Group for the Advancement of Psychiatry: Psychopathological Disorders in Childhood: Theoretical Considerations and a Proposed Classification (Research Rep No 62). New York, Group for the Advancement of Psychiatry, 1966, pp 229–230

Group for the Advancement of Psychiatry: Psychopathological Disorders in Childhood: Theoretical Considerations and a Proposed Classification. New York, Jason Aronson, 1974

Gruber FA, Segalowitz SJ: Some issues and methods in the neuropsychology of language, in Language Development and Neurological Theory. Edited by Segalowitz S, Gruber FA. New York, Academic, 1977, pp 3–19

Gualtieri CT, Koriath U, Van Bourgondien M, et al: Language disorders in children referred for psychiatric services. Journal of the American Academy of Child Psychiatry 22:165–171, 1983

Hadders-Algra M, Touwen BC, Olinga AA, et al: Minor neurological dysfunction and behavioural development: a report from the Groningen Perinatal Project. Early Hum Dev 11:221–229, 1985

Haenel T, Werder H: Zur problematik des psychogenen mutismus im kindes- und jugendalter. Schweizer Archiv für Neurologie, Neurochirurgie und Psychiatrie 12:261–276, 1977

Hagerman RJ, Falkenstein AR: An association between recurrent otitis media in infancy and later hyperactivity. Clin Pediatr 26:253–257, 1987

Hall DM, Hill P: When does secretory otitis media affect language development? Arch Dis Child 61:42–47, 1986

Hall PK, Tomblin JB: A follow-up study of children with articulation and language disorders. J Speech Hear Disord 43:227–241, 1978

Halmi KA, Falk JR, Schwartz E: Binge-eating and vomiting: a survey of a college population. Psychol Med 11:697–706, 1981

Halverson CF, Waldrop MF: Relations between preschool activity and aspects of intellectual and social behavior at age 7. Developmental Psychology 12:107–112, 1976

Hamlett KW, Pellegrini DS, Conners CK: An investigation of executive processes in the problem-solving of attention deficit disorder–hyperactive children. J Pediatr Psychol 12:227–240, 1987

Harlow LL, Newcomb MD, Bentler PM: Depression, self-derogation, substance use, and suicide ideation: lack of purpose in life as a mediational factor. J Clin Psychol 42:5–21, 1986

Harper DC, Richman LC: Personality profiles of physically impaired adolescents. J Clin Psychol 34:636–642, 1978

Hay DA, Prior M, Collett S, et al: Speech and language development in preschool twins. Acta Genet Med Gemellol (Roma) 36:213–223, 1987

Hayley GMT, Fine S, Marriage K, et al: Cognitive bias and depression in psychiatrically disturbed children and adolescents. J Consult Clin Psychol 53:535–537, 1985

Healy K, Conroy RM, Walsh N: The prevalence of binge-eating and bulimia in 1,063 college students. J Psychiatr Res 19:161–166, 1985

Hechtman L, Weiss G: Controlled prospective fifteen year follow-up of hyperactives as adults: non-medical drug and alcohol use and anti-social behavior. Can J Psychiatry 31:557–567, 1986

Henderson SE, Hall D: Concomitants of clumsiness in young school children. Dev Med Child Neurol 24:448–460, 1982

Herbert GW, Wedell K: Communication handicaps of children with specific language deficiency. Paper presented at the annual conference of the British Psychological Society, Southampton, UK, April 1970

Herjanic B, Reich W: Development of a structured psychiatric interview for children: agreement between child and parent on individual symptoms. J Abnorm Child Psychol 10:307–324, 1982

Herjanic B, Herjanic M, Brown R, et al: Are children reliable sources? J Abnorm Child Psychol 3:41–48, 1975

Hermansen A, Jensen HR, Ibsen KK: On children with defective speech. Int J Rehabil Res 8:203–207, 1985

Hermelin B: Images and language, in Autism: A Reappraisal of Concepts and Treatment. Edited by Rutter M, Schopler E. New York, Plenum, 1978, pp 141–154

Hersov L: Emotional disorders, in Child and Adolescent Psychiatry: Modern Approaches, 2nd Edition. Edited by Rutter M, Hersov L. Oxford, UK, Blackwell Scientific Publications, 1985, pp 368–381

Hetherington EM: Divorce: a child's perspective. Am Psychol 34:851–858, 1979

Hewitt LE, Jenkins RL: Fundamental Patterns of Maladjustment: The Dynamics of Their Origin. Springfield, IL, Charles C Thomas, 1946

Hiebert B, Wong B, Hunter M: Affective influences on learning disabled adolescents. Learning Disability Quarterly 5:334–343, 1982

Hingtgen J, Bryson C: Recent developments in the study of early childhood psychosis: infantile autism, childhood schizophrenia and related disorders. Schizophr Bull 5:8–55, 1972

Hoag JM, Norriss NG, Himeno ET, et al: The encopretic child and his family. Journal of the American Academy of Child Psychiatry 10:242–256, 1971

Hogan AE, Quay HC: Cognition in child and adolescent behavior disorder, in Advances in Clinical Child Psychology, Vol 7. Edited by Lahey BB, Kazdin AE. New York, Plenum, 1984, pp 1–34

Holborow PL, Berry PS: Hyperactivity and learning difficulties. Journal of Learning Disabilities 19:426–431, 1986

Holborow PL, Berry PS, Elkins J: Prevalence of hyperkinesis: a comparison of three rating scales. Journal of Learning Disabilities 17:411–415, 1984

Holden EW, Tarnowski KJ, Prinz RJ: Reliability of neurological soft signs in children: re-evaluation of the PANESS. J Abnorm Child Psychol 10:163–172, 1982

Hollingshead AB: Two-factor index of social position. Unpublished manuscript, 1957 [Available from Dr. Hollingshead, Yale Statim, New Haven, CT]

Holroyd J: When WISC verbal IQ is low. J Clin Psychol 24:457, 1968

Hook P, Johnson DJ: Metalinguistic awareness and reading strategies. Bulletin of the Orton Society 28:62–78, 1978

Hoy E, Weiss G, Minde K, et al: The hyperactive child at adolescence: cognitive, emotional and social functioning. J Abnorm Child Psychol 6:311–324, 1978

Hresko WP: The elicited imitation of varying sentence constructions by learning disabled and normal children. Unpublished doctoral dissertation, Temple University, Philadelphia, PA, 1975

Hresko WP: Elicited imitation ability of children from learning disabled and regular classes. Journal of Learning Disabilities 12:456–461, 1979

Hughes HM, DiBrezzo R: Physical and emotional abuse and motor development: a preliminary investigation. Percept Mot Skills 64:469–470, 1987

Hull FM, Mielke PW Jr, Timmons RJ, et al: The national speech and hearing survey: preliminary results. ASHA 13:501–509, 1971

Hulme C, Lord R: Clumsy children: a review of recent research. Child Care Health Dev 12:257–269, 1986

Hunt RD, Cohen DJ: Psychiatric aspects of learning disabilities. Pediatr Clin North Am 31:471–497, 1984

Ierodiakonou CS: Psychological problems and precipitating factors in the stuttering of children. Acta Paedopsychiatrica 37:166–174, 1970

Inamdar S, Siomopoulous G, Osborn M, et al: Phenomenology associated with depressed moods in adolescents. Am J Psychiatry 136:156–159, 1979

Ingram TTS: Specific developmental disorders of speech in childhood. Brain 82:450–467, 1959

Ingram TTS: Report of the dysphasia sub-committee of the Scottish Paediatric Society. Unpublished copy, 1963

Ingram TTS: The classification of speech and language disorders in young children, in The Child With Delayed Speech. Edited by Rutter M, Martin JM. London, Heinemann, 1972, pp 13–31

Inhelder B: Observations on the operational and figurative aspects of thought in dysphasic children, in Normal and Deficient Child Language. Edited by Morehead D, Morehead A. Baltimore, MD, University Park Press, 1976, pp 335–343

Interagency Committee on Learning Disabilities: Learning disabilities: a report to the U.S. Congress. Washington, DC, Department of Health and Human Services, 1987

Irwin R: Ohio looks ahead in speech and hearing therapy. J Speech Hear Disord 13:55–60, 1948

Israel L: Word knowledge and word retrieval: phonological and semantic strategies, in Language Learning Disabilities in School-Age Children. Edited by Wallach G, Butler K. Baltimore, MD, Williams & Wilkins, 1984, pp 230–250

Jacobs SC, Prusoff BA, Paykel ES: Recent life events in schizophrenia and depression. Psychol Med 4:444–453, 1974

Jaenicke C, Hammen C, Zupan B, et al: Cognitive vulnerability in children at risk for depression. J Abnorm Child Psychol 15:559–572, 1987

Jastak JF, Bijou SW, Jastak SR: Wide Range Achievement Test. Wilmington, DE, Guidance Associates, 1976

Jay SM, Routh DK, Brantley JC, et al: Social class differences in children's comprehension of adult language. Journal of Psycholinguistic Research 9:205–217, 1980

Jenkins JJ: Implications of basic research: thoughts behind the conference, in Speech and Language in the Laboratory, School, and Clinic. Edited by Kavanagh J, Strange W. Cambridge, MA, MIT Press, 1978, pp xv–xviii

Jenkins RL: Diagnoses, dynamics, and treatment in child psychiatry. Psychiatric Research Report 18:91–120, 1964

Jenkins RL: Psychiatric syndromes in children and their relation to family background. Am J Orthopsychiatry 36:450–457, 1966

Jenkins S, Bax M, Hart H: Behavior problems in pre-school children. J Child Psychol Psychiatry 21:5–17, 1980

Jerger S, Martin RC, Jerger J: Specific auditory perceptual dysfunction in a learning disabled child. Ear Hear 8:78–86, 1987

Johnson PL, O'Leary KD: Parental behavior patterns and conduct disorders in girls. J Abnorm Child Psychol 15:573–581, 1987

Johnston E, Johnston A: Children's play, in The Piagetian Language Nursery. Edited by Johnston E, Johnston A. Rockville, MD, Aspen, 1984, pp 195–216

Johnston JR: On location: thinking and talking about space. Topics in Language Disorders 2:17–31, 1981

Johnston JR, Ramstad V: Cognitive development in pre-adolescent language impaired children. Br J Disord Commun 18:49–55, 1983

Johnston O, Short H, Crawford J: Poorly co-ordinated children: a survey of 95 cases. Child Care Health Dev 13:361–376, 1987

Jones DJ, Fox MM, Babigian HM, et al: Epidemiology of anorexia nervosa in Monroe County, New York: 1960–1976. Psychosom Med 42:551–558, 1980

Jorm AF, Share DL, Matthews R, et al: Behaviour problems in specific reading retarded and general reading backward children: a longitudinal study. J Child Psychol Psychiatry 27:33–43, 1986

Jurkovic GJ, Prentice NM: Relation of moral and cognitive development to dimensions of juvenile delinquency. J Abnorm Psychol 86:414–420, 1977

Kagan J: Change and Continuity in Infancy. New York, John Wiley, 1971

Kagan J, Moss HA: Birth to Maturity. New York, John Wiley, 1962

Kales A, Soldatos CR, Kales JD: Sleep disorders: insomnia, sleepwalking, night terrors, nightmares, and enuresis. Ann Intern Med 106:582–592, 1987

Kamhi AG: Nonlinguistic symbolic and conceptual abilities of language impaired and normally developing children. J Speech Hear Res 24:446–453, 1981

Kandel DB, Davies M: Epidemiology of depressive mood in adolescents. Arch Gen Psychiatry 39:1205–1212, 1982

Kanner L: Autistic disturbances of affective contact. The Nervous Child 2:217–250, 1943

Kanner L: Irrelevant and metaphorical language in early infantile autism. Am J Psychiatry 103:242–246, 1946

Kanner L: Follow-up study of 11 autistic children originally reported in 1943. Journal of Autism and Childhood Schizophrenia 1:119–145, 1971

Kaplan BJ, McNicol J, Conte RA, et al: Physical signs and symptoms in preschool-age hyperactive and normal children. J Dev Behav Pediatr 8:305–310, 1987

Kaplan SL, Hong GK, Weinhold C: Epidemiology of depressive symptomatology in adolescents. Journal of the American Academy of Child Psychiatry 23:91–98, 1984

Kapp K: Self concept of the cleft lip and or palate child. Cleft Palate J 16:171–176, 1979

Karp N: Issues of disorder definitions according to P.L. 94-142. Paper presented at the National Institute of Mental Health Workshop on Issues in Research on Emotional/Behavioral Disorders Related to Learning Disabilities, Rockville, MD, September 1987

Kashani JH, Simonds JF: The incidence of depression in children. Am J Psychiatry 136:1203–1204, 1979

Kashani JH, Orvaschel H, Burke JP, et al: Informant variance: the issue of parent-child disagreement. Journal of the American Academy of Child Psychiatry 24:437–441, 1985

Kashani JH, Holcomb WR, Orvaschel H: Depression and depressive symptoms in preschool children from the general population. Am J Psychiatry 143:1138–1143, 1986

Kashani JH, Daniel AE, Sulzberger LA, et al: Conduct disordered adolescents from a community sample. Can J Psychiatry 32:756–760, 1987

Kashani JH, Orvaschel H, Rosenberg TK, et al: Psychopathology in a community sample of children and adolescents: a developmental perspective. J Am Acad Child Adolesc Psychiatry 28:701–706, 1989

Kaslow NJ, Rehm LP, Siegel AW: Social-cognitive and cognitive correlates of depression in children. J Abnorm Child Psychol 12:605–620, 1984

Kastrup M: Psychic disorders among pre-school children in a geographically delimited area of Aarhus County, Denmark. Acta Psychiatr Scand 54:29–42, 1976

Kavale KA: A comparison of learning disabled and normal children on the Boehm Test of Basic Concepts. Journal of Learning Disabilities 15:160–161, 1982

Kavale KA, Forness SR: Learning disability and the history of science: paradigm or paradox? Remedial and Special Education 6:12–23, 1985

Kazdin AE, French NH, Unis AS, et al: Assessment of childhood depression: correspondence of child and parent ratings. Journal of the American Academy of Child Psychiatry 22:157–164, 1983

Kean ML: Three perspectives for the analysis of aphasic syndromes, in Neural Models of Language Processes. Edited by Arbib MA, Caplan DC, Marshall JC. New York, Academic, 1982, pp 173–201

Kean ML: The question of linguistic anomaly in developmental dyslexia. Annals of Dyslexia 34:137–151, 1984

Keller E, Gopnik M: The neuropsychology of motor and sensory processes of language, in Motor and Sensory Processes of Language. Edited by Keller E, Gopnik M. Hillsdale, NJ, Erlbaum, 1987, pp ix–xix

Kidd KK, Kidd JR, Records MA: The possible causes of the sex ratio in stuttering and its implications. Journal of Fluency Disorders 3:13–23, 1978

Kindlon D, Sollee N, Yando R: Specificity of behavior problems among children with neurological dysfunctions. J Pediatr Psychol 13:39–47, 1988

King C, Young RD: Attentional deficits with and without hyperactivity: teacher and peer perceptions. J Abnorm Child Psychol 10:483–495, 1982

King R, Jones C, Lasky EZ: In retrospect: a 15-year follow-up of speech-language–disordered children. Language, Speech, and Hearing Services in Schools 13:24–32, 1982

Kinsbourne M, Hiscock M: The normal and deviant development of functional lateralization of the brain, in Infancy and Developmental Psychobiology. Mussen's Handbook of Child Psychology, 4th Edition, Vol 2. Edited by Haith MM, Campos JJ. New York, John Wiley, 1983, pp 157–280

Kirk SA, McCarthy JJ, Kirk WD: The Illinois Test of Psycholinguistic Abilities (ITPA), Revised Edition. Urbana, IL, University of Illinois Press, 1968

Klackenberg G: What happens to children with retarded speech at 3? Longitudinal study of a sample of normal infants up to twenty years of age. Acta Paediatr Scand 69:681–685, 1980

Klein-Konigsberg E: Semantic integration and language learning disabilities: from research to assessment and intervention, in Language Learning Disabilities in School-Age Children. Edited by Wallach G, Butler K. Baltimore, MD, Williams & Wilkins, 1984, pp 251–270

Klerman GL: The evaluation of diagnostic classes: the approach of the NIMH collaborative study. Paper presented at the American Psychiatric Association Invitational Workshop, DSM-III: An Interim Appraisal, Washington, DC, October 1983

Knight-Arest I: Communicative effectiveness of learning disabled and normally achieving 10- to 13-year-old boys. Learning Disability Quarterly 7:237–245, 1984

Koch JLA: Die Psychopathischen Minderwertigkeiter. Dorn, Rauensburg, 1891

Kohlberg L, Yaeger J, Hjertholme E: Private speech: four studies and a review of theories. Child Dev 39:691–736, 1968

Kopp CB: Risk factors in development, in Infancy and Developmental Psychobiology. Mussen's Handbook of Child Psychology, 4th Edition, Vol 2. Edited by Haith MM, Campos JJ. New York, John Wiley, 1983, pp 1081–1188

Kotsopoulos A, Boodoosingh L: Language and speech disorders in children attending a day psychiatric programme. Br J Disord Commun 22:227–236, 1987

Kovacs M: Interview Schedule for Children, 1978 [Available from Dr. Kovacs, Western Psychiatric Institute, Pittsburgh, PA 15213]

Kraemer HC, Pruyn JP, Gibbons RD, et al: Methodology in psychiatric research: report on the 1986 MacArthur Foundation Network I Methodology Institute. Arch Gen Psychiatry 44:1100–1106, 1987

Kraepelin E: Psychiatrie. Leipzig, JA Banth, 1909

Kurita H: Infantile autism with speech loss before the age of 30 months. Journal of the American Academy of Child Psychiatry 24:191–196, 1985

Lahey BB, Schaughency EA, Hynd GW, et al: Attention deficit disorder with and without hyperactivity: comparison of behavioral characteristics of clinic-referred children. J Am Acad Child Adolesc Psychiatry 26:718–723, 1987

Lahey M, Launer PB, Schiff-Myers N: Prediction of production: elicited imitation and spontaneous speech productions of language disordered children. Applied Psycholinguistics 4:317–343, 1983

Landau S, Milich R: Social communication patterns of attention-deficit–disordered boys. J Abnorm Child Psychol 16:69–81, 1988

Landman GB, Levine MD, Fenton T, et al: Minor neurological indicators and developmental function in preschool children. J Dev Behav Pediatr 7:97–101, 1986

Lapointe CM: Token test performance by learning disabled and achieving adolescents. Br J Disord Commun 11:121–133, 1976

Lapouse R, Monk MA: An epidemiologic study of behavior characteristics in children. Am J Public Health 48:1134–1144, 1958

Largo RH, Molinari L, Comenale Pinto L, et al: Language development of term and preterm children during the first five years of life. Dev Med Child Neurol 28:333–350, 1986

Lasky EZ, Klopp K: Parent-child interactions in normal and language-disordered children. J Speech Hear Disord 47:7–18, 1982

Lassman FM, Fisch RO, Vetter DK, et al: Early Correlates of Speech, Language, and Hearing (Collaborative Perinatal Project of the National Institute of Neurological and Communicative Disorders and Stroke). Littleton, MA, PSG Publishing Company, 1980

Lavik NJ: Urban-rural differences in rates of disorder: a comparative psychiatric population study of Norwegian adolescents, in Epidemiological Approaches in Child Psychiatry. Edited by Graham PJ. London, Academic, 1977, pp 223–251

Layton-Thomas L, Baker PS: Description of semantic-syntactic relations in an autistic child. J Autism Dev Disord 11:385–399, 1981

Lee L: Developmental Sentence Analysis. Evanston, IL, Northwestern University Press, 1974

Lerea L, Ward B: The social schema of normal and speech-defective children. J Soc Psychol 69:87–94, 1966

Lerner JA, Inui TS, Trupin EW, et al: Preschool behavior can predict future psychiatric disorders. Journal of the American Academy of Child Psychiatry 24:42–48, 1985

Leslie SA: Psychiatric disorders in the young adolescents of an industrial town. Br J Psychiatry 125:113–124, 1974

Lessing EE, Black M, Barbera L, et al: Dimensions of adolescent psychopathology and their prognostic significance for treatment outcome. Genetic Psychology Monographs 93:155–168, 1976

Lessing EE, Williams V, Gill E: A cluster-analytically derived typology: feasible alternative to clinical diagnostic classification of children? J Abnorm Child Psychol 10:451–482, 1982

Levi G, Capozzi F, Fabrizi A, et al: Language disorders and prognosis for reading disabilities in developmental age. Percept Mot Skills 54:119–122, 1982

Levi G, Musatti L, Piredda L, et al: Cognitive and linguistic strategies in children with reading disabilities in an oral storytelling test. Journal of Learning Disabilities 17:406–410, 1984

Levine MD, Oberklaid F, Ferb T, et al: The Pediatric Examination of Educational Readiness. Pediatrics 66:341–349, 1980

Levine MD, Meltzer LJ, Busch B, et al: Pediatric Early Elementary Examination: studies of a neuro-developmental examination for 7 to 9 year old children. Pediatrics 71:894–903, 1983

Lewis DO, Shanok SS, Pincus JH, et al: Violent juvenile delinquents. Journal of the American Academy of Child Psychiatry 18:307–319, 1979

Lewis DO, Shanok SS, Balla DA, et al: Psychiatric correlates of severe reading disabilities in an incarcerated delinquent population. Journal of the American Academy of Child Psychiatry 19:611–622, 1980

Lewis RB, Kass CE: Labelling and recall in learning disabled students. Journal of Learning Disabilities 15:238–241, 1982

Lillywhite H, Bradley D: Communication Problems in Mental Retardation. New York, Harper & Row, 1969

Lindholm BW, Touliatos J: Behavior problems of children in regular classes and those diagnosed as requiring speech therapy. Percept Mot Skills 49:459–463, 1979

Livingood AB, Cohen-Sandler R: Failures of individuation and communication disorders in children. J Pediatr Psychiatry 5:179–187, 1980

Livingston R, Nugent H, Roder L, et al: Family histories of depressed and severely anxious children. Am J Psychiatry 142:1497–1499, 1985

Loeber R, Dishion TJ: Early predictors of male delinquency: a review. Psychol Bull 94:68–99, 1983

Loftus ER, Palmer JC: Reconstruction of automobile destruction: an example of the interaction between language and memory. Journal of Verbal Learning and Verbal Behavior 13:585–589, 1974

Lolley TL: An investigation of the relationship of voice disorders to classroom behavior and educational achievement. Unpublished doctoral dissertation, University of Maryland, College Park, MD, 1975. Cited in Dissertation Abstracts International 37:917(A), 1975

Loomis S, Alessi NE: Speech/language disorders in a group of child psychiatric inpatients. Paper presented at the 35th annual meeting of the American Academy of Child and Adolescent Psychiatry, Seattle, WA, October 1988

Lorsbach T: Individual differences in semantic encoding processes. Journal of Learning Disabilities 15:476–480, 1982

Lotter V: Epidemiology of autistic conditions in young children. Soc Psychiatry 1:124–137, 1966

Lotter V: Epidemiology of autistic conditions in young children, I: prevalence. Social Psychology 1:163–173, 1967

Louttit CM, Halls EC: Survey of speech defects among public school children of Indiana. Journal of Speech Disorders 1:73–80, 1936

Love AJ, Thompson MG: Language disorders and attention deficit disorders in young children referred for psychiatric services: analysis of prevalence and a conceptual synthesis. Am J Orthopsychiatry 58:52–64, 1988

Lovell K, Hoyle HW, Siddall MQ: A study of some aspects of the play and language of young children with delayed speech. J Child Psychol Psychiatry 9:41–50, 1968

Lowe TL: Other disorders with physical manifestations, in Psychiatry, Vol 2. Edited by Michels R, Cavenar JO Jr. Philadelphia, PA, JB Lippincott, 1985, pp 1–10

Luria AR: The Role of Speech in the Regulation of Normal and Abnormal Behavior. Oxford, UK, Pergamon, 1961

Luria AR, Yudovich F: Speech and the Development of Mental Processes in the Child. London, Staples Press, 1959

Lyle JG: Certain antenatal, perinatal, and developmental variables and reading retardation in middle-class boys. Child Dev 41:481–491, 1970

Lyon R, Watson B: Empirically derived subgroups of learning disabled readers: diagnostic characteristics. Journal of Learning Disabilities 14:256–261, 1981

Maccoby EE, Jacklin CN: The Psychology of Sex Differences. Stanford, CA, Stanford University Press, 1974

Maccoby EE, Jacklin CN: Psychological sex differences, in Scientific Foundations of Developmental Psychiatry. Edited by Rutter M. London, Heinemann, 1980, pp 92–100

MacFarlane JW, Allen L, Honzik P: A Developmental Study of Behavior Problems of Normal Children Between 21 Months and 14 Years. Berkeley, CA, University of California Press, 1954

Mann VA: Longitudinal prediction and prevention of early reading difficulty. Annals of Dyslexia 34:117–136, 1984

Margalit M, Shulman S: Autonomy perceptions and anxiety expressions of learning disabled adolescents. Journal of Learning Disabilities 19:291–293, 1986

Markoski B: Conversational interactions of the learning disabled and non-disabled child. Journal of Learning Disabilities 16:606–609, 1983

Marks IM, Gelder MG: Different ages of onset in varieties of phobia. Am J Psychiatry 123:218–221, 1966

Martin JAM: Syndrome delineation in communication disorders, in Language and Language Disorders in Childhood. Edited by Hersov LA, Berger M, Nicol EA. New York, Pergamon, 1980, pp 77–95

Masten A, Garmezy N: Risk, vulnerability, and protective factors in developmental psychopathology, in Advances in Clinical Child Psychology, Vol 8. Edited by Lahey BB, Kazdin AE. New York, Plenum, 1985, pp 1–52

Matthews RM, Whang P, Fawcett S: Behavioral assessment of occupational skills of learning disabled adolescents. Journal of Learning Disabilities 15:38–41, 1982

McCauley R, Swisher L: Are maltreated children at risk for speech or language impairments? An unanswered question. J Speech Hear Disord 52:301–303, 1987

McConaughy SH, Ritter DR: Social competence and behavioral problems of learning disabled boys aged 6–11. Journal of Learning Disabilities 19:39–45, 1986

McCord J: Parental behavior in the cycle of aggression. Psychiatry 51:14–23, 1988

McCune-Nicolich L, Carroll S: Development of symbolic play: implications for the language specialist. Topics in Language Disorders 2:1–15, 1981

McDermott JF: Anxiety disorder in children and adults: coincidence or consequence? Integrative Psychiatry 3:158–161, 1985

McGee R, Silva PA, Williams S: Behavior problems in a population of seven-year-old children: prevalence, stability, and types of disorder: a research report. J Child Psychol Psychiatry 25:251–259, 1984

McHale A: An investigation of personality attributes of stammering, enuretic and school phobic children. Br J Educ Psychol 37:400–401, 1967

McKinney JD: The search for subtypes of specific learning disability. Journal of Learning Disabilities 17:43–50, 1984

McKinney JD: The search for subtypes of specific learning disability, in Annual Progress in Child Psychiatry and Child Development 1985. Edited by Chess S, Thomas A. New York, Brunner/Mazel, 1985, pp 542–559

McKinney JD, Speece DL: Academic consequences and longitudinal stability of behavioral subtypes of learning disabled children. J Educ Psychol 78:369–372, 1986

McLeod J: Educational underachievement: toward a defensible psychometric definition. Journal of Learning Disabilities 12:322–330, 1979

McWilliams BJ, Matthews HP: A comparison of intelligence and social maturity in children with unilateral complete clefts and those with isolated cleft palates. Cleft Palate J 16:363–372, 1979

McWilliams BJ, Musgrave RH: Psychological implications of articulation disorders in cleft palate children. Cleft Palate J 9:294–303, 1972

Mead GH: Mind, Self and Society. Chicago, IL, University of Chicago Press, 1934

Mehrhof E, Rousey CL: Speech difficulties symptomatic of destructive behavior toward self or others. J Nerv Ment Dis 152:63–67, 1971

Mendelson W, Johnson M, Stewart MA: Hyperactive children as teenagers: a follow-up study. J Nerv Ment Dis 153:272–279, 1971

Mendlewicz J, Rainer JD: Adoption study supporting genetic transmission in manic-depressive illness. Nature 268:327–329, 1977

Meyer A: The life-chart, in Contributions to Medical and Biological Research. Edited by Welch WH. New York, Paul B Hoeber, 1919, pp 1128–1133

Michelson L, Susgai DP, Wood RP, et al: Social Skill Assessment and Training With Children. New York, Plenum, 1983

Michelsson K, Noronen M: Neurological, psychological and articulatory impairment in five-year-old children with a birthweight of 2000 g. or less. Eur J Pediatr 141:96–100, 1983

Milich R, Dodge KA: Social information processing in child psychiatric populations. J Abnorm Child Psychol 12:471–489, 1984

Milisen R: The incidence of speech disorders, in Handbook of Speech Pathology and Audiology. Edited by Travis L. Englewood Cliffs, NJ, Prentice-Hall, 1971, pp 619–633

Miller FJW, Court SDM, Knox EG, et al: The School Years in Newcastle Upon Tyne. London, Oxford University Press, 1974

Miller L: Problem solving and language disorders, in Language Learning Disabilities in School-Age Children. Edited by Wallach G, Butler K. Baltimore, MD, Williams & Wilkins, 1984, pp 199–229

Miller LC, Barrett CL, Hampe E: Phobias of childhood in a prescientific era, in Child Personality and Psychopathology: Current Topics, Vol 1. Edited by Davids A. New York, John Wiley, 1974, pp 89–134

Miller ML, Chiles JA, Barnes VE: Suicide attempters within a delinquent population. J Consult Clin Psychol 50:491–498, 1982

Miller RG, Palkes HS, Stewart MA: Hyperactive children in suburban elementary schools. Child Psychiatry Hum Dev 4:121–127, 1973

Mills A, Streit H: Report of a speech survey: Holyoke, Massachusetts. Journal of Speech Disorders 7:161–167, 1942

Mitchell J, McCauley E, Burke PM, et al: Phenomenology of depression in children and adolescents. J Am Acad Child Adolesc Psychiatry 27:12–20, 1988

Moller H: Stuttering, pre-delinquent, and adjusted boys: a comparative analysis of personality characteristics as measured by the WISC and the Rorschach Test. Unpublished doctoral dissertation, Boston University, Boston, MA. Cited in Dissertation Abstracts International 21:1461–1462, 1960

Moore DR, Chamberlain P, Mukai LH: Children at risk for delinquency: a follow-up comparison of aggressive children and children who steal. J Abnorm Child Psychol 7:345–355, 1979

Moore SR, Simpson RL: Teacher-pupil and peer verbal interactions of learning disabled, behavior-disordered, and nonhandicapped students. Learning Disability Quarterly 6:273–282, 1983

Moran MR, Byrne MC: Mastery of verb tense markers by normal and learning disabled children. J Speech Hear Res 20:529–542, 1977

Moretti MM, Fine S, Haley G, et al: Childhood and adolescent depression: child-report versus parent-report information. Journal of the American Academy of Child Psychiatry 24:273–280, 1985

Morley ME: The Development and Disorders of Speech in Childhood. Edinburgh, E & S Livingstone, 1957

Morley ME: The Development and Disorders of Speech in Childhood, 2nd Edition. Edinburgh, E & S Livingstone, 1965

Morley ME: Receptive/expressive developmental aphasia. Br J Disord Commun 8:47–53, 1973

Morris NT, Crump WD: Syntactic and vocabulary development in the written language of learning disabled and non-learning disabled students at four age levels. Learning Disability Quarterly 5:163–172, 1982

Muma JR, Laeder RL, Webb CE: Adolescent voice quality aberrations: personality and social status. J Speech Hear Res 11:576–582, 1968

Murphy DA, Pelham WE: Attention deficit disorder, in Recent Developments in Adolescent Psychiatry. Edited by Hsu LKG, Hersen M. New York, John Wiley, 1989, pp 233–268

Myers JK, Lindenthal JJ, Pepper MP: Life events, social integration, and psychiatric symptomatology. J Health Soc Behav 16:421–427, 1975

Myers JK, Weissman MM, Tischler GL, et al: Six-month prevalence of psychiatric disorders in three communities. Arch Gen Psychiatry 41:959–967, 1984

Myklebust HR: Auditory Disorders in Children. New York, Grune & Stratton, 1954

National Center for Health Statistics: Prevalence of selected impairments: United States—1977 (DHEW Publ No PHS-82-1562). Washington, DC, U.S. Government Printing Office, 1981

National Institute of Mental Health: Pharmacotherapy of children (special issue). Psychopharmacol Bull, April 1973

National Institute of Neurological Diseases and Stroke: Human Communication and Its Disorders: An Overview (monograph no 10). Bethesda, MD, National Institute of Neurological Diseases and Stroke, 1972

Neeper R: Toward the empirical delineation of learning disability subtypes. Unpublished doctoral dissertation, University of Georgia, Athens, GA, 1985

Neeper R, Greenwood RS: On the psychiatric importance of neurological soft signs, in Advances in Clinical Child Psychology, Vol 10. Edited by Lahey BB, Kazdin AE. New York, Plenum, 1987, pp 217–258

Neils J, Aram DM: Family history of children with developmental language disorders. Percept Mot Skills 63:655–658, 1986

Nelson LK, Kamhi AG, Apel K: Cognitive strengths and weaknesses in language-impaired children: one more look. J Speech Hear Disord 52:36–43, 1987

Nelson OW: An investigation of certain factors relating to the nature of children with functional defects of articulation. Journal of Educational Research 47:211–216, 1953

Newcorn JH, Halperin JM, Healey JM, et al: Are ADDH and ADHD the same or different? J Am Acad Child Adolesc Psychiatry 28:734–738, 1989

Nezu AM: A problem-solving formulation of depression: a literature review and proposal of a pluralistic model. Clinical Psychology Review 7:121–144, 1987

Nicolosi L, Harryman E, Kresheck J: Terminology of Communication Disorders, 2nd Edition. Baltimore, MD, Williams & Wilkins, 1983

Ninio A: Picture book reading in mother-infant dyads belonging to two subgroups in Israel. Child Dev 51:587–590, 1980

Nippold MA, Sullivan MP: Verbal and perceptual analogical reasoning and proportional metaphor comprehension in young children. J Speech Hear Res 30:367–376, 1987

Noel M: Referential communication abilities of LD children. Learning Disability Quarterly 3:70–75, 1980

Offord DR, Boyle MH, Szatmari P, et al: Ontario child health study, II: six-month prevalence of disorder and rates of service utilization. Arch Gen Psychiatry 44:832–836, 1987

Olatawura MO: Encopresis: a review of 32 cases. Acta Paediatr Scand 62:358–364, 1973

Ollendick TH: Discrepancies between verbal and performance IQs and subtest scatter on the WISC-R for juvenile delinquents. Psychol Rep 45:563–568, 1979

Olsen J, Wong B, Marx R: Linguistic and metacognitive aspects of normally achieving and learning disabled children's communication process. Learning Disability Quarterly 6:289–304, 1983

Orton ST: Reading, Writing and Spelling Problems in Children. New York, WW Norton, 1937

Orvaschel H: Maternal depression and child dysfunction: children at risk, in Advances in Clinical Child Psychology, Vol 6. Edited by Lahey BB, Kazdin AE. New York, Plenum, 1983, pp 169–197

Orvaschel H, Puig-Antich J, Chambers W, et al: Retrospective assessment of prepubertal major depression with the Kiddie-SADS-E. Journal of the American Academy of Child Psychiatry 21:392–397, 1982

Ounsted M, Moar VA, Scott A: Factors affecting development: similarities and differences among children who were small, average, and large for gestational age at birth. Acta Paediatr Scand 75:261–266, 1986

Overall JE, Pfefferbaum B: An investigation of the consistency of diagnostic concepts among five child and adolescent psychiatrists. Multivariate Behavioral Research 17:435–445, 1982

Pajurkova EM, Orr RR, Rourke BP, et al: Children's word-finding test: a verbal problem-solving task. Percept Mot Skills 42:851–858, 1976

Paradise JL: Otitis media during early life: how hazardous to development? A critical review of the evidence. Pediatrics 68:869–873, 1981

Parisi D: Grammatical disturbances of speech production, in The Cognitive Neuropsychology of Language. Edited by Coltheart M, Sartori G, Job R. Hillsdale, NJ, Erlbaum, 1987, pp 201–219

Parnas J, Teasdale TW, Schulsinger H: Continuity of character neurosis from childhood to adulthood: a prospective longitudinal study. Acta Psychiatr Scand 66:491–498, 1982

Pasamanick B, Knobloch H: Brain damage and reproductive casualty. Am J Orthopsychiatry 30:298–305, 1960

Patterson CJ, Cohn DA, Kao BT: Maternal warmth as a protective factor against risks associated with peer rejection among children. Development and Psychopathology 1:21–38, 1989

Patterson GR: An empirical approach to the classification of disturbed children. J Clin Psychol 20:326–337, 1964

Patterson GR: Coercive Family Process. Eugene, OR, Castalia, 1982

Patterson J: Characteristics of play activities in two hyperactive children. Unpublished manuscript, University of New Mexico, Albuquerque, NM, 1981

Paul R, Cohen DJ: Outcomes of severe disorders of language acquisition. J Autism Dev Disord 14:405–421, 1984

Paul R, Feldman C: Communication deficits in autism. Paper presented at the Institute for Communication Deficits in Autistic Youth, Columbia University, New York, 1984

Paul R, Cohen DJ, Caparulo BK: A longitudinal study of patients with severe developmental disorders of language learning. Journal of the American Academy of Child Psychiatry 22:525–534, 1983

Pearce JB: The recognition of depressive disorder in children. Journal of the Royal Society of Medicine 71:494–500, 1978

Pearl R, Cosden M: Sizing up a situation: LD children's understanding of social interactions. Learning Disability Quarterly 5:371–373, 1982

Pennington BF, Smith SD: Genetic influences on learning on disabilities and speech and language disorders. Child Dev 54:369–387, 1983

Perlmutter BF, Crocker J, Cordray D, et al: Sociometric status and related personality characteristics of mainstreamed learning disabled adolescents. Learning Disability Quarterly 6:20–30, 1983

Peters JE, Romine JS, Dykman RA: A special neurological examination of children with learning disabilities. Dev Med Child Neurol 17:63–78, 1975

Peterson DR: Behavior problems of middle childhood. Journal of Consulting Psychology 25:205–209, 1961

Petrie I: Characteristics and progress of a group of language disordered children with severe receptive difficulties. Br J Disord Commun 10:123–133, 1975

Pfeffer CR, Solomon G, Plutchik R, et al: Suicidal behavior in latency-age psychiatric patients: a replication and cross validation. Journal of the American Academy of Child Psychiatry 21:564–569, 1982

Piaget J: The Origins of Intelligence in Children. New York, International Universities Press, 1952

Piaget J: The Language and Thought of the Child. London, World Publishing, 1955

Piattelli-Palmarini M: Language and Learning: The Debate Between Jean Piaget and Noam Chomsky. Cambridge, MA, Harvard University Press, 1980

Pierce S, Bartolucci G: A syntactic investigation of verbal autistic, mentally retarded and normal children. Journal of Autism and Childhood Schizophrenia 7:121–134, 1977

Pihl RO, McLarnon LD: Learning disabled children as adolescents. Journal of Learning Disabilities 17:96–100, 1984

Pirozzolo FJ, Campanella DJ, Christensen K, et al: Effects of cerebral dysfunction on neurolinguistic performance in children. J Consult Clin Psychol 49:791–806, 1981

Porter JE, Rourke BP: Socioemotional functioning of learning-disabled children: a subtypal analysis of personality patterns, in Neuropsychology of Learning Disabilities: Essentials of Subtype Analysis. Edited by Rourke BP. New York, Guilford, 1985, pp 257–280

Power MJ, Benn RT, Morris JN: Neighbourhood, school and juveniles before the courts. British Journal of Criminology 12:111–132, 1972

Poznanski EO, Zrull P: Childhood depression: clinical characteristics of overtly depressed children. Arch Gen Psychiatry 23:8–15, 1970

President's Commission on Mental Health of Children: Report of the President's Commission on Mental Health of Children, Vol 1. Washington, DC, American Psychiatric Association, 1980

Prins DT: Personality, stuttering severity and age. J Speech Hear Res 15:148–154, 1972

Prizant BM, Audet LR, Burke GM, et al: Communication disorders and emotional/behavioral disorders in children and adolescents. J Speech Hear Disord (in press)

Pronovost W: A survey of services for the speech and hearing handicapped in New England. J Speech Hear Disord 16:148–156, 1951

Puig-Antich J, Weston D: The diagnosis and treatment of major depressive disorder in childhood. Ann Rev Med 34:231–245, 1983

Pyle RL, Mitchell JE, Eckert ED, et al: The incidence of bulimia in freshman college students. International Journal of Eating Disorders 2:75–85, 1983

Quay HC: Dimensions of personality in delinquent boys as inferred from the factor analysis of case history data. Child Dev 35:479–484, 1964

Quay HC: Personality patterns in preadolescent delinquent boys. Educational and Psychological Measurement 26:99–110, 1966

Quay HC: Patterns of aggression, withdrawal, and immaturity, in Psychopathological Disorders of Childhood. Edited by Quay HC, Werry JS. New York, John Wiley, 1972, pp 1–29

Quay HC: Classification, in Psychopathological Disorders of Childhood, 2nd Edition. Edited by Quay HC, Werry JS. New York, John Wiley, 1979, pp 1–42

Quay HC, Peterson DR: Manual for the Behavior Problem Checklist, 1979 [Available from Dr. Peterson, 39 N. Fifth Ave, Highland Park, NJ 08904]

Quay HC, Peterson DR: Manual for the Revised Behavior Problem Checklist, 1983 [Available from Dr. Quay, Box 248074, University of Miami, Coral Gables, FL, 33124]

Quinn P, Rapoport J: Minor physical anomalies and neurological status in hyperactive boys. Pediatrics 53:742–747, 1974

Radosh A, Gittelman R: The effect of appealing distractors on the performance of hyperactive children. J Abnorm Child Psychol 9:179–189, 1981

Randall D, Reynell J, Curwen M: A study of language development in a sample of three-year-old children. Br J Disord Commun 9:3–16, 1974

Raph JB, Nicolich LM: Emergence of symbolic function in play and language. Unpublished manuscript, Rutgers University, New Brunswick, NJ, 1978

Rapin I: Conductive hearing loss effects on children's language and scholastic skills: a review of the literature. Ann Otol Rhinol Laryngol 88 (suppl 60):3–12, 1979

Rapin I, Allen DA: Syndromes in developmental dysphasia and adult aphasia. Res Publ Assoc Res Nerv Ment Dis 66:57–75, 1988

Regier DA, Allen G (eds): Risk factor research in the major mental disorders (DHHS Publ No ADM-81-1068). Bethesda, MD, National Institute of Mental Health, 1981

Regier DA, Myers JK, Kramer M, et al: The NIMH Epidemiologic Catchment Area Program: historical context, major objectives, and study population characteristics. Arch Gen Psychiatry 41:934–941, 1984

Reid DK, Hresko WP: A developmental study of the relation between oral language and early reading in learning disabled and normally achieving children. Learning Disability Quarterly 3:54–61, 1980

Rescorla L: Language delay at 2. Paper presented at the Boston University Conference on Language Development, Boston, MA, October 1984

Rescorla L: Preschool psychiatric disorders: diagnostic classification and symptom patterns. Journal of the American Academy of Child Psychiatry 25:162–169, 1986

Rett A: Rett syndrome: history and general overview. Am J Med Genet 25 (suppl 1):21–25, 1986

Rey JM, Bashir MR, Schwarz M, et al: Oppositional disorder: fact or fiction? J Am Acad Child Adolesc Psychiatry 27:157–162, 1988

Richman LC: Behavior and achievement of cleft palate children. Cleft Palate J 13:4–10, 1976

Richman LC: Parents and teachers: differing views of behavior of cleft palate children. Cleft Palate J 15:360–364, 1978

Richman LC, Harper DC: School adjustment of children with observable disabilities. J Abnorm Child Psychol 6:11–18, 1978

Richman LC, Harper DC: Self identified personality patterns of children with facial or orthopedic disfigurement. Cleft Palate J 16:257–261, 1979

Richman LC, Lindgren SD: Verbal mediation deficits: relation to behavior and achievement in children. J Abnorm Psychol 90:99–104, 1981

Richman N: Disorders in pre-school children, in Child and Adolescent Psychiatry: Modern Approaches, 2nd Edition. Edited by Rutter M, Hersov L. Oxford, UK, Blackwell Scientific Publications, 1985, pp 336–350

Richman N, Stevenson JE: Language delay in 3-year-olds: family and social factors. Acta Paediatrica Belgica 30:213–219, 1977

Richman N, Stevenson JE, Graham PJ: Prevalence of behaviour problems in 3-year-old children: an epidemiological study in a London borough. J Child Psychol Psychiatry 16:277–287, 1975

Richman N, Stevenson JE, Graham PJ: Pre-school to School: A Behavioural Study. London, Academic, 1982

Riddle KD, Rapoport JL: A 2-year follow-up of 72 hyperactive boys. J Nerv Ment Dis 162:126–134, 1976

Roberts JE, Sanyal MA, Burchinal MR, et al: Otitis media in early childhood and its relationship to later verbal and academic performance. Pediatrics 78:423–430, 1986

Robins E, Guze SB: Establishment of diagnostic validity in psychiatric illness: its application to schizophrenia. Am J Psychiatry 126:983–987, 1970

Robins LN: Deviant Children Grown Up. Baltimore, MD, Williams & Wilkins, 1966

Robins LN: Deviant Children Grown Up, Revised Edition. Huntington, NY, Robert E Krieger, 1974

Robins LN, Ratcliff KS: Risk factors in the continuation of childhood antisocial behavior into adulthood. International Journal of Mental Health 7:96–116, 1978–1979

Robins LN, Helzer JE, Croughan J, et al: National Institute of Mental Health Diagnostic Interview Schedule: its history, characteristics, and validity. Arch Gen Psychiatry 38:381–389, 1981

Robins LN, Helzer JE, Weissman MM, et al: Lifetime prevalence of specific psychiatric disorders in three sites. Arch Gen Psychiatry 41:949–958, 1984

Rodd LJ, Braine MDS: Children's imitations of syntactic constructions as a measure of linguistic competence. Journal of Verbal Learning and Verbal Behavior 10:430–443, 1971

Rosenbek JC, Wertz RT: A review of fifty cases of developmental apraxia of speech. Language, Speech, and Hearing Services in Schools 3:23–32, 1972

Rosenblatt D: Play, in Developmental Psychiatry. Edited by Rutter M. Baltimore, MD, University Park Press, 1980, pp 292–305

Rosenthal TL, Alford GS, Rasp LM: Concept attainment, generalization, and retention through observation and verbal coding. J Exp Child Psychol 13:183–194, 1972

Roth FP, Clark DM: Symbolic play and social participation abilities of language-impaired and normally developing children. J Speech Hear Disord 52:17–29, 1987

Rourke BP: Socioemotional disturbances of learning disabled children. J Consult Clin Psychol 56:801–810, 1988

Rousey CL (ed): Psychiatric Assessment by Speech and Hearing Behavior. Springfield, IL, Charles C Thomas, 1974

Rudel RG: Learning disability: diagnosis by exclusion and discrepancy. Journal of the American Academy of Child Psychiatry 19:547–569, 1980

Rudel RG, Denckla MB, Broman M: The effect of varying stimulus context on word-finding ability: dyslexia further differentiated from other learning disabilities. Brain Lang 13:130–144, 1981

Ruess AL: A comparative study of cleft palate children and their siblings. J Clin Psychol 21:354–360, 1965

Russell GFM: Anorexia and bulimia nervosa, in Child and Adolescent Psychiatry: Modern Approaches, 2nd Edition. Edited by Rutter M, Hersov L. Oxford, UK, Blackwell Scientific Publications, 1985, pp 625–637

Rutter M: Sex differences in children's responses to family stress, in The Child in His Family. Edited by Anthony E, Koupernki C. New York, John Wiley, 1970, pp 165–196

Rutter M: Psychiatry, in Mental Retardation: An Annual Review, Vol 3. Edited by Wortis J. New York, Grune & Stratton, 1971, pp 186–221

Rutter M: Maternal Deprivation Reassessed. Harmondsworth, UK, Penguin, 1972

Rutter M: Emotional disorder and educational underachievement. Arch Dis Child 49:249–256, 1974

Rutter M: Helping Troubled Children. New York, Plenum, 1975

Rutter M: Protective factors in children's responses to stress and disadvantage, in Primary Prevention of Psychopathology, Vol 3: Social Competence in Children. Edited by Kent MW, Rolf JE. Hanover, NH, University Press of New England, 1979, pp 49–74

Rutter M: Changing Youth in a Changing Society: Patterns of Adolescent Development and Disorder. Cambridge, MA, Harvard University Press, 1980

Rutter M: Epidemiological-longitudinal approaches to the study of development, in The Concept of Development. Minnesota Symposia on Child Psychology, Vol 15. Edited by Collins WA. Hillsdale, NJ, Erlbaum, 1982, pp 105–144

Rutter M: Psychopathology and development: links between childhood and adult life, in Child and Adolescent Psychiatry: Modern Approaches, 2nd Edition. Edited by Rutter M, Herzov L. Oxford, UK, Blackwell Scientific Publications, 1985, pp 720–742

Rutter M: The developmental psychopathology of depression: issues and perspectives, in Depression in Young People. Edited by Rutter M, Izard C, Read P. New York, Guilford, 1986, pp 3–30

Rutter M: Psychosocial resilience and protective mechanisms. Am J Orthopsychiatry 57:316–331, 1987a

Rutter M: The role of cognition in child development and disorder. Br J Med Psychol 60:1–16, 1987b

Rutter M: Age as an ambiguous variable in developmental research. International Journal of Behavioral Development 12:1–34, 1989a

Rutter M: Isle of Wight revisited: twenty-five years of child psychiatric epidemiology. J Am Acad Child Adolesc Psychiatry 28:633–653, 1989b

Rutter M, Brown GW: The reliability and validity of measures of family life and relationships in families containing a psychiatric patient. Social Psychology 1:38–53, 1966

Rutter M, Garmezy N: Developmental psychopathology, in Handbook of Child Psychology, 4th Edition, Vol 4. Edited by Mussen P. New York, John Wiley, 1983, pp 775–911

Rutter M, Giller H: Juvenile Delinquency: Trends and Perspectives. New York, Guilford, 1984

Rutter M, Gould M: Classification, in Child and Adolescent Psychiatry: Modern Approaches. Edited by Rutter M, Hersov L. Oxford, UK, Blackwell Scientific Publications, 1985, pp 304–324

Rutter M, Hersov L: Child Psychiatry: Modern Approaches. Oxford, UK, Blackwell Scientific Publications, 1977

Rutter M, Madge N: Cycles of Disadvantage: A Review of Research. London, Heinemann, 1976

Rutter M, Martin JAM (eds): The Child With Delayed Speech. London, Heinemann, 1972

Rutter M, Quinton D: Psychiatric disorder: ecological factors and concepts of causation, in Ecological Factors in Human Development. Edited by McGurk H. Amsterdam, North-Holland, 1977, pp 173–187

Rutter M, Graham P, Yule WA: Neuropsychiatric Study in Childhood. Lavenham, UK, The Lavenham Press, 1970a

Rutter M, Tizard J, Whitmore K: Education, Health, and Behavior. London, Longman, 1970b

Rutter M, Cox A, Tupling C, et al: Attainment and adjustment in two geographical areas, I: the prevalence of psychiatric disorder. Br J Psychiatry 126:493–509, 1975a

Rutter M, Shaffer D, Shepherd M: A Multiaxial Classification of Child Psychiatric Disorders. Geneva, World Health Organization, 1975b

Rutter M, Graham P, Chadwick OFD, et al: Adolescent turmoil: fact or fiction? J Child Psychol Psychiatry 17:35–56, 1976a

Rutter M, Tizard J, Yule W, et al: Research report: Isle of Wight studies, 1964–1974. Psychol Med 6:313–332, 1976b

Rutter M, Maughan B, Mortimore P, et al: Fifteen Thousand Hours: Secondary Schools and Their Effects on Children. London, Open Books; Cambridge, MA, Harvard University Press, 1979

Ryan ND, Puig-Antich J, Ambrosini P, et al: The clinical picture of major depression in children and adolescents. Arch Gen Psychiatry 44:854–861, 1987

Sameroff AJ, Chandler MJ: Reproductive risk and the continuum of caretaking casualty, in Review of Child Development Research, Vol 4. Edited by Horowitz F, Hetherington EM, Scarr-Salapatek S, et al. New York, Russell Sage Foundation, 1975, pp 187–244

Sampson OC: Reading and adjustment: a review of the literature. Educational Research 8:184–196, 1966

Sander EK: When are speech sounds learned? J Speech Hear Disord 37:55–63, 1972

Santostefano S: Anxiety and hostility in stuttering. J Speech Hear Res 3:337–347, 1960

Sato S, Dreifuss FE: Electroencephalographic findings in a patient with developmental expressive aphasia. Neurology 23:181–185, 1973

Savich PA: Anticipatory imagery ability in normal and language-disabled children. J Speech Hear Res 27:494–501, 1984

Schiefelbusch R: Language disabilities of cognitively involved children, in Principles of Childhood Language Disabilities. Edited by Irwin J, Marge M. Englewood Cliffs, NJ, Prentice-Hall, 1972, pp 209–237

Schonhaut S, Satz P: Prognosis for children with learning disabilities: a review of follow-up studies, in Developmental Neuropsychiatry. Edited by Rutter M. New York, Guilford, 1983, pp 542–563

Schubert DSP, Wagner ME, Schubert HJP: Effects of sibling constellations, in Developmental-Behavioral Pediatrics. Edited by Levine MD, Carey WB, Crocker AC, et al. Philadelphia, PA, WB Saunders, 1983, pp 225–229

Schwartz G, Merten D: The language of adolescence: an anthropological approach to the youth culture. American Journal of Sociology 72:453–468, 1967

Schwartz S: Language disabilities in infantile autism: a brief review and comment. Applied Psycholinguistics 2:25–31, 1981

Schweckendiek W, Danzer C: Psychological studies in patients with clefts. Cleft Palate J 7:533–539, 1970

Segalowitz SJ (ed): Language Functions and Brain Organization. New York, Academic, 1983

Seidel VP, Chadwick OFD, Rutter M: Psychological disorders in crippled children: a comparative study of children with and without brain damage. Dev Med Child Neurol 17:563–573, 1975

Selkirk EO: Phonology and Syntax: The Relation Between Sound and Structure. Cambridge, MA, MIT Press, 1984

Semel EM, Wiig EH: Comprehension of syntactic structures and critical verbal elements by children with learning disabilities. Journal of Learning Disabilities 8:53–58, 1975

Serbin LA, O'Leary KD: How nursery schools teach girls to shut up. Psychology Today 9:57–58, 1975

Sermas CE, Cox MD: The stutterer and stuttering: personality correlates. Journal of Fluency Disorders 7:141–158, 1982

Shafer SQ, Shaffer D, O'Connor PA: Hard thoughts on neurological "soft signs," in Developmental Neuropsychiatry. Edited by Rutter M. New York, Guilford, 1983, pp 133–143

Shaffer D: Suicide in childhood and early adolescence. J Child Psychol Psychiatry 15:275–291, 1974

Shaffer D: The clinical management of bedwetting in children, in Handbook of Clinical Assessment of Children and Adolescents, Vol 2. Edited by Kestenbaum CJ, Williams DT. New York, New York University Press, 1988, pp 689–710

Shaffer D, Fisher P: The epidemiology of suicide in children and adolescents. Journal of the American Academy of Child Psychiatry 20:545–565, 1981

Shaffer D, Chadwick OFD, Rutter M: Psychiatric outcome of localized head injury in children, in Outcome of Severe Damage to the Central Nervous System. CIBA Foundation Symposium No 34 (NS). Edited by Porter R, Fitzsimons D. Amsterdam, Elsevier North-Holland, Excerpta Medica, 1975, pp 191–210

Shaffer D, Campbell M, Cantwell DP, et al: Child and adolescent psychiatric disorders in DSM-IV: issues facing the child psychiatry work group. J Am Acad Child Adolesc Psychiatry 28:830–835, 1989

Shapiro T, Sherman M: Long-term follow-up of children with psychiatric disorders. Hosp Community Psychiatry 34:522–527, 1983

Shectman A: Age patterns in children's psychiatric symptoms. Child Dev 41:683–693, 1970

Sheridan MD: The importance of spontaneous play in the fundamental learning of handicapped children. Child Care Health Dev 1:3–17, 1975

Sheridan MD, Peckham CS: Hearing and speech at seven. Special Education 62:16–20, 1973

Sheridan MD, Peckham CS: Follow-up at 11 years of children who had marked speech defects at 7 years. Child Care Health Dev 1:157–166, 1975

Sheridan MD, Peckham CS: Follow-up at 16 years of school children who had marked speech defects at 7 years. Child Care Health Dev 4:145–157, 1978

Sherrill DD: Peer, teacher, and self perceptions of children with severe functional articulation disorders. Unpublished doctoral dissertation, University of Nebraska, Teachers College, Omaha. Cited in Dissertation Abstracts International 28:507–508, 1967

Shervanian C: Speech, thought, and communication disorders in childhood psychosis: theoretical implications. J Speech Hear Disord 32:303–313, 1967

Shriberg L, Kwiatkowski J, Best S, et al: Characteristics of children with phonologic disorders of unknown origin. J Speech Hear Disord 51:140–161, 1986

Siegel LS, Lees A, Allan L, et al: Non-verbal assessment of Piagetian concepts in pre-school children with impaired language development. Educational Psychology 1:153–158, 1981

Siegel LS, Saigal S, Rosenbaum P, et al: Predictors of development in preterm and full-term infants: a model for detecting the at-risk child. J Pediatr Psychol 7:135–148, 1982

Silva PA: A comparison of the predictive validity of the Reynell Developmental Language Scales, the Peabody Picture Vocabulary Test and the Stanford-Binet Intelligence Scale. Br J Educ Psychol 56:201–204, 1986

Silva PA, Williams SM: Developmental language delay from three to seven years and its significance for low intelligence and reading difficulties at age seven. Dev Med Child Neurol 25:783–793, 1983

Silva PA, Justin C, McGee R, et al: Some developmental and behavioural characteristics of seven-year-old children with delayed speech development. Br J Disord Commun 19:147–154, 1984

Simonds JF, Heimburger RE: Psychiatric evaluation of youth with cleft lip-palate matched with a control group. Cleft Palate J 15:193–201, 1978

Snow K: Articulation proficiency in relation to certain dental abnormalities. J Speech Hear Disord 26:209–212, 1961

Snow ME, Hertzig ME, Shapiro T: Expression of emotion in young autistic children. J Am Acad Child Adolesc Psychiatry 26:836–838, 1987

Snowling MJ: Phonemic deficits in developmental dyslexia. Psychol Res 43:219–234, 1981

Soensken PA, Flagg CL, Schmits DW: Social communication in learning disabled students: a pragmatic analysis. Journal of Learning Disabilities 14:283–286, 1981

Solomon AI: Personality and behavior patterns of children with functional defects of articulation. Child Dev 32:731–737, 1961

Sommers R, Kane A: Nature and remediation of functional articulation disorders, in Communication Disorders: Remedial Principles and Practice. Edited by Dickson S. Glenview, IL, Scott Foresman, 1975, pp 106–193

Speece DL, McKinney JD, Appelbaum MI: Longitudinal development of conservation skills in learning disabled children. Journal of Learning Disabilities 19:302–307, 1986

Spekman NJ: Dyadic verbal communication abilities of learning disabled and normally achieving fourth- and fifth-grade boys. Learning Disability Quarterly 4:139–151, 1981

Spencer EM: An investigation of the maturation of various factors of auditory perception in pre-school children. Unpublished doctoral dissertation, Northwestern University, Chicago, IL, 1958

Spitzer RL, Williams JBW: Classification of mental disorders and DSM-III, in Comprehensive Textbook of Psychiatry III, Vol 1. Edited by Kaplan

HI, Friedman AM, Sadock BJ. Baltimore, MD, Williams & Wilkins, 1980, pp 1035–1072

Spriesterbach DC: Psychosocial Aspects of "the Cleft Palate Problem," Vol 1. Iowa City, IA, University of Iowa Press, 1973

Sproat R: Competence, performance, and agrammatism: a reply to Grodzinsky. Brain Lang 27:160–167, 1986

Stark RE, Mellits ED, Tallal P: Behavioral attributes of speech and language disorders, in Genetic Aspects of Speech and Language Disorders. Edited by Ludlous CH, Cooper JA. New York, New York Academy Press, 1983, pp 37–52

Stavrakaki C, Vargo B, Roberts N, et al: Concordance among sources of information for ratings of anxiety and depression in children. J Am Acad Child Adolesc Psychiatry 26:733–737, 1987

Stevenson HW, Newman RS: Long-term prediction of achievement and attitudes in mathematics and reading. Child Dev 57:646–659, 1986

Stevenson JE, Richman N: The prevalence of language delay in a population of three-year-old children and its association with general retardation. Dev Med Child Neurol 18:431–441, 1976

Stevenson JE, Richman N: Behavior, language and development in three-year-old children. Journal of Autism and Child Schizophrenia 8:299–313, 1978

Stewart JM: Multidimensional scaling analysis of communicative disorders by race and sex in a mid-south public school system. J Commun Disord 14:467–483, 1981

Stewart JM, Martin ME, Brady GM: Communicative disorders at a health-care center. J Commun Disord 12:349–359, 1979

Stoner SB, Glynn MA: Cognitive styles of school-age children showing attention deficit disorders with hyperactivity. Psychol Rep 61:119–125, 1987

Sturge C: Reading retardation and antisocial behavior. Unpublished master's thesis, University of London, London, 1972

Szatmari P: Some methodologic criteria for studies in developmental neuropsychiatry. Psychiatr Dev 2:153–170, 1985

Szmukler G, McCance C, McCrone L, et al: Anorexia nervosa: a psychiatric case register study from Aberdeen. Psychol Med 16:49–58, 1986

Tager-Flusberg H: The conceptual basis for referential word meaning in children with autism. Child Dev 56:1167–1178, 1985

Tallal P, Dukette D, Curtiss S: Behavioral/emotional profiles of preschool language-impaired children. Development and Psychopathology 1:51–67, 1989a

Tallal P, Ross R, Curtiss S: Familial aggregation in specific language impairment. J Speech Hear Disord 54:167–173, 1989b

Tant JL, Douglas VI: Problem solving in hyperactive, normal and reading disabled boys. J Abnorm Child Psychol 10:285–306, 1982

Tarnowski KJ, Prinz RJ, Nay SM: Comparative analysis of attentional deficits in hyperactive learning-disabled children. J Abnorm Psychol 95:341–345, 1986

Tarver SG: Underselective attention in learning-disabled children: some reconceptualizations of old hypotheses. Exceptional Education Quarterly 2:25–35, 1981

Tarver-Behring S, Barkley RA, Karlsson J: The mother-child interactions of hyperactive boys and their normal siblings. Am J Orthopsychiatry 55:202–209, 1985

Teja JS, Malhotra HK, Verma SK: The child with speech problems. Indian Journal of Psychiatry 14:207–211, 1972

Templin MC: Certain Language Skills in Children. Institute of Child Welfare Monograph No 26. Minneapolis, MN, University of Minnesota Press, 1957

Terrell B, Schwartz R, Prelock P, et al: Symbolic play in normal and language impaired children. J Speech Hear Res 27:424–429, 1984

Thorley G: Hyperkinetic syndrome of childhood: clinical characteristics. Br J Psychiatry 144:16–24, 1984

Tittle CR, Villemez WJ, Smith DA: The myth of social class and criminality: an empirical assessment of the empirical evidence. American Sociological Review 43:643–656, 1978

Tomblin JB: Children's language disorders, in Processes and Disorders of Human Communication. Edited by Curtis J. New York, Harper & Row, 1978, pp 246–271

Tonge WL, James DS, Hillam SM: Families Without Hope. London, Headley Brothers, 1975

Trapp EP, Evan J: Functional articulatory defect and performance on a nonverbal task. J Speech Hear Disord 25:176–180, 1960

Travis LE: Handbook of Speech Pathology. Englewood Cliffs, NJ, Prentice-Hall, 1957

Trites RL, Dugas E, Lynch G, et al: Prevalence of hyperactivity. J Pediatr Psychol 4:179–188, 1979

Tuomi S, Ivanoff P: Incidence of speech and hearing disorders among kindergarten and grade one children. Special Education in Canada 51:5–8, 1977

Udwin O, Yule W: Imaginative play in language disordered children. Br J Disord Commun 18:197–205, 1983

U.S. Office of Education: Definition and criteria for defining students as learning disabled. Federal Register 42:65082–65085, 1977

U.S. Public Law 94-142, Education of the Handicapped Act, 1975

Varbiro K, Engelmayer A: Traumatic fear experience as an etiological factor in the formation of stuttering. Magyar Pszichologiai Szemle 29:223–238, 1972

Verhulst FC, van der Lee JH, Akkerhuis GW, et al: The prevalence of nocturnal enuresis: do DSM-III criteria need to be changed? A brief research report. J Child Psychol Psychiatry 26:989–993, 1985

Verhulst FC, Althaus M, Berden GF: The child assessment schedule: parent-child agreement and validity measures. J Child Psychol Psychiatry 28:455–466, 1987

Vetter DK: Language disorders and schooling. Topics in Language Disorders 2:13–19, 1982

Vogel S: A qualitative analysis of morphological ability in learning disabled and achieving children. Journal of Learning Disabilities 16:416–420, 1983

Voorhees J: Neuropsychological differences between juvenile delinquents and functional adolescents: a preliminary study. Adolescence 16:57–66, 1981

Vygotsky LS: Thought and Language. Cambridge, MA, MIT Press, 1962

Wadsworth J, Burnell I, Taylor B, et al: The influence of family type on children's behaviour and development at five years. J Child Psychol Psychiatry 26:245–254, 1985

Wagner CO, Gray LL, Potter RE: Communicative disorders in a group of adult female offenders. J Commun Disord 16:269–277, 1983

Walsh RN, Greenough WT (eds): Environment as Therapy for Brain Dysfunction. New York, Plenum, 1976

Wang WS-Y: Human Communication: Language and Its Psychobiological Bases: Readings from Scientific American. San Francisco, CA, WH Freeman, 1982

Wasserman GA, Green A, Allen R: Going beyond abuse: maladaptive patterns of interaction in abusing mother–infant pairs. Journal of the American Academy of Child Psychiatry 22:245–252, 1983

Watson CG: Personality adjustment in boys with cleft lips and palates. Cleft Palate J 1:130–138, 1964

Weber JL: The speech and language abilities of emotionally disturbed children. Can Psychiatr J 10:417–420, 1965

Wechsler D: The Wechsler Pre-School and Primary Scale of Intelligence (WPPSI). New York, Psychological Corporation, 1967

Wechsler D: Wechsler Intelligence Scale for Children—Revised Manual (WISC-R). New York, Psychological Corporation, 1974

Weiland J, Legg D: Formal speech characteristics as a diagnostic aid in childhood psychosis. Am J Orthopsychiatry 34:91–94, 1964

Weinberg W, Rutman J, Sullivan L, et al: Depression in children referred to an educational diagnostic center: diagnosis and treatment. J Pediatr 83:1065–1072, 1973

Weingartner H, Rapoport JL, Buchsbaum MS, et al: Cognitive process in normal and hyperactive children and their response to amphetamine treatment. J Abnorm Psychol 89:25–37, 1980

Weissman MM: Advances in psychiatric epidemiology: rates and risks for major depression. Am J Public Health 77:445–451, 1987

Weissman MM, Myers JK, Harding PS: Psychiatric disorders in a U.S. urban community: 1975–1976. Am J Psychiatry 135:459–462, 1978

Weissman MM, Wickramaratne P, Merikangas KR, et al: Onset of major depression in early adulthood: increased family loading and specificity. Arch Gen Psychiatry 41:1136–1143, 1984

Weissman MM, Wickramaratne P, Warner V, et al: Assessing psychiatric disorders in children: discrepancies between mothers' and children's reports. Arch Gen Psychiatry 44:747–753, 1987

Weller EB, Weller RA: Clinical aspects of childhood depression. Pediatr Ann 15:843–847, 1986

Welner Z, Reich W, Herjanic B, et al: Reliability, validity and parent-child agreement studies of the Diagnostic Interview for Children and Adolescents (DICA). J Am Acad Child Adolesc Psychiatry 26:649–653, 1987

Wepman J: Auditory Discrimination Test (1958), Revised Edition. Chicago, IL, Language Research Associates, 1973

Werner EE, Smith RS: Vulnerable but Invincible: A Longitudinal Study of Resilient Children and Youth. New York, McGraw-Hill, 1982

Werry JS, Quay HC: The prevalence of behavior symptoms in younger elementary school children. Am J Orthopsychiatry 41:136–143, 1971

Werry JS, Reeves JC, Elkind GS: Attention deficit, conduct, oppositional, and anxiety disorders in children, I: a review of research on differentiating characteristics. J Am Acad Child Adolesc Psychiatry 26:133–143, 1987

West DJ, Farrington DP: Who Becomes Delinquent? London, Heinemann, 1973

Wetherby AM: Ontogeny of communicative functions in autism. J Autism Dev Disord 16:295–316, 1986

White House Conference on Child Health and Protection: Special Education. New York, Century, 1931

Whitehouse C: Token test performance by dyslexic adolescents. Brain Lang 18:224–235, 1983

Wierzbicki M: Similarity of monozygotic and dizygotic child twins in level and lability of subclinically depressed mood. Am J Orthopsychiatry 57:33–40, 1987

Wiig EH: Language disabilities of adolescents. Br J Disord Commun 11:3–17, 1976

Wiig EH, Semel EM: Comprehension of linguistic concepts requiring logical operations by learning disabled children. J Speech Hear Res 16:627–636, 1973

Wiig EH, Semel EM: Productive language abilities in learning-disabled adolescents. Journal of Learning Disabilities 8:578–586, 1975

Wiig EH, Semel EM: Language Assessment and Intervention for the Learning Disabled. Columbus, OH, Charles E. Merrill, 1980

Wiig EH, Semel EM, Crouse A: The use of English morphology by high-risk and learning disabled children. Journal of Learning Disabilities 6:457–465, 1973

Wiig EH, Semel EM, Nystrom LA: Comparison of rapid naming abilities in language-learning disabled and academically achieving 8 year olds. Language, Speech, and Hearing Services in Schools 13:11–23, 1982

Wiig EH, Becker-Redding U, Semel EM: A cross-cultural, cross-linguistic comparison of language abilities of 7- to 8- and 12- to 13-year-old children with learning disabilities. Journal of Learning Disabilities 16:576–585, 1983

Wilchesky M, Reynolds T: The socially deficient LD child in context: a systems approach to assessment and treatment. Journal of Learning Disabilities 19:411–415, 1986

Williams DE, Melrose BM, Woods CL: The relationship between stuttering and academic achievement in children. J Commun Disord 2:87–98, 1969

Williams DM, Darbyshire JD, Vaghy DA: An epidemiological study of speech and hearing disorders. J Otolaryngol 9 (suppl 7):5–24, 1980

Wilson BC, Risucci DA: A model for clinical-quantitative classification. Generation 1: application to language-disordered preschool children. Brain Lang 27:281–309, 1986

Wilson FB, Lamb MM: Comparison of personality characteristics of children with and without vocal nodules based on Rorschach protocol interpretation. Acta Symbolica 5:43–55, 1974

Wing L: The handicaps of autistic children: a comparative study. J Child Psychol Psychiatry 10:1–40, 1969

Wing L, Yeates SR, Brierly LM, et al: The prevalence of early childhood autism: comparison of administrative and epidemiological studies. Psychol Med 6:89–100, 1976

Wirls CJ, Plotkin RR: A comparison of children with cleft palate and their siblings on projective test personality factors. Cleft Palate J 8:399–408, 1971

Wolff PH, Waber D, Bauermeister M, et al: The neuropsychological status of adolescent delinquent boys. J Child Psychol Psychiatry 23:267–279, 1982

Wolff S: Symptomatology and outcome of pre-school children with behaviour disorders attending a child guidance clinic. J Child Psychol Psychiatry 2:269–276, 1961

Wolff S: Dimensions and clusters of symptoms in disturbed children. Br J Psychiatry 118:421–427, 1971

Wolfus B, Moscovitch M, Kinsbourne M: Subgroups of developmental language impairment. Brain Lang 10:152–171, 1980

Wolkind S, Rutter M: Children who have been "in care": an epidemiological study. J Child Psychol Psychiatry 14:97–105, 1973

Wolpaw T, Nation JE, Aram D: Developmental language disorders: a follow-up study. Illinois Speech and Hearing Journal 12:14–18, 1979

Woods CL: Social position and speaking competence of third-grade and sixth-grade stuttering boys. Unpublished doctoral dissertation, University of Iowa, Iowa City, IA, 1969. Cited in Dissertation Abstracts International 30:4413(B), 1970

World Health Organization: Mental Disorders: Glossary and Guide to Their Classification in Accordance with the Ninth Revision of the International Classification of Diseases. Geneva, World Health Organization, 1978

Wren C: Identifying patterns of processing disorder in six-year-old children with syntax problems. Br J Disord Commun 17:83–92, 1982

Wright NE, Thislethwaite D, Elton RA, et al: The speech and language development of low birth weight infants. Br J Disord Commun 18:187–196, 1983

Wyatt GL: Mother-child relationship and stuttering in children. Unpublished doctoral dissertation, Boston University, Boston, MA, 1958. Cited in Dissertation Abstracts International 19:881, 1958

Wylie HL, Franchack P, McWilliams BJ: Characteristics of children with speech disorders seen in a child guidance center. Percept Mot Skills 20:1101–1107, 1965

Yanagawa M: On the etiology of stuttering and personality tendencies in mothers and children. Japanese Journal of Child Psychiatry 15:22–28, 1973–1974

Yoss KA, Darley FL: Developmental apraxia of speech in children with defective articulation. J Speech Hear Res 17:399–416, 1974

Zeitlin H: The Natural History of Psychiatric Disorder in Childhood. New York, Oxford University Press, 1986

Zentall SS: Production deficiencies in elicited language but not in the spontaneous verbalizations of hyperactive children. J Abnorm Child Psychol 16:657–673, 1988

Zentall SS, Gohs DE: Hyperactive and comparison children's response to detailed vs global cues in communication tasks. Learning Disability Quarterly 7:77–87, 1984

Zinkus PW, Gottlieb MI: Patterns of auditory processing and articulation deficits in academically deficient juvenile delinquents. J Speech Hear Disord 48:36–40, 1983

Author Index

279

Wolfus, B., 3, 156, 172
Wolkind, S., 133, 135, 195
Wolpaw, T., 21, 228
Woods, C.L., 13, 222
World Health Organization, 42, 115
Wren, C., 3
Wright, N.E., 55
Wyatt, G.L., 222
Wylie, H.L., 13, 222

Yanagawa, M., 14, 222
Yoss, K.A., 56
Young, R.D., 80
Yudovich, F., 7
Yule, W., 8

Zeitlin, H., 142, 144
Zentall, S.S., 17
Zinkus, P.W., 17, 222
Zrull, P., 144

Subject Index

291

Social Inst. paper
- pg 178
- pg. 186